Diane
Dupuy
1989

DARE TO DREAM

DARE TO DREAM

The Story of the Famous People Players

DIANE DUPUY
WITH LIANE HELLER

KEY PORTER BOOKS

Canadian Cataloguing in Publication Data

Dupuy, Diane.
Dare to dream

ISBN 1-55013-122-2

1. Famous People Players. 2. Puppets and puppet-plays — Canada. 3. Black box theaters — Canada. 4. Mentally handicapped — Canada. I. Heller, Liane. II. Title.

PN1979.B57D86 1988 791.5'3'0880826 C88-094333-5

Key Porter Books Limited
70 The Esplanade
Toronto, Ontario
Canada M5E 1R2

Cover photo: Rick Bostick
Editor: Sarah Swartz, The Editorial Centre
Phototypesetting: Computer Composition of Canada, Inc.

All photos, except where indicated, are courtesy of Famous People Players and are either taken by Ken Bell or are family photos.

The publisher gratefully acknowledges the assistance of the Ontario Arts Council.

Printed and bound in Canada

88 89 90 91 92 6 5 4 3 2 1

Contents

Acknowledgements ... ix

Introduction ... 1

Beginnings ... 7

Birth of a Dream
May 1968–June 1974 ... 33

Struggling to Stay Alive
June 1974–January 1975 ... 55

Breakthrough in Las Vegas
February 1975–October 1975 ... 81

A Company of Professionals
November 1975–December 1978 ... 115

A Growing Circle of Friends
January 1979–April 1980 ... 141

The Road to China
May 1980–November 1982 ... 162

"Special People"
November 1982–December 1984 ... 189

Magic on Broadway
January 1985–December 1986 ... 211

Epilogue ... 237

This book is dedicated to the Famous People Players family, to my family and especially to my loyal and trusted friends, Seymour Heller and Judi Schwartz.

"Great spirits always encounter violent opposition from mediocre minds." Albert Einstein.

Acknowledgements

In the fourteen years since the founding of the Famous People Players, I have learned more than I could teach. I have been the student. The players have been the teachers. They taught me to love myself. They taught me to forgive. They have given me the inner fulfillment I was missing in my life. They are the guardian angels who silently bring empathy to the puppets that they bring to life. The players remind me of monks as they quietly pull their hoods over their faces before going on stage. They're making a commitment, a vow that says "I am a person; I'm me. I'm here to overcome my handicap, to find out and learn about my abilities, not to be reminded of my disabilities."

As a Canadian I have watched as Americans put a man on the moon and as submarines explored the depths of the oceans — both for progress and for the enhancement of our future. But I am referring to a different kind of progress — progress of helping people right here on earth — because by helping others, we help ourselves.

We watched a man, who is blind, sail the world, battling the waves like Don Quixote. Why? So that we'll learn to see. We watched the Man in Motion wheel himself around the world, and up the Great Wall of China. Why? So that we'll learn to run to help others. We watched a man with one leg run against time. Why? So that we'll learn to explore the depths of our emotions. So, as we say in the theatre: Ladies and Gentlemen, let me introduce the people who, just when my life needed a touch of color added a whole rainbow with their love:

Honorable John B. Aird, John Armstrong, Darlene Arsenault and J.W. Armstrong, David Balinsky, Lt. Col. Kenneth Bell, Tony Bennett, Gord and Ted Billinger, Henry Botchford, Lloyd Bochner, Reg Bovaird, Marian Bradshaw, Judi Brake, Bob Bratina, David Broadfoot, Lesley Brown, Peter Brophey, Ronnie Brown, Marian Brayton, Else Buck, Michelle Busby and Jim Bull, James Carnrite, Dr. Frank Cashman, Joseph Cates, Sandra Ciccone, Floyd Chalmers, Charles & Eileen Clarke, Charleen Clarke, Stephen & Mary Colhoun, Ida Colalillo, Wally Crouter, Joe Cruden and Bill Cully, Marc Daniels, William Daniel, Annastasia Danyliw, Victor Davies, Dr. Paul Devenyi, Ron Dick, Maria Didia, Benny D'Onofrio, Judge Patrick W. Dunn, Jeanine, Joanne & Bernard Dupuy, June Eggleton, Sam Ellis, Gino Empry and Trevor Eyton, Gill & Joe Fodor, Hap Freeman, Don Francks and Herb Gardner, Hans Gerhandt and Mark Goldstaub, John Haddad, Kim Hansen, Joan Harrison, Don Harron, Lyman Henderson, Pat Hennessey, Helen Honickman and A.H. Hotchmer, Catherine Hurley, Robert Jani and Ron James, Ingrid Kidd, June, Ed & Greg Kozak, Patrick J. Keenan, Bob King, Maureen Kitts, Zigfreid "Ziggy" Kirchmeyer and Lucy Kraus, Ann Laitin, Jack Lemmon, Stephen Lewis, Deborah Lim, Dr. & Mrs. Lim, Hal Linden, and Joe Logemmari and Barry London, Ann-Margret, Sandy Mandel, Jack McAndrew, the Honorable Pauline & Don McGibbon, Lyman MacInnis, Lois Maxwell, Catherine McKinnon, Renee Morrison, Ed Mirvish, Renato Marulli, James Macdonald and Wilt Melnick, Anne Murray and Mrs. Grant Murray, Paula & Wally Neil, Dr. Than Nwe, Knowlton Nash, Newman's Own and Leslie Neilson, Martin O'Malley, Dr. J. Pakula, Dini Petty, Therese Picco, Geoff Pickering, Mike Platz, Victor Polley, Lucile Pratt and Aliceson Pounder, Warren Quinn,

Doug Riley, Norman Riley, the late Dr. Alan Roeher, Stanley Robinson, Deborah Rossen, Peter Rosen, Sandy Rake, the late Claire Rossen and Muriel Rubin, Nick Santini, Leo Schwartz, Ronald Secker, Bob Simpson, Paul Skaife, Roger Smith, Tom Sullivan, Dorothy & Bob Spencer, Dolly Tarshis, Ian Taylor, Charles & Diana Tisdall, Alex Trebek, Alan Thicke, Gordon Thomson, Lorraine Thomson, Mary Thompson, Neil Thompson, Mary C. Thornton, Ida Triggiani and Dr. Tyrone Turner, Frank Verlizzo, Andrey Watson, Jack Webster, Ben Wicks, Bill Wittman and Pauline Watson.

The people whose names do not grace this page are, like Liberace and Paul Newman, Silent Humanitarians.

Note: Some of the names of members of Famous People Players and other individuals involved in their story have been changed, at their request or because of the nature of events described.

DARE TO DREAM

Introduction

The face in the dressing room mirror is deathly pale, and under the bright lights the lines of anxiety seem etched in stone.

I know it's my own reflection I'm seeing, but for some reason it looks like the face of a stranger.

Maybe it's just being here.

Yes, that feels strange; so strange that I can hardly believe it's me sitting here, endlessly waiting, waiting, waiting for that curtain to rise — on a dream? Or on a nightmare?

Opening night, October 26, 1986, the Lyceum theatre, Broadway. What *are* you doing here, Diane Dupuy? How did you and your Famous People Players get yourselves from a two-minute show for the cleaning staff in a Toronto church basement to opening night at the Lyceum, already a legend when Broadway was still just the name of a street?

My own bewilderment stares back at me from the mirror, and I feel a great need to reach out and touch that stranger, to offer her some sort of reassurance that would change that puzzled, troubled frown to a smile.

If only there were a way to tell her that all those months of turmoil — and all those years of struggle — weren't about to end in disaster. If only there were a way to prove to her that she wasn't deluding herself with the belief that performers who once had trouble finding centre stage could conquer a stage that once held the likes of Judy Holliday and Helen Hayes.

If only there were a way to promise her that the Famous People Players would take Broadway by storm tonight and wake up tomorrow morning knowing that never again would anyone or anything place a barrier between themselves and their dreams.

Tonight's performance could be a total disaster. Or, even if it isn't, these tough New York critics could turn thumbs down on the Famous People Players and close the show overnight. Sure, we were a success with Liberace in Las Vegas, and at Radio City Music Hall, and on tour in China, and at the National Arts Centre in Ottawa. But Broadway is different. Broadway is like taking on Mount Everest when you've scaled only a few little hills.

Well, if you fall, so what? You just pick yourself up and start over. True enough, for most performers. But for the Famous People Players it wouldn't be just another show bombing out on Broadway. We'd also be facing such comments as, "They did very well, considering that they're retarded" and "Shouldn't we be just a little more realistic about our expectations of the mentally handicapped?"

Once again, we'd have to shoulder the weight of the usual oppressive labels: "retarded," "mentally handicapped," "mentally disabled," and many other supposedly up-to-date terms that shove people into narrow little slots, curb their potential, crush their spirits.

The whole idea of this Broadway run was to end all that once and for all. That's why nowhere in our program is there a single word that suggests that the performers are in some way "different" from other people — except for their talent. Other handicaps aren't the focus of that sort of attention. There aren't any programs announcing the appearance of "Stevie Wonder, America's greatest blind singer and composer." There is no assumption that the audience is going to enjoy Stevie's performance more because they pity him for being blind.

It just doesn't work that way. Stevie Wonder sells millions of records because he's a great performer, and if the Famous

People Players make it on Broadway, it'll be because they too are great performers.

But if we don't make it, you can be sure that — program or no program — all the little patronizing remarks are going to come creeping back into our lives like so many old nightmares. That's the unfairness of it: If you succeed, it's because you're good; if you fail, it's because you're "retarded."

I feel a great deal of responsibility for the company and the people in it. After all, I'm the one whose faith in the Famous People Players was so great that I kept insisting we go for the brass ring of Broadway. I'm the one who kept turning a deaf ear to anyone who suggested that our show, while entertaining and amusing, wasn't quite the right stuff for Broadway. I'm the one who kept telling the performers that we would be a hit, that we *had* to be a hit.

In my soul, I truly feel that my belief in the performers' enormous personal and artistic potential was what motivated me to push as hard as I did for us to gain this opportunity. Sure, I was doing it for myself, too, in the sense that when the Famous People Players soar, I soar. But if they fell from such a dizzying height as Broadway, might they come to believe that I was trying to use them, that it was my selfish ambition that forced them to reach for something they ultimately couldn't achieve? Might they come to hate me? Oh, God! I couldn't bear that!

"Dora Doom," I silently address my mirror image, "you sure deserve that nickname. Here you are, creating all that devastation from something that hasn't happened!"

No, it hasn't happened; not yet, anyway. But what if it does? What if it does? I feel my anguish rise again and as tears fill those huge dark eyes in front of me, I have to look away from the mirror.

"Hi there, dearie!"

I turn to face the impish grin of Greg Kozak, his small body already swathed in the black velvet hooded jumpsuit he'll wear on stage tonight. The hood, when it's down around his shoulders — as it is now — makes him look like a mischievous little elf. But when he pulls the hood over his face on stage, he'll become a magician who pushes and pulls a puppet under the incandescent brilliance of ultraviolet light and yet remains invisible to the audience.

Black-light theatre! The puppets, painted in dazzling fluorescent colors, are the stars that shine in the dark and seem to the audience to cavort, dance, and fly, even — with no visible means of support. But the real magic makers are performers like Greg: In the camouflage of their jumpsuits, they can't be seen by the audience, and in the dark confinement of their hoods, they themselves can barely see where they're going. Yet, without them, the puppets are only objects of painted foam rubber, fabric and wood; not the characters of a fairy tale come to life.

Greg's anxious voice breaks into my silent musing: "What's the matter, dearie?"

"Yeah, what's wrong, Mrs. Dupuy?" Renato Marulli is right behind Greg. "Did something happen?" He claps a hand to the side of his face, shaking his head with the same tragic air my grandmother displayed when she was upset with my brother Robert and me. "Oh, my God! Something terrible happened, didn't it, Mrs. Dupuy?"

Sandra, Darlene, Debbie . . . They're all in the dressing room now, all the performers, circling me like distraught mother hens, their voices a chorus of worry: "What did we do?"

"Did they cancel the show?"

"Am I in trouble? I got my props set up, just about . . . ."

"What's going on?"

"Do we have to go home?"

Then, suddenly, the voices die away. They just stand there, looking at me expectantly, waiting for me to allay their fears, or at least tell them what — if anything — they have to fear.

"Look, this is *it*," I blurt out, tears springing to my eyes again. "There's nothing I can say or do now. It's all up to you. I love you, and if it doesn't go well tonight, I hope you'll still love me . . . ."

"We're going to be *great*, Diane!" bellows Darlene.

"Sure, dearie" — that's Greg — "the Mets'll take it at Shea Stadium, and the Famous People Players will take it in the Lyceum theatre!"

"Now lookit, Mrs. Dupuy," says Renato, crashing a huge fist down on the makeup table, sending tubes of lipstick and cans of hairspray flying in all directions. "We're gonna do it! We *gotta do it*!!"

I'm speechless with awe at the intensity of their passion, their confidence. We fall into each other's arms, hugging like a family come together one last time before the war begins.

"Okay, everybody, let's go check our props!" shouts Debbie Lim, her petite, delicate appearance a sharp contrast to her authoritative voice. "We've got a show to do!"

"No kidding?" retorts Greg, his arm around Debbie as they lead the way out of the dressing room and into the future, which is as much a question mark as ever; yet not half as frightening as it was before we shared that moment of closeness.

I walk over to the small window at the opposite end of the room, picking my way through an obstacle course of boots, sneakers, sweat pants, and tote bags. Normally, I'd be annoyed at the sight of all this clutter, but tonight my mind can focus only on the performance that is now — what is it? — twenty minutes away. Please, God, let it be all right, I pray, staring out at the driving rain, which has been with us ever since we started the previews ten days ago.

It's only when I hear a cheerful voice behind me — "No problem, Diane!" — that I realize I've said that prayer aloud. "You remember what I told you?" asks Sam Ellis, production supervisor, as he comes to join me at the window. "If it's raining, you're gonna have a hit."

We stand side by side for what seems an eternity; finally, Sam glances at his watch, pats my shoulder comfortingly, and heads out the door. "Coming?" he asks over his shoulder.

"Yeah, I'm going out front in just a second."

I suppose I should fix my makeup before I venture out into the audience. After all that crying, I've probably got mascara streaks down to my chin.

There. That's better. Matter of fact, Dupuy, you don't look half bad, all things considered. Now, if only you could get rid of these butterflies . . . .

"Five minutes, Diane."

Now who is it? "Oh, hi, Mickey." I walk over to Mickey Fox, the house property man, who's leaning against the dressing room door. His face is the very picture of serenity. He's seen it all, hasn't he? All the hits, all the flops . . .

"Mickey, everybody keeps saying it's going to go well, but I just can't seem to believe it. What do you think's going to happen?"

Mickey is silent for a moment, scuffing his shoe against the floor as he carefully considers his answer.

"I wish I could tell you, but I'm afraid it's just not possible," he says, and he ushers me out into the hallway, letting the door slowly swing shut behind us. "The die is cast, my dear. The die is cast."

Beginnings

For three generations, my family has been drawn to the arts: painting, music, design, and theatre, especially on my mother's side. My mother's parents, Guido and Zena Gioberti, were born in Ascoli Piceno, a small Italian town famous for its exquisite and unique ceramics. My grandfather, a skilled woodcarver, also had a keen ear for music and could play just about any instrument; my grandmother was a gifted seamstress.

When the Giobertis emigrated to Canada, settling in Hamilton, Ontario, Guido was nineteen and Zena was only fifteen years old. At first, life in Canada was tough for the young couple. There was no market for my grandfather's woodworking skills, so he drove a jitney — a cross between a taxi and a bus. For a ride of a few blocks you paid ten cents, while a longer trip might cost a whole quarter.

As the Depression set in, the jitney trade dwindled, and my grandparents went to work in a tailor shop. Except for the few years my grandmother stayed home to raise Mom and her sisters, my grandparents worked together in the shop all their lives.

Along with their work, Guido and Zena Gioberti shared a love of music. My grandfather's versatility made him a welcome member of the Italo-Canadian Band. Later, he helped form what was to become the first Boy Scout band in Canada.

Music was very much part of life in the Gioberti household, and my grandparents loved listening to opera. One day, grandfather brought home a record featuring a young baritone whose voice was so glorious that he and my grandmother decided to send him a telegram of congratulation. But nowhere on the record was a single mention of his name. It took my grandfather weeks, but he finally tracked down the mystery singer — Leonard Warren.

On the eve of the nervous young singer's debut at the Metropolitan Opera House, he received the Giobertis' telegram: "This is just the beginning of a brilliant career!" Warren, deeply moved, wrote back, and the correspondence continued. And by the time Warren started touring, he and my grandparents were such good friends that it was only natural for him to stay at their house when the tour reached Hamilton. (Years later, Mom and Dad carried on the family tradition, inviting Warren to stay with them whenever he was singing in the Toronto-Hamilton area.)

As a teenager, my mother often sang along with the operatic arias she heard on records at home. But she never dreamed that, in her forties, she would be performing arias herself. While my mom was wardrobe mistress of the Hamilton Opera, the vocal coach decided that everyone who worked for the opera should sing in the chorus. After hearing her fine soprano voice, he encouraged Mom to develop her talent, and Warren insisted on arranging lessons for her in New York with his singing coach. Mom went on to sing with the Hamilton Opera in *La Bohème*, *Carmen* and *Madama Butterfly.* Today, if you visit the Famous People Players prop room, don't be surprised if you hear a lovely voice singing Verdi to the accompaniment of a sewing machine!

Mom's first job was as a saleswoman in the drapery department of a department store, where she soon caught the eye of a young display artist. The inventive suitor introduced himself by dropping a note on Mom's sales counter: "Good morning, Mary Sunshine! Sincerely, Stanley Thornton." There was some tension between the two families — Italian Catholic on one side, English-Irish Protestant on the other — but they finally accepted the inevitable. In 1943 Mary Gioberti and Stanley Thornton were married.

I was born September 8, 1948.

"I'm in heaven when I see you smile, my Diane," my mother sang softly to me; then she said, "Smile for me, my Diane." And I did — or so the story goes!

My earliest memories are of our house. When I was little, it sometimes seemed like a fairy-tale castle to me, located as it was at the top of a hill, with flowering trees in the front yard. I loved my room, which had a walk-in closet where I hid when I wanted to get away from everyone; I scooted right to the back and covered myself with clothes while Mom, Dad, and my cousins ran around the house shouting for me: "Diane! Diane! Where are you, Diane?" But they never found me in there, and I never came out until I was ready.

When I was a little older, just before I started school, I was allowed to go visit Dad in his shop called "Stanley Signs," where he created signs, window displays, and holiday decorations. I loved to stay all day, endlessly fascinated with the colors, the brushes, and the characters — like Elsie the Cow and the Planters Peanut Man — which he reproduced, in meticulous detail, for grocery store displays. His specialty was Christmas trees for banks and other big businesses: He painted them gold, blue, white, every color of the rainbow — the whole shop shone with glittering paint, sparkles, and fabulous heaps of tinsel. Dad worked away, stopping every so often when one of a long line of visitors dropped in to have coffee and chat about what was going on in the neighborhood. "Stanley Signs is the crossroads of life," Dad would say to me. "Sooner or later, everybody comes through here. Right, Pumpkin?"

With a rainbow palette of color, endless supplies of paper, and lots of encouragement from Dad to paint exactly what I wanted, I was in heaven. The only time I didn't like being at Dad's shop was when he made me clean all the brushes and wipe paint off the floor at the end of a day's work; sometimes I cried and begged to go home, but he always made me stay until all the cleaning was done. I didn't understand it then, but when Dad became tyrannical in that way, it was the dark side of his personality emerging. Sometimes he lost his temper quite suddenly; if he didn't like my table manners, he might smack me and send me to the basement until after dinner. As a child, I didn't really know what I had done wrong; all I could see was this big face yelling at me to go down to the basement. And for me, that face was like the big green face of the Wicked Witch of the West from *The Wizard of Oz.*

But the basement itself didn't scare me at all. Dad kept all the lights out, but that didn't bother me; I just walked in a circle, over and over, until my eyes adjusted to the dark. Then, I pretended I was a fairy princess, Robin Hood, a great actress, or the Lone Ranger. It was down in that basement that I decided to become famous. Someday, I promised myself, everybody was going to applaud me. In that basement, I discovered that I could create a world of my own — a world of magic and dreams — from my imagination. Everything could be transformed just by making up a story.

Then came my sixth birthday. And school. I'll never forget my first day at Sacred Heart School because the Sister who was our teacher immediately slapped me in the face. I don't know why she did it; I must have done something wrong, but to this day I have no idea what it was.

A little while later, she went around the classroom with a box of crayons — the sharp points so temptingly new — and asked each of us to choose one. I must have tried to take two, because she said very sternly, "One, Diane!" So I picked black. Then she handed out pieces of paper with circles on them, and told us to color them, following the lines. But at Dad's shop there was no such thing as coloring within the lines; I always just drew what I wanted, so I did the same thing in the classroom. To me, it looked prettier that way. But our teacher didn't share my creative viewpoint. "I said *follow* the lines, Diane!"

At recess, when I approached a group of kids to play, they all circled me, chanting:

She's got eyes as big as the world,
She's got eyes as big as the world,

Skinny! Skinny!
She's got eyes as big as the world,
Retard! Retard!
She's got eyes as big as the world,
Freak, freak! Retard!

I was stunned. I went home that afternoon in a daze, thinking about that horrible word: retard. Retards were weirdos who were kept hidden away. They were people from whom you ran away if you saw them on the street.

And that's what the kids at school thought I was: a "retard." I just couldn't get over it; I walked up the stairs into the house, flopped down on the couch, and just lay there. After a while, Mom came home.

"What's the matter, Diane?" she asked, hugging me.

"Nothing."

"How was school? Did you like it?"

"It was fine, Mom."

She knew something was wrong, but she couldn't get a word out of me. I was too ashamed about being called a "retard." At the time, I was just a kid who had been told she was different from the others, and being different was obviously something very bad. It would be years before I figured out that the word was a label people use to describe someone whom they consider less than normal. It would be years before I realized that "normal" was not quite the exalted state it was cracked up to be. It would be years before I realized that children use words like "freak" and "retard" to describe anyone who doesn't quite fit into their accepted pattern of appearance or behavior: someone who is skinnier than the others, or fatter, even someone who chooses a black crayon for a drawing (rather than a red or blue one) and then has the nerve to color outside the lines everyone else is following.

Not only was I an outcast amongst my peers, but I had academic problems as well. At school, it was, "Diane Thornton, the number one goes here, the number two goes there, and the number three goes over here," as our teacher pointed to three spaces next to each other on the blackboard. "Now, come up here and put the numbers in their places. Right now! Do you hear me, Diane?" I obediently trotted up to the board and promptly put all three numbers in one space. Sister screamed at me and the kids laughed. After school, their taunts and jeers were waiting for me again.

Later in the year, the school held a parent-teacher evening, and Sister brought out one of my arithmetic tests to show Mom and Dad. There had been 22 questions on the test, and I had made 20 mistakes. Mom and Dad kept saying, "Diane, look at all these mistakes. What's wrong with you?" Sister kept saying, "Yes, Diane, what's wrong? Please tell us; we can't help you if you don't tell us what's wrong."

All I could think was: What about the two answers I got right? Why doesn't anybody talk about them?

Maybe if I had spoken those thoughts it might have helped. But I couldn't tell them — or maybe I didn't know how to tell them — that they were hurting me by talking only about what I'd done wrong and not even mentioning my right answers, even though there were only two.

I just shut off. At school, and at home, if anyone asked me about failing a test, I went silent. "Diane, why can't you get good marks like your cousins?" Mom or Dad would ask me.

Silence.

The whole idea of failure turned me to ice. It was bad, like being called "retard."

But in the inner world I had created, I could be anything I wanted, and my favorite personality was the Lone Ranger. If I failed a test and got scolded or punished, if the kids made fun of me after school, I just climbed on my imaginary horse, Silver, and galloped all the way home, shouting, "Hi-yo, Silver!" I imagined going after bank robbers, or saving a whole town from the bad guys.

Some people might say I was avoiding the painfulness of reality by withdrawing from it. But there was something more to my ability to live in my imagination. I knew it, and so did my parents. Despite their disappointment in my schoolwork, they sensed that my daydreams weren't only an escape. They were part of me, and probably always would be. "You're just like your father," Mom said. "A dreamer." That was true; Dad was the one who created magic out of paper and paints.

The Christmas I was six, Mom gave me what was to be the greatest gift of my life, although I didn't know it at the time. I only knew that it was something none of the other kids had, something with which I could indulge my favorite pastime: playing make-believe. It was a puppet theatre.

The theatre was made of cardboard, and there were only three puppets — Punch, Judy, and Elsie the Cow — but it became all my dreams rolled into one. Being behind that theatre was like being inside my imagination. I could summon anyone I wanted. I could make people cry at the sight of Punch hitting Judy; I could make them laugh at Elsie the Cow dancing to the Sleeping Beauty music from my Walt Disney record; I could make them cheer and applaud. As awful as it was to be different in the eyes of the kids at school, it was wonderful to be different in the eyes of an audience. They loved it. They loved *me.*

I put on shows in the backyard for my cousins and the kids on the block. I put on shows for Mom and Dad; shows for all the relatives when there was a party at our house; and shows just for myself, in the basement, with only a dim light shining as I turned on the record player and made all the puppets dance to the beautiful words of a Disney song:

When you wish upon a star,
Makes no difference who you are . . .

Mom helped me in other ways, too. For example, she became president of the Parent-Teacher Association at our school. Everyone loved the parties she organized, and she always looked beautiful, wearing a hat that set off her large, expressive eyes, presiding over the huge silver teapot. My classmates even gave up tormenting me on the days of those parties, and I think that's why Mom got involved in the PTA in the first place.

Eventually, I discovered that I wasn't a failure at everything in school — just most things. I finally started to follow the lines when coloring, and I was very good at reading aloud. As I read to the class about Dick and Jane, I became those characters; they came to life from the pages of the book, and even my teacher was impressed.

But I never made friends at school in the first few years. Mom's tea parties at school, the readings in class — none of it worked. The kids took notice of me for a moment, but that never extended to a friendship.

Luckily, I already had a best friend: my brother, Robert.

From the day Mom brought him home — I had just turned four — I loved that kid. I remember holding him in my arms and feeding him his bottle. I was never jealous of him for being the baby and getting more attention from Mom and Dad. As soon as he was old enough to play, we became inseparable friends. Sometimes we spent whole days in the nearby ravine, where I made a broom of leaves and branches, swept the path, and made a little house.

It was with Robert that I discovered my latent talent as an orchestrator. I was a choir girl; my friend Horst was an altar boy; and Robert felt excluded. "I wish I could be an altar boy, too," he told me one day. Suddenly, I was transformed into a little business negotiator. I knew I could get that gig for Robert. I started, like any sensible theatrical agent, by bolstering my client's ego. One day I took Robert to St. Joseph's Chapel, near our house. During the Mass, I pointed to one of the altar boys assisting the priest and whispered, "You should be up there, Robert. You'd do a much better job than that kid."

"Yeah!" replied Robert. "So what should I do?"

Well, get yourself backstage, of course! "Robert," I said, "you go back there and tell the priest you want to be an altar boy."

"I'm scared! You come with me!"

I took Robert by the hand, led him to the vestry, and implored the priest to accept him: "My little brother is very shy, but he wants to be an altar boy more than anything in the world." Robert won the audition; the priest took him on and started giving him instruction. In the interval, the priest was appointed to a new church, and his first day on the job happened to coincide with Robert's debut; consequently, there was a full house of parishioners, curious about their new priest.

I remember sitting in the front pew, biting my nails — the nervous agent hoping her protégé's first show would be a hit. There he is, looking so solemn . . . . Now the priest is praying, and Robert is supposed to pick up that big book, the Epistle. And move it from the left side of the altar to the right side . . . . What's he doing? He's just standing there, frozen! He's got stage fright! Come on, Robert, pick up that book! Oh, good, the priest is whispering in his ear. . . . He's going to pick up the book now. . . . Oh, no! It's too heavy for him! He's going to drop it! He's going to . . .

Crash!!!

That was Robert's less than auspicious debut as an altar boy. Unlike the theatre, which is cruelly unforgiving of mistakes, the clergy is much more understanding — especially of weeping young altar boys begging for another chance. Robert kept his job, got over his stage fright, and became a wonderful altar boy.

Another time, my classmates and I were lined up for confession. Everybody was whispering in line: We all knew you were supposed to say what you'd done wrong, but nobody could figure out exactly what to say. "I know what to do," I said, and they all turned around. "You go in and tell the priest you stole seven pencils from the office, and I'll tell him I took five paper clips, and you say you got a whole box of chalk from Sister's desk, and . . ."

They took my advice; the priest told them to say seven Hail Marys (eight for the one who supposedly took the chalk) and that was that!

But I still didn't make any friends at school, and, worse than that, my marks were slipping lower and lower. Finally, disaster struck: I failed Grade Three. The comments I got from my cousins were bad — "How could you *do* that, Diane?" And the spanking I got from Dad was worse. But worst of all was the news that I was going to repeat Grade Three at a private school, Loretto Academy. It sounded like prison. And I was sure that, if the kids at Sacred Heart had made my life miserable, they would be that much meaner at a private school — especially since I was going to be a year behind the other nine-year-olds.

I couldn't have been more wrong.

The first day I arrived at Loretto, I stopped outside the school to dismount from Silver. "Good boy! Good boy!" I told him, patting his nose.

"Who are you talking to, dear?"

I turned around, startled, and saw one of the nuns standing there. Uh-oh. Now I'm going to get it, I thought. But I was wrong; she was smiling. I decided to give it a chance.

"Um . . . this is my horse, Silver."

"That's wonderful! So you must be the Lone Ranger," she said. "I'm Mother Bertillo. What's your other name?"

"Diane Thornton, Mother."

"All right, Diane, now here's what we're going to do," she said, and her whole face lit up with that lovely smile. "We're going to take Silver over here and tie him to this tree while you come inside with me and do your studies, and he'll be right here when you get out of school."

I just couldn't believe it! Mother Bertillo wasn't going to give me a lecture about making up stories. Right from the beginning, she respected that I was a dreamer and needed my dreams.

It was as if I were starting school all over again, but this time everything was different. Mother Bertillo made everything fascinating — even arithmetic! I loved her stories about Jesus and the saints because they were so magical. She helped us to imagine St. Francis talking to the animals, St. Patrick taming the snakes, and Jesus breaking the bread and fishes to feed hundreds of hungry people with leftovers. Even the sad stories were beautiful — Joan of Arc; Jesus falling beneath the cross three times — because Mother Bertillo never tried to frighten us. She explained things in such a way that we understood that sometimes you have to suffer for something in which you believe.

Because of Mother Bertillo's imaginative teaching, and the small size of the classes, I started to do much better in school. I even started to make friends, especially the twins, Susan and Kitty. They didn't look a bit like twins; in fact, they were so unalike that it was hard to even see them as sisters. Susan was tall, thin and red-haired with lots of freckles, while Kitty was a short, plump brunette. Susan was always tidy and got good grades. But Kitty didn't do well in school, and she was always getting her face dirty and her hair tangled at recess. I liked them both, because they were so different, and we spent a lot of time together.

Everything was going well in my life; so well that I didn't even notice the threatening clouds on the horizon — until the storm hit.

In the winter of 1958, Robert and I began to notice that Dad was spending more and more time at his shop or on out-of-town trips, as Mom called them. One terrible night, I awoke from a nightmare and ran downstairs. The front door was open, and I could see Dad in a car with a strange woman. They were kissing.

For months Mom and Dad continued trying to behave as if nothing was wrong, but by spring Dad wasn't even coming home on weekends. Sometimes Robert and I awoke late at night to hear Mom crying. Finally, in September — just after I started Grade Four — they separated.

From the moment she and Dad split up, Mom became father, mother, and provider — with a vengeance. She left for work early, came home late, and still managed to cook us wonderful meals, keep the house spotless, create fabulous costumes for our parties, and treat us to the most magical birthdays any child could imagine.

Since Robert and I had birthdays only two days apart, we often had double birthday parties, and one of the most memorable was the year I turned eleven and Robert, seven. Mom threw a surprise party for us and invited all our classmates and friends on a hayride out in the country. There was a huge cake with about twelve layers; there was a barbecue with foot-long hot dogs. And in the evening, there was singing in front of the campfire. I got all my favorite books: a huge pile of Nancy Drew mysteries (Nancy Drew had joined the Lone Ranger as my ideal in crime-fighting excellence).

Mom had a great job as manager of Beube's, Hamilton's most exclusive sportswear shop, but whenever she had an opportunity to make some extra money she jumped at the chance. There had been a man coming into Beube's to clean and wax the floors at night. Mom took over his job, and I remember sometimes waiting for her while she was doing the floors. We sat on a sofa in the main salon as she laid down the heavy coats of wax and then, tiptoeing along the narrow carpet that flanked the room, we carefully made our way out of the store. Mom made it seem like a game, and she had the same attitude when she started to do all the alterations in the store herself instead of hiring a seamstress. The workload was so heavy that she was often up past midnight, hemming a skirt or altering the waistline of a dress, but she made us believe that she was having a great time. She never once said to us, "Do you know how hard I have to work to get you these gifts?"

I'm afraid Robert and I took terrible advantage of her at times, playing our pranks and getting into our scrapes. She once scolded us for burning a hole in the living room rug after setting a heap of newspapers on fire during a game of cowboys and Indians. We were upset that she yelled at us but we didn't realize what it was going to cost to get that rug repaired. Mom didn't put it to us that way; she just let us know what we had done was wrong, without laying on any additional burden of guilt.

But doing something wrong while I was with Dad was an entirely different matter. When Robert and I went to his shop, we had to show him our homework. I was still doing fairly well in school at that point, thanks to Mother Bertillo's influence, but I did have my weak areas, especially spelling. Robert, on the other hand, made almost no mistakes in any of his subjects, so the brunt of Dad's particular method of discipline always fell on me. Over and over, he made me spell out correctly the words I had gotten wrong, with a smack of his metal ruler on my hand at the sound of each letter: *R* (whack!) *E* (whack!) *C* (whack!) *E* (whack!) *I* (whack!) and so on, until I had spelled "received" to his satisfaction.

I hated being hit like that, but I loved Dad; Robert and I both loved him and wanted to see him as much as we could. Mom made it clear that we could see Dad whenever we wanted. I lived for the mornings Dad said to me, "You're going to be a winner, Pumpkin!" And I lived for the afternoons he took Robert and me down to the TH&B Railway: "Do you know what TH&B stands for, Pumpkin? Tramps, Hobos and Bums!" We laughed and laughed all the way to the soda fountain, where Dad treated us to giant milkshakes and hamburgers. One time, he even built us a model railway, complete with hills and bridges for the trains, and on it was a huge sign: TRAMPS, HOBOS AND BUMS RAILWAY.

Dad took us swimming, too, every Saturday from 6 to 10 P.M. at the Hamilton YMCA. I don't think we spent more than 30 seconds out of the water during the entire four hours, and when we reluctantly hauled ourselves out of the pool, our fingers were wrinkled like prunes and our eyes were the color of ripe cherries from all the chlorine. But we didn't care; we would have stayed till midnight if we had been allowed. After the swim, Dad always walked right to our front door, but he didn't come inside.

Both my brother and I dreamed of a time when Dad would come back and live with us. In fact, we even tried to make it happen. The Christmas after he and Mom separated, we decided that if we got Dad an extra special gift, he might come home. "Here's what we're going to do, Robert," I said, and Robert got a suspicious look on his face, as if he knew that when I said "we," it meant I was going to come up with the idea and he was going to carry it out.

"We're going to take this cup," I continued, pulling a bronze mug out of the china cabinet, "and go around to all our neighbors and tell everyone that you want to sing a Christmas carol for them."

"But I don't *want* to sing by myself. Why don't you sing, too?" he asked.

"Oh, but Robert," I argued, "it's going to break their hearts when they see a little boy singing in the living room all by himself, and they'll give us enough money to get something really nice for Dad so he'll come home."

Robert gave in at that bit of emotional blackmail, and we agreed to set out on our fund-raising campaign that very evening. At the first door, the lady told us to come back later because she had guests in the house. "Oh please," I begged, "my brother really wants to sing for you, and it'll only take a second."

"All right, Diane," she said, ushering us into the living room. There were six people sitting on sofas sipping tea, and as Robert stood in the center of the room with the mug clutched in his hand, they all went quiet. For some reason, this struck me as incredibly funny, and I started giggling just as Robert began to sing.

"Silent . . . teeheehee . . . night." Now Robert was laughing, too. "Holy . . . heeheehee . . . night," he warbled, all the way through the first verse of the carol. There wasn't a second verse. The lady quickly bundled us out of there, sticking a five-dollar bill into the mug as we scooted.

Robert was terribly embarrassed, but I remember throwing myself down in the snow and rolling around with delight, shouting, "We got the money! We got the money!" We bought Dad a beautiful silk tie, and he loved it. But he didn't come home.

When I realized that even a great present wasn't going to bring Dad back to us, it was as if I had just lost the most important part of my life. It was a deep hurt which I felt nothing could ever heal, and it was an awful emptiness I would spend my whole life trying to fill.

When my marks started slipping again, in Grade Five, there were more slaps on the hand with the ruler from Dad. And even worse than that was the verbal punishment. He would yell at me, tell me I was stupid, and predict that I would never amount to anything.

So I retreated within myself again; now fantasies once again became my refuge. There had been a few months when I hadn't even bothered to bring Silver to school with me — the kids at Loretto hadn't teased me, so I hadn't needed a quick getaway — but now I needed him again. And if it wasn't the Lone Ranger and Silver, it was my puppets.

But reality was about to bring change into my life — in the form of an adventure. Mom had been doing so much sewing in her job at Beube's that she decided to go into business for herself. In less than a month she rented a store, got a bank loan — with the help of the store owner, who also gave her six months' free rent — and opened Fashion Court, just after Christmas of 1959.

It didn't take Mom long to turn Fashion Court into a thriving business: Hamilton's first haute couture salon. She worked like crazy — ten, twelve hours a day — fixing up the store, designing everything from tailored suits to evening gowns, and sewing far into the night to keep up with the demands from a growing number of clients. Eventually, her fashions became so popular that she had to hire some staff.

Her energy was boundless, and today, at 73, she's the same way. She'll put in a nine-hour day designing costumes and props at the Famous People Players warehouse and then spend the evening making dresses for my daughters to wear to a party. When she makes up her mind to accomplish something, there is absolutely nothing that will stand in her way.

It was the spring of 1960 and I was eleven years old when Mom realized she could no longer afford to maintain both a home and a business. She decided to rent out the house, which Dad had agreed she should have after their separation, and moved us all into a big, airy flat over the Fashion Court building.

Moving day was sad. It was hard for Robert and me to leave our enchanted house in the ravine with all its hiding places. It was particularly hard for me to give up my magical retreat in the basement, where I had spent so many hours conjuring my favorite daydreams of fame and fortune.

But perhaps it turned out for the best. Although I would never forget our house and our street, I was leaving behind a lot of trouble and pain along with the happier memories. And if my attraction to the world of fantasy was something I needed in my life, I also needed more of a direct involvement with the real world — with people — and living above Fashion Court certainly gave me that.

Mom made our new home look stunning: a huge, open-concept room divided into kitchen, living room, and sleeping areas. There was black-and-gold straw paper on the walls, black lacquer on the window seats, and a high-gloss black floor set off by a thick white carpet. It wasn't like any of my friends' houses, and that's why I liked it so much. It made me feel special, unique. And I really needed that feeling.

The summer was wonderful. My friend Susan and I were nuts about movies and musicals. We went to the Palace and the Capitol, which really were like palaces, with ornate balconies all in red-and-gold plush, frescoes of angels and cherubs, and heavy velvet curtains. We would sit there before the curtains rose and pretend we were the visiting royalty, waving our arms regally as if to say, "Let the show begin!"

I loved all the movies: the biblical films like *The Robe* and *The Ten Commandments*, the Westerns (the heroes all reminded me of the Lone Ranger) and the Doris Day movies because she was so beautiful with her blonde hair and her peaches-and-cream complexion. But my very favorite was Audrey Hepburn. I wanted to go away to finishing school, the way she did in *Sabrina*, and then return to marry Humphrey Bogart. I especially identified with Holly Golightly in *Breakfast At Tiffany's*. For years I imagined having a cat called Cat and an apartment with a bathtub sawed in half. And I even used to get up early on Saturday to practise stretching my neck so I would look more like Audrey Hepburn.

Even more than the movies, I adored musicals, which were very popular; the touring companies of the Broadway productions often came through Hamilton. Susan and I used to run through the flat pretending to be Judy Holliday in *Bells Are Ringing*, or the sailors in *South Pacific*. We sang at the top of our lungs: "There ain't nothing like a dame!" or my favorite, "Honeybunch, tall and thin . . ."

When Mom heard me singing, she thought I was so good that she took me down to a Hamilton theatre company to audition for its production of *The Flower Drum Song*, which calls for a few children in bit parts. There were hundreds of kids with their mothers, and I was amazed when I was chosen to go into the finals.

Only ten of us left! I put my whole heart into my rendition of "Honeybunch," but I didn't get a part, and I was too disappointed to even cry. Mom kept telling me there would be other chances, and reminding me how well I had done to get all the way to the finals, but I just couldn't see it that way. To me, it was the monster again — failure — and that was the end of my aspiring career as a singer-actress.

For a few weeks, I even stopped going to the movies, and delved into books instead. I had graduated from Nancy Drew mysteries to anything and everything by Robert Louis Stevenson, because he wrote about pirates and adventures at sea. (I think I reread *Treasure Island* three times!) Since I wasn't going to be a singer on Broadway (and if, by some quirk of fate, I didn't grow up to become the Lone Ranger or a detective like Nancy Drew), perhaps I would have an illustrious future as a pirate.

But my abrupt change in career planning didn't keep me away from the movies for long, especially with the first "Gidget" movies coming to Hamilton that summer, with Sandra Dee and Cliff Robertson, who played the supercool surfing bum, the Great Kahuna. Susan and I were both madly in love with Cliff Robertson, and I've got to admit I felt a little flutter when I finally met him recently. He was even better looking than I remember him in the movies!

It was the best summer ever, but as I started Grade Six, I realized there were going to be problems again — with my schoolwork. I tried to memorize the spelling rules and the long division tables, but they just wouldn't stay in my head. They weren't at all like the words to a Broadway song or the great speech Holly's boyfriend makes at the end of *Breakfast At Tiffany's.* He tells her that everywhere she goes, she builds a barrier around herself — and everywhere she goes, she only bumps into herself. That made a lot more sense to me than how to divide 7,000 by 39.

The worse my marks got, the more Dad lost his temper; and the angrier he became, the more poorly I did in school. It was a vicious circle, and the situation got even worse when Dad began drinking heavily. Sometimes I could even smell liquor on his breath when Robert and I went to see him in the morning: He was becoming an alcoholic. I became afraid to go and see him because he was always flying into such a rage about my bad homework. One day, just to avoid being the one who got into all the trouble, I told Dad that Robert had punched Susan while she and I were playing (omitting that Susan and I provoked Robert by mocking him and refusing to let him join our game, as we were doing more and more that year).

Dad grabbed my brother by the arm with such force that I thought his tiny elbow would be wrenched from the socket. Then he started hitting Robert so hard that I was afraid he would kill him. "That'll teach you to go around punching people!" he bellowed.

Crying and screaming, I begged Dad, "Please don't hurt my brother!" He finally let us go, and I took Robert home to change his clothes. Luckily, Mom wasn't home, and neither of us ever told her about it.

I was still crying when I got to school, and my whole face had broken out in a rash. The instant Mother Bertillo saw me, she put her arms around me and took me into the chapel to ask what was wrong. I found myself blurting out everything about Dad's drinking and the frightening way he was behaving. I even told her I felt at fault for what Dad had done to Robert. Mother Bertillo hugged and consoled me. She told me I was not to blame and she explained that Dad was a very troubled man who needed help and prayer to realize he had a problem. She was so kind and understanding that I started to feel better.

But my marks didn't improve accordingly: I failed Grade Six. On the last day of school, there was a special concert in the auditorium, and I had been asked to do a recitation. I picked a poem called *Beautiful Things* from our school reader: The words described what makes life worth living — the beauties of nature, the love of friends and family — and my life had been such a roller coaster after my parents' separation that I poured all my volatile emotions into that reading.

At the end, there was a tremendous ovation, and, as I left the stage, Mother Bertillo took me in her arms and hugged me. "Diane, I saw a great talent emerge in you when you were on that stage," she said. "But now I have to do something that's really going to hurt you. I have to fail you." Another grade I had failed: My heart fell. It was painful to find out about it that way, but I never held a grudge against Mother Bertillo because I loved her so much.

Since my mother couldn't afford to send me back to Loretto for another year, the following year brought yet another school — St. Patrick's — and another collection of bullies, who followed me home almost every day, tripping me and hitting me whenever they caught up. But, just as the kids at Sacred Heart had stopped picking on me when I read stories aloud in class, the bullies eased off when I got to Grade Seven and gave a puppet show to the class.

Punch and Judy were a great hit with my class — especially the violence:

"Oh, Punch, how could you do this to me and the baby? I hate you! I hate you!"

"Judy, Judy, Judy, I'm getting tired, Judy, Judy. Bring me my dinner or else . . ."

"Or else what?"

I brought their heads together to signal the start of the battle, as the kids let out a tremendous cheer.

I didn't mind the bullies anymore because they were applauding me. I felt happy to be making others happy. But I didn't do any more puppet shows at school.

Soon after the show, I packed Punch and Judy away in their theatre and put them in a box under my bed: I was starting to feel that puppets might be a bit childish. But I never threw them away. I knew that, someday, I would want them again: the seed was planted. Not only does being a performer give people happiness; it gives the performer respect for himself as well.

One day, when I was at Mass with my classmates, I suddenly noticed that the priest's voice was hardly audible; when I went to receive Communion, I took huge steps because the floor seemed to be going uphill.

I thought the horrible sensation would pass, but it just got worse. Miss Thompson began a lesson, and I heard her very faintly call my name. "Something's wrong with the floor!" I said, starting to cry, and the echoes of the kids' laughter reached me as if from a great distance. I couldn't explain what was wrong, so I sat down, and Miss Thompson went on with the class.

At lunchtime, I walked home — very slowly because of all the ripples in the sidewalk — and went into the kitchen. Maybe I'm just hungry, I thought, and I poured myself a huge bowl of Wheat Chex. Then the nausea hit me in huge waves; I began vomiting, and the next thing I knew, I was in bed. The doctor was in the room, talking to my mother. I could hardly make out what he was saying, but it was something about a virus in my inner ear that had affected my balance. For two weeks I lay in bed trying not to move: With the slightest turn of my head, the room would start spinning. Finally, one morning, I heard something pop in my right ear and all the sound came back.

But I never did recover the use of my left ear; the virus had caused nerve damage. I've learned to compensate for it — I turn my right side toward people when they're talking to me — but

I'm terrified that something might happen to my right ear because then I'd be completely deaf.

Shortly after my illness, I received another shock to my equilibrium, this time an emotional rather than a physical blow. Mom told Robert and me that we couldn't visit Dad anymore — he was moving to Arizona.

Some people might say the move was a blessing, given the way he had been treating us. But emotion has a way of destroying the most logical argument. I couldn't feel relieved that Dad was going away. Despite the abuse to which he had subjected us, there had also been good times. When Dad wasn't drinking, he was more fun than anyone in the world. I loved him, and I knew I would miss him terribly.

Other than the puppet show, my two years at St. Patrick's had been dismal. I had been indifferent to what was going on in the classroom, vulnerable to the mockery of bullies, withdrawn in my behavior. But something happened in Grade Eight to bring out the fight in me.

One of our classmates had epilepsy, and she sometimes had seizures in the middle of a lesson. She collapsed on the floor, her body writhing until her skirt tangled around her shoulders, her underwear revealed. The kids always laughed, and the very first time I heard the laughter, I couldn't stand it. I jumped to my feet and yelled, "Stop laughing at her! There's nothing funny about it at all!"

I didn't care that they turned on me because of my outburst; I didn't even care that they called me "fink" the time I ran to get our teacher, who was out of the classroom, and told him the kids had been ridiculing her again. I had great difficulty defending myself against them, but it seemed natural to protest their treatment of someone else.

The real change came when I went to Central, a huge high school with more than 1,000 students. Grade Nine marked the beginning of a tremendous shift in my personality. I became much more assertive, self-confident, and rebellious. At Central, my schoolwork was worse than ever, but I just didn't care anymore. If a teacher said, "You know, Diane, you're going to fail if you persist in this attitude," I would just shrug. My attitude did not endear me to the teachers. But the other kids thought I was really cool, and I began to see that, since I clearly wasn't going to be a major force as a student, I could exert influence in other ways.

For example, I became a big organizer for school parties and dances. I had a great time putting together the decorations and helping to choose the music for all the functions at Central. My best friend Joan and I were the best dancers in the school. We even started dancing outside school. In our corduroy outfits adorned with treble clefs, made by Mom, and white dancing boots, we went to the Hamilton shopping malls and convinced the rock bands who played there on Saturdays to let us dance as part of their show.

When it came to my subjects, I majored in detention. One day I was to read aloud a history report about Ponce de León, who had supposedly discovered the Fountain of Youth. I had enjoyed reading a book about him, but I had nothing written. So I just made it up, pretending I was reading from the blank sheets of paper in my hand.

"I am truly impressed, Diane," said Mr. Wong, our teacher. "I never expected anything of this quality from you. Please, read it to the class again."

I was lost. There was no way I could repeat what I had just invented, so it was another detention and another failing grade. But now that I was a social success at school, the failures became meaningless to me. And when I flunked Grade Nine, I made up my mind never to go back. Mom tried to talk me out of my decision, but it was like arguing with a brick wall. When I was 16, my formal education was over, and I felt free. I took a number of odd jobs and eventually became a salesclerk in the bra department at Eaton's.

The independence was wonderful — at least, as much independence as $49.00 a week would buy me — but something was missing in my life. I hadn't seen my father — or even exchanged a letter with him — since he had moved to Arizona five years before, and, the year I left school, I decided to visit him for a week.

The tall man waving from behind the velvet-roped barrier in the arrival lounge at Phoenix Airport was slightly balding and a little bit pudgy around the middle, but, to me, he was the handsomest man in the world. Clutching my suitcase, I raced toward him, nearly knocking over the barricade in my eagerness to reach him.

"Dad!" I threw my arms around him, dropping the suitcase in the path of two elderly women.

Dad bent to pick up the bag, flashing his sunniest smile. "I'm so sorry, ladies," he said contritely, "but, you see, this is my daughter who's come all the way from Canada to see me, so I hope you'll excuse our exuberance."

"Oh, how nice!" they clucked, completely disarmed.

In that brief exchange, any doubts about seeing my father were banished. Dad was clearly his old self again: charming, articulate, full of life — and, most of all, delighted to see me!

"Let's have a look at you, Pumpkin," he said. "Wait a second; you're too grown up to be called Pumpkin anymore. The pumpkin has turned into a princess." His happy laugh rang out like bells. "Eh, Miss Priss?" And that became my new nickname, a sort of secret code between us, because only we knew that Miss Priss meant Princess.

"Oh, Dad, I'm so happy to see you!" Tears of joy welled in my eyes.

"Now, now, none of that," he said, leading the way to his car. "We're going to have a great time!"

Dad's promise was an understatement: It was the best week of my life. We went to Tombstone, which felt like walking into every Western movie I had ever seen. All the streets and buildings had been carefully preserved in 19th-century style: the old post office, the general store, the stagecoach. There were women walking around in long dresses, and men in full cowboy gear, complete with ten-gallon hats and string ties. There was even a re-creation of the legendary shootout at the O.K. Corral, just like a scene from *High Noon*, the Earp brothers and Doc Holliday versus Ike Clanton, Sheriff Behan, Kid Claiborne and the McLowry clan.

And we wandered through the desert, where tumbleweeds blew like ghosts across the path of the car, where stubbly sagebrush pierced the flatness that seemed to go on forever. Every once in a while, we stopped at a little watering hole; there was even one saloon, near Tucson, where the spittoon was obviously still in working order, and where the bartender still slid the icy glasses of beer down the length of the long mahogany bar. "Drinks on the house!" Dad commanded, and everyone in the bar cheered. "This here's Miss Priss, all the way from Canada, and we're off to see the world together!"

I fell in love with Arizona — the incredible beauty of vermilion stone against azure sky in Red Rock Canyon; the barren goldness of the desert; the cool, dark green of the mountains. Exploring it with Dad was a dream come true; it was as if I were *really* the Lone Ranger, only now there were two of us.

The best part was when we finally reached the Grand Canyon. Open-mouthed in wonder, I gazed for the first time on the splendor of an endless expanse of jutting rock disappearing into the horizon and soaring a mile or more into the clouds. "It really is God's country, Dad," I said. "It's a miracle."

Dad was silent for a moment, and there was a contemplative look on his face, as if he were searching for just the right words. "I don't know if you realize how much I've missed you, Diane," he finally said, his eyes full of tenderness. "You and Robert are the most important people in my life, and I hope you believe me; I never meant for the trouble between your mother and me to hurt either of you."

My trip was so idyllic that, when I returned home, my job at Eaton's seemed pretty boring by comparison. My sales dropped off, and finally — just before Christmas — I was given two weeks' notice. It seemed a sign, so I wrote to Dad, and asked him if I could come and live with him permanently. The answer was yes, and despite Mom's protests, I set out for Phoenix early in 1967.

But nothing was the same when I went to live with Dad. He was drinking again and he had moved from a comfortable house to a small, run-down apartment behind his shop in a rough neighborhood. As he drank more and more, he began ignoring his work and taking out his frustration and unhappiness on me. Curses, punches, and kicks became the norm.

When his abuses became too much to bear I got a job in Phoenix and moved out, taking an apartment with another girl. One afternoon, Dad called me at work, asking me for $50.00.

"I haven't got any extra money, Dad," I protested.

"Either I get that money," he said coldly, "or the immigration authorities will be informed that you're working in this country illegally." With that, he hung up. I scraped together the money, but the following week he wanted $60.00. I was too terrified to argue with him, even when I was forced to leave the apartment for lack of rent money. Luckily for me, my roommate sent me to a group of her friends, who let me live in their house for free. When I thought I'd worn out my welcome, I moved to another place, and another. Everywhere I went, people put a roof over my head and shared their food with me: I'll never forget their generosity.

Strangely enough, it wasn't Dad's incessant demands for money that finally drove me out of Phoenix and back home. Just before Christmas, I was called to the security room of the store. There was money missing from the till: Had I taken it? "No," I answered, surprised. The supervisor told me a lie-detector test would prove my innocence, and I agreed to submit to it. After all, I had nothing to hide.

I was left alone in the room with a polygraph operator who hooked me up to some wires and asked me a few questions. When it was over, I jumped to my feet, saying, "See? I didn't take the money!" He just shook his head and showed me the ascending lines on the graph.

"I would never steal from anyone!" I sobbed. "All these months I've been giving my father money, and I never had anything left for myself. But I never stole anything, no matter how bad things got." Tears streamed down my face. "Don't you believe me?"

"Yes, I do believe you," he said. When the supervisor came back into the room, he repeated his belief in my innocence, adding that a lie-detector test is not always accurate. But the supervisor didn't agree and ordered me to leave the store immediately.

I grabbed my purse and ran out of the building, still crying with shame and anger, and marched straight over to the immigration center in the main government building. There, I confessed everything. I wasn't thrown in jail, but I was given 120 days to go back to Canada.

I'm not sure why I didn't go home immediately — I must have had some sort of emotional breakdown. I don't remember much of anything during the months that followed. All I recall is that my friends took care of me and let me stay with them as long as I wanted.

One afternoon, early in May, I suddenly realized that I belonged back in Hamilton. I called Mom and told her I was coming home.

Birth of a Dream

MAY 1968 - JUNE 1974

Things had changed while I was away. Mom had sold Fashion Court and was now working at Creed's, one of Toronto's most exclusive fashion centers. She welcomed me to her new house with open arms. It was smaller than our old place, but Mom's artistic touches made it lovely, with inviting sofas and chairs and perfectly co-ordinated drapes and carpets. And for me, a wonderful little room all done in bright colors.

I was happy to be home, but I felt disjointed; it was as if all the spirit had gone out of me. Here I was, twenty years old, a high school dropout with no boyfriend, no job, no prospects for the future. I spent several weeks feeling good and sorry for myself.

One afternoon, as I was looking for a pair of shoes in the hall closet, I tripped over a piece of cardboard. It was my puppet theatre! And, in a box next to the theatre, were my old friends Punch and Judy. The old puppet theatre was too small for my body — I hadn't used it since I was fourteen — and I wondered if Mom might have some ideas about making a new one. Maybe I could even put on some shows in a shopping mall. By the time Mom came home I was already rehearsing. Mom was so happy to see me interested in something again that she threw herself into my new project with all the enthusiasm of a New York impresario.

She designed the new puppet theatre to come apart into sections that would fit into her Volkswagen Beetle, and she found a carpenter to build it. When the theatre was ready, she painted big, wild flowers on it and a sign at the top — LOVE — in huge letters. Gradually, she helped me add to my puppet collection: a dog, a crow, a witch doctor, a mouse, and a swan. Then came a Mountie and a uniformed policeman I could use to arrest Punch after he beat up Judy. Mom added her own touches: big mustachio for the policeman; extra feathers for the swan; a fluffy brown fur coat for the dog; even a new scarlet uniform for the Mountie, complete with gold braid and brass buttons. Then she encouraged me to find an agent who would book shows for me in shopping centers and at birthday parties. When I went to get my picture taken for the agent's files, Mom even designed a new hairstyle for me — long, but swept back off my forehead.

When it came time for my first show, at a shopping center in Ancaster, Mom drove me there and back and cheered every one of my six shows. For this debut performance as a professional puppeteer, I played Bobby Vinton's "Mr. Lonely" on my old phonograph and had the fluffy brown dog act out the title part. The kids loved the sight of the mournful little dog, hanging his head in sorrow, and for each show the crowd got bigger. I was impressed by all the attention; by all the applause and money, too. Seventy-five dollars seemed a fortune to me, especially since it was for doing something I loved. I didn't say anything to Mom on the way home afterward, but I silently thanked her for helping me to pick up the pieces and start feeling whole again.

My little business was slow getting off the ground. I only had a few bookings at parties and in malls that summer. So I decided to get a regular job in a department store in Hamilton.

One day, just before lunch, a petite, friendly-looking, dark-haired girl about my own age came in looking for a bra. We started chatting, and it was one of those rare first meetings when you feel you've known the person all your life. That's the way it was with Judi Schwartz: we became friends instantly. Today, eighteen years later, we're still best friends.

As for the job, I was fired within a month. I convinced Judi to take a week's vacation with me in Arizona, but I never once mentioned my father. And when we returned from Phoenix, I was determined not to sit around pitying myself as I had done before: I immediately went to Toronto and got myself a job at the Holt Renfrew department store downtown.

However, I knew I wasn't going to find fulfillment in the belt department at Holt Renfrew. I lasted a year in the job, but my sales were never high, and, in the spring of 1970, I was first in line for a series of layoffs at the store. The day I left, I got on the phone to the promotions manager at Eaton's, urging him to hire me to perform with my puppets in the toy department. By noon I was in his office, and by 2 P.M. I had a job.

Of course, it wasn't a full-time job, just three days of shows during the store's Easter sales. I was afraid Mom would be upset, but she turned out to be my biggest fan. After watching most of my shows at Eaton's, she became my chief ally in a plan to expand my puppetry career.

I had my eye on the Canadian National Exhibition, but I thought I needed something a bit more contemporary to capture the attention of the "Ex" crowd. At the time, the newspapers were full of stories about Prime Minister Trudeau's not-so-secret dates with Barbra Streisand in New York, and I thought the two of them would make great subjects for a puppet skit. Mom designed the puppets' costumes: Trudeau had a magnificent burgundy velvet smoking jacket (and, of course, a rose for his lapel) and Streisand was all decked out in a sailor outfit, like the one she wore in *Don't Rain On My Parade*. The song I chose was "Lover Come Back To Me," and, after I had rehearsed it until I was seeing it in my sleep, I wangled an audition with David Garrick, the manager of the CNE.

Mr. Garrick almost fell out of his seat laughing, and I was hired: sixteen shows a day for three weeks, and the whopping sum of $500.00, plus all the "Ex" food I could eat. I did a Punch-and-Judy routine, which was a great hit with the kids, but I think it was the Trudeau-Streisand duet that got me all the attention: *The Toronto Star* even carried a front-page picture of me holding the Trudeau and Streisand puppets. I'm on to something, my devious little mind told me, so I added a few other puppets of local personalities, all designed by Mom, such as TV weatherman Percy Saltzman and TV talk show host Elwood Glover.

During one of my shows, I noticed a familiar face in the front row; the man was laughing and applauding with great enthusiasm. Gee, I *know* him, I thought. After the show, he came over and introduced himself: It was Bill Cosby! We talked about puppetry, which he enjoys immensely, and he told me about an art form called black-light theatre. I had never heard of it before, but Bill told me it looked like magic and was amazing to watch.

Curious, I went to the library and looked it up. Black-light theatre had originated in Japan and spread to Europe, especially Czechoslovakia, where puppetry had been a flourishing art form for centuries. The technique used ultraviolet lights set in front of the stage to illuminate life-size puppets, each of which was manipulated by as many as three people. These puppets were painted in fluorescent colors. When the house lights were dimmed, the ultraviolet light caught the fluorescence, making the puppets appear to glow in the dark. The performers dressed entirely in black, with hoods over their heads, so the ultraviolet light wouldn't reveal their presence on stage. Using a number of heavy black boxes as springboards, the performers could jump up and down in sequence to make the puppets appear to gallop, leap, swim — even fly. It sounded wonderful, but I didn't take my research any further at the time. The CNE was just coming to an end, and there was another big job waiting for me.

Because of the attention I got at the "Ex," I was invited to do a series of shows in shopping malls in Calgary and Edmonton, Alberta, and Winnipeg, Manitoba. My first tour! And the money sounded like a fortune: fifteen hundred dollars. I was on the road until late 1971 and I remember being lonely in hotel rooms. But I had my $1,500, which I managed to stretch out until the summer of 1972 with the help of occasional puppetry bookings. I was invited back to the CNE that summer and my work continued slowly that year.

Just before Christmas, I got a call from a woman who introduced herself as Audrey Watson. She asked if I was available to do a show for a group of children who were mentally handicapped at Surrey Place Centre, for which she co-ordinated volunteer services.

I don't want to do this, I thought. How did they get my name, anyway? These kids are going to be a bunch of crazies. They'll knock down the theatre. They'll ruin the show. I can't possibly do this. My mind raced to my memories of the kids shouting, "Retard! Retard!" when I was six. "Yes, I'd be delighted to do it," I shocked myself by saying.

There were about 50 children in the audience, and, during my performance, one of them had a seizure. Nobody laughed. They all went to help her, straightening her clothing and making sure she hadn't hurt herself falling. As for their reaction to the show, I had never had such a great audience. They laughed, cheered, and clapped all the way through, especially during a particularly difficult sequence in which Punch has to catch a ball. Their delight made me feel it had been worthwhile to put all that effort into perfecting the trick. I suddenly thought to myself: Just who is retarded here? These kids helped the girl who had a seizure; these kids loved my show and made me feel good. It was the so-called normal kids who laughed at the epileptic girl in my Grade Eight class.

After the show, I struck up a conversation with Audrey, who asked me if I was interested in finding out more about the mentally handicapped. "How did you know?" I asked, and she smiled as she signed me up for a volunteer course.

Part of the course involved spending a day at an institution in Orillia, where we went one Saturday in February 1973. I was absolutely horrified at what I saw. There were no doors on the washrooms. People were herded from place to place. And, worst of all, there were no smiles from patients or staff. Drab colors, depression, and gloom everywhere. It made me sad and angry. I wanted to somehow change the situation — I wanted to save these people.

It was as if I were on my imaginary horse Silver again, riding like crazy to save a whole town. Only now the feeling was all caught up with my puppets and the pleasure they gave the children at Surrey Place, and the misery of the people in the institution in Orillia. There was a clue in all this, a clue to something I could accomplish for others, and for myself.

This idea kicked around in my mind for weeks, but, in the meantime, my attention turned to finding more work. At the time, Judi was working at the Artists' Workshop in the Poor Alex Theatre in Toronto. She had started there as a receptionist, just after we came back from Arizona. I still remember that before her interview, she felt nervous. "Judi," I told her, "you just go in there and say, 'Where do I hang my coat?' " She took my advice and got the job, working her way up to manager.

So one day in early spring of 1973, I walked in to the Artists' Workshop and said, "Hey, Judi, where do I hang my coat?"

My job wasn't very glamorous: running errands and cleaning the ceramics oven for $40.00 a week and some free courses. Then, one afternoon, I noticed that a company called Black Box Theatre was rehearsing at the Poor Alex. The name reminded me of the material I had read in the library. Sure enough, the company turned out to be a black-light theatre troupe which had been established four years earlier by a Czechoslovakian named Mikulas Kravjansky.

I spent a month working with them in my spare time. Mostly, I helped carry props, so I didn't find out much more about the technique. But I sat very quietly in the back of the theatre, watching them rehearse. It was magic, just as Bill Cosby had said. It was explosive. Glowing colors; the puppets flying, spinning, somersaulting through the air with no visible means of support. It was as if the pictures I had created in my mind as a child of six had suddenly come to life before my eyes.

One day, a friend, Joseph Fodor, called me at work and asked if I would go out with a friend of his. I was skeptical but finally agreed. (It's only in retrospect that I realize how some phone calls have changed my life.) That evening I was still scolding myself for saying yes when my landlady told me my "gentleman caller" had arrived. There at the front door stood a tall, good-looking, dark-haired man who introduced himself as Bernard Dupuy. What a dreamy accent, I thought.

Bernard escorted me to his car with a flair that gave new meaning to the title "gentleman," but suddenly I froze in mid-step. "What's *that*?" I said, pointing to what looked like a spaceship on wheels.

"That's my car," he said, and paused, smiling mischievously. "Oh, you mean what *kind* of car? It's a Citröen Maserati." Then he lifted the gull-wing door to let me in.

"How did you get a car like this?"

"Simple. I work for the company." We both cracked up, and we were still laughing when we got to the elegant French restaurant. After dinner we went dancing, and at the end of the evening I sat in my room basking in a luxurious sensation that was entirely new to me: a warm, secure feeling that this was a man on whom I could depend. I'd never met anyone like Bernard before: kind, a bit shy, but full of quiet self-confidence. And he must have felt the same chemistry, because we kept seeing each other, almost every night.

My romance was wonderful, but my career was on hold. Sometimes it takes a kick in the can from a friend to get you going. One day Judi called me into her office at the Artists' Workshop and said: "I'm going to do you the biggest favor of your life. You've got too much talent to be a gofer around here, and you're fired."

It was the autumn of 1973. There weren't any promotional events for which I could do puppet shows at department stores, and I was tired of serving hot dogs between shows at kids' birthday parties. I wanted something more and decided to see a Manpower counsellor. She knew about my show at Surrey Place and told me about a job opening for a receptionist in the fund-raising office of the National Program for the Mentally Handicapped.

I got the job, which began with taking phone messages and developed into research work. I didn't mind the work —

especially talking to people on the phone — but it bothered me that I had no contact with people who were retarded. They never seemed to be in that office. There were posters everywhere showing them operating assembly-line machinery in sheltered workshops. I thought about that, as I had been thinking about the Surrey Place puppet show, the trip to Orillia, and the black-light theatre I had seen at the Poor Alex. And I wondered: Why can't the retarded do something other than assembly-line or janitorial work? Why can't they do something wonderful and magical, something fulfilling like black-light theatre? A strange new sensation overcame me, a sense that my life was coming into focus.

I had always seen everything as larger than life, because, to me, everything *was* larger than life: like a movie, or a play — or a puppet show. I dreamed up stories in my head; out in the world, I acted them out. The process was what I call magic, and I wanted to share it.

It was my instinct for survival that led me back to my childhood fantasies, back to my puppets. But life had to be more than playing with puppets in my bedroom. I was an adult who wanted to live in the real world — for all its pain and suffering. Maybe I could do something to alleviate the hurt: share the magic of my dreams with the world; use my capacity for seeing life as a drama — my puppet show — to make the world a better place for others.

But who were these others with whom I could share dreams of a better world. Where would I find them? How?

By some miracle, I did find them. I can only call it a miracle, because I have no other way of explaining the amazing feeling of *belonging* that surged through me when I brought my puppet show to those children at Surrey Place. Those children made me feel like less of an outsider; they made me feel that my vision of life as a drama was special and worthwhile; they made me want to devote my vision to people like them; they made me want to share my magic with people like them. Special people.

That night I noticed a newspaper advertisement for Liberace's show at the O'Keefe on November 12. The caption under a photo of Liberace at the keyboard of his grand piano read "Direct from Las Vegas." Thinking about Las Vegas and its image of fabulous stage shows, and contemplating the delightful smile of Liberace — his smile looked so spontaneous that even the fuzziness of the photo couldn't dim its brilliance — I decided to go to his show.

The next day, I managed to get four tickets. Mom wasn't free that night, but Bernard came, as well as my brother Robert and my friend Ann Laitin from the Artists' Workshop.

"Liberace?" asked Bernard. "Isn't he for little old ladies with blue hair?"

"Oh, come on, Bernard," I said. "It'll be fun; we can get all dressed up. And besides, I've got an idea about Liberace."

"What kind of idea?"

"Oh, nothing, really," I replied evasively.

I took the same approach when I asked Ann and Robert to come to the concert. I only told them I thought it would be an enjoyable experience. We could all put on our formals — long gowns for the women, fancy suits for the guys — and have a great time going to the elegant O'Keefe Centre.

From my seat at the back of the auditorium, it looked like Liberace was far away; a distant mirage of color, glitter and incandescence. His show was unlike anything I'd ever seen. His grand, sweeping gestures over the keyboard of the huge, gleaming white piano produced a sound of such brilliance and dazzling speed that I just sat there, transfixed. His smile was so full of joy and enthusiasm that, even sitting in the back row, I could feel the warmth of his personality and his love for the music that cascaded from his piano, illuminated by a gorgeous, ornately wrought candelabra.

After the show I whispered to Ann, "Let's go backstage and meet him."

"I don't think we can do that," she said nervously. "The backstage area is off limits to the public."

"Let's try, anyway." We nonchalantly strolled toward the

security guard standing at the door to the backstage area and offered him $10.00 if he would let us go back and meet Liberace.

"Nope," was his clipped reply.

Undaunted, we tried again; this time, we offered him $20.00. "Look, ladies," he said, "this isn't going to work. No visitors are allowed back there, and I'm not going to lose my job over it."

Rebuffed, we walked over to the lounge, where Robert and Bernard were sitting over drinks. I didn't say a word to them about our attempt to get backstage; I just sat there, trying to figure out a way to meet Liberace. "Look over there," Bernard said. "They're setting up a buffet for a party; doesn't it look fabulous?"

I stared at the roped-off reception area for a few minutes, and as I was about to look away, Liberace was suddenly there, all decked out in a sequined suit and a collection of diamond rings that would have done justice to the front window of Tiffany's. As the orchestra began to play, he gallantly offered his hand to the wife of Hugh Walker, general manager of the O'Keefe Centre, and the two of them whirled across the floor in a fabulous grand waltz.

Without even thinking what I was doing, I hiked up my long red skirt, climbed over the roped barrier, walked across the dance floor, and, tapping Mrs. Walker on the shoulder, asked "May I cut in?"

The next thing I knew, I was dancing with Liberace, but my mouth was going at least twice as fast as my feet: "I'm so pleased to meet you, Mr. Liberace," I began. "You see, I work for Des O'Connor at the London Palladium (I had seen the famed Palladium show when it came to the O'Keefe two years before), and we're planning to create a life-size puppet of you when Des gets back from his tour, and it'll be really great under black-light because everything will glow — the candelabras, the puppet, the piano. It'll be like real magic."

Liberace was enchanted. When the waltz was over, he took my arm and led me over to Hugh Walker. After the introductions, I started my rapid-fire monologue again; I went on and on about the life-size Liberace puppet that was soon going to be created and waxed eloquent about the glories of the black-light technique. I didn't let anyone get a word in edgewise. I was certain that if Walker or Liberace began questioning me, I would soon be exposed as a dissembler who had never set foot in the London Palladium, let alone been employed there.

When I finally finished my high-speed descriptions, Liberace turned to his manager, Seymour Heller. "This is wonderful, Seymour," he said. "Why don't you give the young lady your card."

Heller complied, and I grasped that card as if it were made of pure gold. "Now, you hang on to that card," Liberace told me. "And keep in touch with Seymour."

Card in hand, I bolted from the reception area before I could be found out. Bernard, Robert, Ann, and I laughed all the way up Yonge Street, but the whole time I was thinking that Liberace himself had told me to keep in touch. I even had his manager's card. On this promise — faint as it was — I felt sure that I could achieve my dream of a black-light theatre company composed of people who were mentally handicapped. It was as if Liberace, in his brief conversation with me, had become a living inspiration — a mentor — whose personality and performing style would be the subject of our first show. I even had a name for the company: Famous People Players — a perfect way of describing a troupe that would use lifesize puppets of well-known people like Liberace.

The next morning I bought a recording of Liberace's greatest hits; I loved them all, but most of all I loved the song "Aruba Liberace." It was fast, lively, and upbeat. Playing that record and recalling my talk with Liberace galvanized my imagination and intensified my faith in my dreams.

I thought about my shows at the Canadian National Exhibition, and all the excitement I had generated by taking wood-and-fabric versions of Trudeau and Streisand and making them do a little pas de deux to the tune of "Lover Come Back To Me." And I realized what made people enjoy that number so much:

The real Trudeau and Streisand would never get up on a stage and dance to that song. But it was funny and entertaining to see the puppets act out such a fantasy, especially after all the gossip about them that had appeared in the newspapers.

I imagined bringing other famous people on stage in much the same way, as puppets of themselves, acting out fantasies based on their personal style but impossible for them to perform in real life. But this time I would use the black-light technique so the characters could achieve even more magic. Liberace, in a magnificent rhinestone-encrusted suit, would swoop from the wings of the theatre to the keyboard of a gleaming white grand piano. And he wouldn't just *play* that piano. He would dance with it, turn handsprings over the keys, and twirl it upside-down in midair, tickling the ivories with his toes while standing on his head. As the music built into the dazzling chords, scales, and arpeggios of the typical Liberace performance, dozens of dancing, cartwheeling, somersaulting musical notes would soar out of the piano, his own notes literally coming to life.

The notes, the piano, the piano bench and the candelabra — as well as Liberace himself — would be puppets that seemed to dance and fly on their own. But the puppeteers, dressed in black and invisible under the fluorescent light, would be the ones making all this magic happen. And these performers would be people who are retarded. But no one in the audience would know this until the performers removed their black hoods and took their bows at the end of the show.

The Famous People Players would be like nothing that has ever been imagined in the theatre: a unique form of entertainment created by a unique group of performers. It would be more than a puppet show; it would be a black-light extravaganza of color, movement, and music, brought to the stage by people who had spent their lives in the shadows. The company would be a way to bring these people out of the shadows, to change the world's perception of the mentally retarded.

I decided not to tell anyone the full extent of my dream. I felt that doing so would give people the impression that I was a Don

Quixote tilting at windmills. I wanted to be a Don Quixote who won, not lost; I wanted people to believe in me and help me, not dismiss me as a daydreamer.

In January 1974 I mapped out a basic plan of action. I decided to gather together a group of young people in their late teens and early twenties, who were retarded and who had an interest in the theatre. It was very important to me that Famous People Players be established as a professional theatre company — to free people who are retarded from financial as well as occupational dependency. So the performers couldn't be children. But I wanted them to be young enough and open enough to respond to this entirely new experience. I sensed, after my visit to Orillia, that it would be impossible for me to reach older people who had spent a lifetime in institutions. I thought I would have a better chance working with teen-agers, helping to prevent institutional apathy and inertia from making their lives a vacuum. I also wanted to include in the company a smaller group of nonretarded people who were interested in theatre and, more importantly, enthusiastic about the concept of Famous People Players. Together, we would find somewhere to rehearse — maybe even get a place donated — and create a black-light puppet show. The Liberace number I had imagined would be perfect. I could see the marquee: THE FAMOUS PEOPLE PLAYERS PRESENT A TRIBUTE TO LIBERACE!

I knew I would need some kind of financial support. I remembered reading a newspaper article about a new government program called Opportunities for Youth, which provided funds to young people to create jobs for themselves and other young adults in their communities. It was only a three-month program, but I was convinced that by the end of the third month the Famous People Players would be so famous that theatres would be lining up to book us.

Smartly attired in a tailored skirt and jacket (I knew how to dress for a part), I went to see the Toronto representative of the youth program, Sybil Powell. She listened attentively as I described my success as a puppeteer — especially at the CNE — and smiled when I showed her the photograph of me with the Trudeau and Streisand puppets.

"What I'd like to do is the same idea, only with the black-light technique," I said.

"What's that?"

The words just came flying out of my mouth: "Oh, you paint all the puppets in fluorescent colors, and you turn on the ultraviolet lights so you can't see the puppeteers because they're wearing black and have black hoods on their heads. So you can do anything with the puppets: make them dance, even make them fly. It's like magic."

"I see."

"But these puppets will all be of famous people, like Liberace, and they'll be life-size."

"That sounds wonderful!"

"And, you see, I'm employed in the fund-raising office of the National Program for the Mentally Retarded. I have this idea that I would like to try, which would give young people who are mentally retarded something meaningful to do with their time."

"That's very interesting."

"So I thought it would be great to have this black-light theatre company to train young people who are mentally retarded so they could participate in a creative program in their community — and earn money at the same time.

"I — You see, they could become self-sufficient! It would be a great opportunity for youth — that's the name of your program, right? So this would be an opportunity for *you* to give a chance to young people who could never have this sort of opportunity otherwise!"

Uh-oh, I thought; I've pushed too hard. I leaned forward to say something more, but Sybil interrupted me with a delighted smile.

"I think your idea is wonderful, Diane," she said. "It's a great plan, and I'm going to try to help you in any way I can."

She spent more than an hour giving me the practical advice I desperately needed. I should know exactly who the participants were going to be and any staff I needed to help train them. I should have a place to rehearse and support for my project from the community. "You can call me any time you want, and when you've got everything in place, come back and fill out an application," she said. "I can't promise you'll get the money, but I think you have a very good chance."

A very good chance? To some people that wouldn't be much to fly on, but a faint promise to some was money in the bank to me. I set a course toward the forbidding mountains: the resistance I knew awaited me among the experts in the field of mental retardation.

I started phoning schools for the retarded, training centers, and volunteer organizations in the Toronto area. I tried my best to play up my experience with the mentally retarded (as limited as it was), my background as a puppeteer, and the wonderful response I had received during my puppet show at Surrey Place. With support from the youth program, I could use my experience to give young people who are retarded an exciting new career.

The response was polite but firmly negative: It was a nice idea, but it just wouldn't be practical. The more I tried to convince them, the less they wanted to hear.

"These young people have to be prepared for some kind of future, Miss Thornton," a staff person at one training center told me after I tried to counter her refusal. "Just what kind of future would you be offering them?"

"Well, their future would be a lot brighter if they were doing more than putting colored pencils into boxes," I retorted.

"I'm sorry, but there are certain realities involved in working with these people that you don't seem to understand," she said in dismissal. "I'm afraid I must get back to work now."

School after school, expert after expert; it was like crashing into a mountain of opposition. I knew I couldn't go through the mountain; I had to find a way over it.

I banged on the doors of all the training centers again; wangled appointments with directors of municipal, provincial, and national associations for the mentally retarded; hunted for potential sidekicks with expertise in black-light puppetry or choreography; subjected everyone I knew to a nonstop recitation of my progress and frustrations; banged on still more doors; wrote dozens of letters demanding the support of everyone from Toronto Mayor David Crombie to singer Anne Murray; called Sybil several times a day; banged on more doors. I kept up this mad pace from early morning to past midnight. Every night. Every day.

My first success was finding an ally, a copilot for the journey over the mountains of resistance and doubt. I tried Judi first, but she had landed a job as curator of the art collection at Hart House, a cultural and recreational center on the University of Toronto campus.

"I'll tell you one thing," she remarked after I asked her to give up her job at Hart House and join me. "You sure have a lot of chutzpah."

"What's that word? It sounds like somebody sneezing."

"It's a Yiddish word, and it means something in between confidence and arrogance, with a big scoop of nerve thrown in."

"That sounds a lot like me," I laughed. "Sure you won't quit Hart House?"

"Not a chance," Judi said. "Better try someone else."

I thought of Ann Laitin, who had gone along with my escapade at Liberace's concert. Her spunk and idealism really appealed to me, and she was also a wonderful trained dancer. She was very young (eighteen, compared to *this* old lady of twenty-four!), but I instinctively felt that she was the person to come along for the ride. I was right, because she jumped at the idea.

Her comparative youth also made her role as my assistant easier for both of us. If she had been my age, she might not have put up with: "Here's what we're going to do (meaning her, not me!). We're going to write another letter to Anne Murray's manager." Ann didn't see me as a dictator, but as a friend or an elder sister who had an idea that was worth her effort. We were like Lucy Ricardo and Ethel Mertz in "I love Lucy." Lucy would come up with some harebrained scheme, and Ethel was the first one to get in on the action.

While Ann wrote letters I went back to banging on doors. Finally, I got a little chink open in one of those doors — to the office of Dr. Allan Roeher, executive vice-president of the Canadian Association for the Mentally Retarded.

Like the other professionals in the field, he was initially skeptical. It was a wonderful idea, "but even with this funding from the government, these young people would have to return to some sort of training program later," he said. "It just isn't a long-term solution."

"Oh, yes it is, Dr. Roeher," I argued. "Don't you see? These people would have a career! They would be professional performers!"

"But Diane, surely you know that the entertainment business is full of pitfalls, even for nonretarded people. How can you speak in terms of careers?"

"Well, I got an audition with you, didn't I?" (I had buttonholed him in the corridor at work, in the fund-raising office, which he was visiting one day in late January 1974.)

He had to laugh at that. "True enough," he said. "Why don't you come to my office next week and we'll discuss it further."

The next morning, at 8:45, I was waiting for Dr. Roeher outside his office. He couldn't get rid of me. Every time he glanced at his watch, I pleaded, "Just a few more minutes." I painted the picture of the tribute to Liberace in the most glowing terms I could summon. I explained, for what seemed like the hundredth time, how strongly my puppet show had appealed to the children at Surrey Place. I told him about the black-light experts I had just found: Eric Kalinsky, a design student who had built black-light puppets and props, and Leigh Alexander, a dancer and dance teacher who had performed in black light. I didn't add that they had only said, "Maybe." I told him about Ann and me, how dedicated we were to making the project work and finding the right support. "The right support," I repeated, and, lifting my big dark eyes toward his face, delivered the coup de grâce: "We need you, Dr. Roeher. We need your help if we're going to share this experience with these young people. Please say you'll believe in us."

Dr. Roeher smiled. "I do believe you're sincere, Diane, and that's all I'm going to tell you right now. You'll have to give me a few days to think it over."

In the middle of all this mayhem, Bernard and I got engaged. Our love had just grown, like the most natural thing in the world. Being with Bernard was like being with someone I had known all my life. His quiet humor and strength were perfect foils for my raw energy. He was a great listener and I probably invented the perpetual soliloquy. He was practical and self-assured, while I was a dreamer and a worrywart. In January, when he asked me to move in with him, I was certain he was the man I wanted to share my life.

On Valentine's Day, Dr. Roeher phoned me at work to tell me he would support Famous People Players. I burst into the apartment and headed for the phone, but Bernard stopped me.

"Bernard, I've been trying to reach Ann all day!" I yelled. "Dr. Roeher's giving us a letter of support!"

"Okay," he said, waving a velvet jeweler's box under my nose. "I'll give this to you later."

The phone call forgotten, I reveled in the sparkle of the lovely diamond ring. But what sparkled even more brightly than the ring were Bernard's eyes as he slipped the diamond on my finger.

By the time we got to Hamilton to share a bottle of champagne with Mom, my romantic mood had been erased by thoughts of Famous People Players. I know this sounds odd, but it's the way I am. My mind moves around like — well, like a pilot trying to navigate a tornado. The people in my life have always understood this; they've always been my private ground-control crew. Bernard is the stability and security I need as a foundation for my soaring imagination. Judi is the patience and logic I seek when I need to give vent to my worries. And with Mom, it's always been a bit of ribbing and a lot of practical help.

"Oh, Diane, couldn't you just do a few puppet shows and be a housewife?" she asked as Bernard and I sat in her living room that Valentine's Day.

"No, Mom," I growled. "This is not going to be a puppet show. This is going to be a black-light theatre company, and if you'd like to help . . ."

"You're going to need my help," she said placidly. "Oh, I suppose I could make a few costumes, paint a few puppets. Make it look a *little* more professional."

"It's *going* to be professional," I barked. But I was secretly delighted by Mom's offer, and she knew it.

After Dr. Roeher sent us his letter of support, the provincial and municipal associations weren't far behind. Our local Member of Parliament also endorsed our project and, to our delight, so did Anne Murray. "The benefits of such a project can be rewarding for all of us," she said in her letter.

We had all the staff we needed. Although Leigh wasn't going to work on the project until the following year — she was pregnant — she promised to cosign our application. And we did have another staff person, along with Ann and Eric. She was a friend of Ann's, Vivian Mitchell, and she had worked with people who are retarded in summer camps and recreational programs. I didn't care so much about her credentials. What was more important to me was her enthusiasm for the project.

We even had a place to rehearse, courtesy of Dr. Roeher, who arranged for us to use a lecture room and office on the second floor of the building where he worked.

But the most important element of Famous People Players was still missing: the future stars of the show. And if I had thought I was facing a mountain in January, it was Mount Everest by March.

The major obstacle was the parents of the teen-agers who are retarded, whom I met in special schools or training centers. These parents were worried about their kids' future: What was going to happen to them after the program was over? And what about their pensions?

The parents were skeptical. And I had to have their consent. Even though these "children" of theirs were over eighteen — the minimum age for participation in Opportunities for Youth — the parents were still their legal guardians.

I am adamantly opposed to the idea of a lifelong pension: I believe that giving people a way to rise above others' expectations is much better than paying them to stay exactly as they were. But I can now understand that the parents simply wanted an answer to a very basic question: If something happened to us, how would we know for certain that our kids would be provided with an income?

As it turned out, we were able to work out a solution. On a disability pension, you're allowed to earn additional money up to a certain maximum. Sybil Powell (whose knowledge of how to maneuver around bureaucratic obstacles was invaluable) suggested we pay the performers for two months instead of three so they could stay on their pensions. I resisted this plan, agreeing only when it became clear that we weren't going to get any participants otherwise. At least, I consoled myself, these people will still experience something entirely new: receiving a salary for making magic instead of making pencil cases.

Parents weren't the only problem. The staff in the special schools and training centers were also skeptical. At one school the staff social worker suggested I put on some puppet shows with the seven- and eight-year-olds. "You don't understand," I said. "This is going to be a professional black-light theatre company."

"That's just not possible," she said coldly. "I'm sorry, I can't help you."

I'm not going to give up, I told myself. I'm going to find the Famous People Players if I have to go to every school and training center in Canada. I know they're out there, somewhere.

I didn't have to go that far. At the beginning of April, I found out about a place where I might just find the young people I wanted. The place was the Haney Centre, and one of the teachers, Doreen Crystal, told me that several of the trainees would be interested in a theatre project of the kind I was proposing.

"How many would be interested?" I asked.

"Oh, I don't know, maybe eight or nine," she said. "Maybe more. I think something in the theatre would appeal to them. Why don't we arrange for a time for you to talk to them about it."

"Well, I'd just like to do the final paperwork on our grant," I said, praying she didn't know we had yet to submit our application.

"Oh, that's fine," she said. "You just let me know when you would like to come and talk to the people."

Another episode of the Lucy and Ethel show: "Here's what we're going to do," I told Ann.

"Oh, yeah?"

"We're going to get the application from OFY, and we're going to fill it out, and we're going to say that we have nine participants who are mentally retarded whose names we will give them later . . . ."

"But we don't have them, Diane."

"Well, yes we do. The teacher at the Haney Centre said there would be nine people interested. Eight or nine."

"But that's not the same thing as having them," Ann said. "And what about the parents? You were so worried about the parents."

"Look, we'll take care of the parents later," I said. "So do you want to do this thing or not?"

"Of course I do."

The next morning we submitted our application for an OFY grant, which was accepted in less than two weeks. (I suspect that Sybil pushed through the application so I would stop my relentless phoning!) Our grant was for $18,000, including salaries of $70.00 a week for performers and staff, and $86.00 a week for me, as project leader. I decided not to take my salary and instead use it to buy materials, such as wood, fluorescent paint, and fabrics for the puppets.

In May I went to the Haney Centre and, for the first time, stood in front of a group of people who are mentally retarded and talked to them about my dream. That is, I squirmed my way through a very uncomfortable speech about the wonders of black-light theatre and the great time we were all going to have putting on a show. Waves of laughter floated toward me. I noticed that the people who weren't giggling and shouting seemed much better co-ordinated than the others and I decided these were the ones I wanted. But the well-co-ordinated teenagers were either going to camp for the summer or were uninterested in the project. So I got the worst of the gigglers, the ones who couldn't sit still for one second and had terrible coordination and speech impediments that made it impossible to understand a word they were saying. My heart sank, but I tried to keep smiling as I counted them. Eleven.

An impish voice interrupted my frantic thoughts. "Heydeerie, howya doon?"

"What's your name?" I asked the slight, puckish teen-ager.

"Grzzzk."

"Pardon me?"

"Grigozik."

"Slow down," I said. "I can't understand what you're saying."

"His name is Greg," one of the others put in.

"I want to hear him say it," I insisted. "What . . . is . . . your . . . name . . . please."

"Greg . . . Ko . . . zak," he said, mimicking me.

Slowly, painstakingly, I collected all their names, which took more than an hour. Another hour passed before they understood that they were to come to the association office, not the Haney Centre. I finally had to write the address and the date the program was to begin on eleven pieces of paper for them to take home to their parents.

Struggling to Stay Alive

JUNE 1974 - JANUARY 1975

On June 1, the first day of our Famous People Players project, Ann, Vivian, and I waited for an hour in the carpeted lecture room before we heard what sounded like a herd of elephants coming up the stairs. The first crisis happened before they reached the top of the stairs.

"Oh, my God, this is it! I'm not going to make it! My appendix!" yelled one of the boys, collapsing on the top step.

"Quick, call an ambulance!" I shrieked to Ann.

As she raced to the office to call an ambulance, the boy picked himself up and leaned against the wall, laughing. There was nothing wrong with him. While the others thundered up the stairs, I shouted to Ann to call off the ambulance, then grabbed the "comedian" by the shoulders: "You scared me!"

He looked at me blankly.

"I said you scared me! Why did you do that?"

"I don't know," he said, his tongue slowly protruding from the corner of his mouth while his eyes wandered somewhere above my head, as if he might find the answer there.

"What do you mean, you don't know?" I asked, angry now. "You played a trick on me, and now we've got to call the ambulance back and tell them not to come. Why did you do that?"

"I don't know, Miss," he said, and he looked as if he were about to cry. "I'm scared."

"There's nothing to be scared about . . . . What's your name again?" and I put my arm around him as we walked up the stairs and into the association's main office.

"Larry." I noticed him squirming under my arm.

"Larry what? And what's the matter with you now?"

"I don't want to go this way. Nobody else did."

"Where did they go?"

"That way." He pointed out the door and down a hall.

"Well, this is the way to the rehearsal room," I said, indicating a door at the opposite end of the main office. But Larry broke away from me and headed down the hall, which eventually led to the rehearsal room, but by a much longer and more circuitous route.

"It's easier to go the other way," I said.

His answer was lost in the cacophony that erupted as I opened the door to the rehearsal room. One of the girls, Alice, was locked in a passionate embrace with one of the boys; two others were rolling around on the floor, punching each other. Another girl, Daphne, in a flowered housedress which looked like it belonged to her mother, was sobbing her eyes out. The others were leaping around the room, shrieking with laughter. And in the doorway to our small office stood Ann, Vivian, and Eric, helplessly staring at this bedlam.

I was about to shut them up with a loud yell when suddenly Larry plodded over to one of the laughing boys — no, it was a girl wearing men's pants and a plaid work shirt — and pointed at her, shouting "Retard!" in a voice of such force that the others stopped dead, stunned into silence. The girl burst into hysterical tears and rushed from the room. "Ann, try and keep them quiet," I shouted over my shoulder as I raced after her.

By the time I got downstairs, the girl was lying face down on the sidewalk, sobbing loudly as the startled pedestrians walked around her. As I approached, I could hear that she was muttering something that sounded like, "Label . . . label . . ."

"What label?" I asked. She hauled herself up to a sitting

position and looked at me with such misery in her eyes that I almost started crying myself.

"What Larry called me."

I pulled her to her feet, then pushed her down on the front stoop and sat next to her. Somehow, I thought, I've got to make some sense of all this. "What's your name?"

"Irene."

"Irene what?"

"Irene Lawrence."

"Okay, Irene. I'm Diane. Diane Thornton. Now, what's the label that Larry called you? You mean when he said 'retard'?"

"Yes."

"Why is that a label?"

"I don't know." Her eyes started wandering as Larry's had earlier.

"Never mind 'I don't know,' " I said. "Tell me what a label is."

"It goes on jars in the supermarket."

"Who told you that?"

"The teacher at the center."

"What else did the teacher say about labels?"

"I don't know." Her tongue was beginning to poke out the side of her mouth. I asked her if the teacher had been talking about being mentally retarded.

"She said we shouldn't use that word." Irene's eyes filled with tears.

"What word? Retarded?"

"Don't say that! It's a label, she said. We have to get rid of that label." Irene was crying now, and so was I.

"Irene," I said, "we're going to get rid of the label. You and I and all of us."

"How?"

"We're going to put together the Famous People Players and we're going to be so good that nobody will say you're mentally retarded. They're going to say you're professionals."

We went back upstairs, and talked: It was a day of innocence and discovery, of overcoming fears and exploring dreams. I told them about the kids in school calling me "retard" and how bad it made me feel, because I was afraid of what it meant.

Larry and the others explained why they had avoided the main office: They hated the signs and the posters that used the term "mentally retarded."

"The term 'mentally retarded' exists," I said, "and not to talk about it — to go down a long corridor to avoid it on the signs and posters — is making it worse. We have to talk about it."

Vivian said something about accepting yourself as you are. "Yes," I said, "but that's not enough. You want to be better than you are. What's better?"

"It's better to be like a 'norm,' " said Larry. "I want to be like a 'norm.' Do I look like a 'norm,' Diane?"

"No, you don't, Larry, and that's part of what we're going to do — act like 'norms' — and we're going to be like the pioneers who built the railroad and the first highways. We're going to forge a path for others to follow, and it'll be hard work, but we're going to do it for the people who come after."

"We're gonna be great!" shouted Frank Pritchard, tossing back his luxuriant dark hair (he looked surprisingly like Paul McCartney).

"Yes, we are!" said Ann, supporting me.

"Hey, Ann," Frank said, "you and I make one good couple. Someday we gotta go out on a date." Everyone laughed.

"I want to show you something," I said, waving the card Seymour Heller had given me. "See this? It's Liberace's manager in Hollywood, and Liberace's going to come and see us because we're going to make a big puppet of him — as big as us. Our show will be all in bright colors, and we're going to be pianos and musical notes, and nobody's going to see us till the very end of the show when we come out to take our bows and, boy, will that audience applaud!"

Everyone got excited, and the screaming and yelling started again; the only person who made no noise was Sandra Ciccone, a small, dark-haired girl who just stood there passively. I noticed she was menstruating. Apparently no one had told her what to do during her period. I went with her to the bathroom to show her how to use a sanitary pad and told her to buy more of them and keep two or three in her purse.

When we returned, the noise had stopped; Frank was just coming into the room with a cup of coffee for Ann. Right behind him was Keith Edwards, with a coffee which he shyly presented to me.

"What we have to do now," I said, "is learn to behave like professionals. Part of that means behaving like 'norms,' doing things like washing and shaving and taking care of ourselves. And we have to rehearse our show so we can go to the Canadian National Exhibition, and we *can* go because I'm going to talk to the manager, Dave Garrick."

They started cheering and yelling again, but my voice was louder: "Look, we can't act this way if we're going to be professionals. We have to behave like professionals, and perform like professionals, and then everyone who sees the show will be amazed that it's done by the mentally retarded."

This challenge seemed to appeal to them: Alice stopped flirting, Larry stopped chattering, and even Sandra responded with a little smile.

"What's the show going to be?" asked Mike.

I played my recording of "Aruba Liberace" and described the number we would create to accompany the music: the dancing musical notes, the cavorting Liberace puppet, and the elegant white piano. "We'll start working on it first thing tomorrow morning," I said.

But my optimism was ill-founded. The chaos of Day One had been only a sample of what was to come.

The next day — and many days that followed — was taken up with working on the performers' personal problems. Ann and I had hoped they would have some basic theatre skills, but they didn't even know how to take care of themselves in the most basic ways. Many of them didn't wash; most of them wore clothes that made them look elderly; none of them, it seemed, had ever been told about the benefits of deodorant.

Teaching the performers about hygiene and grooming became an ongoing process. I'd tell Larry to use deodorant; he would nod enthusiastically. Then he would show up the following day smelling like a basket of dirty laundry. And the instruction would start all over again.

On the positive side, the performers were letting me get to know them as individuals. Irene, for all her masculine attire, was a sensitive, emotional girl. Mike was probably the most "normal" of the group. He had attended a public school, but his reading and writing problems had caused his teachers to classify him as retarded. Greg was an energetic, mischievous teen-ager with a great sense of humor and an insatiable interest in sports: If you named a hockey or baseball star, Greg could recite the player's statistics without a pause. Tom Ashton was an irrepressibly good-natured, overweight teen-ager who was eager to get involved — sometimes *too* eager.

The people who represented our biggest challenge were Alice and Daphne. Day after day I would try to convince Daphne to stop dressing like a middle-aged housewife; day after day she would throw a tantrum in response. Often she would work herself up into such a fit that we were forced to call her parents to come and take her home for the rest of the day.

As for Alice, it was impossible to convince her that having sex in the rehearsal room was not an acceptable pastime. One day, just as we were preparing to start rehearsals — Eric, with Mom's help, had built the Liberace puppet, the piano and bench, the candelabra and maracas, and the musical notes — I saw Alice pulling Frank on top of her in the far corner of the room.

"Alice!" I shouted. There was no response; I had to literally pry them apart. "Look, I've told you before that professionals don't have sex on the job." She looked at me blankly. "If you want to have sex, you keep it private and outside working hours. Do you understand?"

"Yes," she said. But by the next day she was right back to flirting with another guy.

Then there was the perennial problem of getting a full cast to work each day. One of them would inevitably forget the route and end up riding the subway for hours, until a public transit employee called the performer's parents.

With all these difficulties, it was a miracle that we actually started rehearsals. When we did, the results were as disheartening as our endless attempts to teach the performers about grooming and hygiene.

Ann, Eric, and I worked on the Liberace puppet (it took three people to manipulate the life-size puppet); Greg was on the piano bench; Frank did the piano; Mike was on the maracas; Tom insisted on doing the candelabrum; and the others were musical notes. It was all very organized, until we started trying to put these elements together.

Every attempt was fraught with difficulty. Greg would bring the piano bench on stage upside-down. Then we'd have a 10-minute discussion that ended with Greg saying "Okay, dearie, we'll do it now," after which he'd bring the bench in upside-down again. Tom would shake the candelabrum so violently that the foam candles drooped and flapped back and forth like leaves in the wind. Frank would wheel the piano past center stage and out past stage right. I'd tell him to stop, scream at him, plead with him, but there was no stopping him at center stage. After a few days of this, the cardboard piano legs would come off, and Eric would have to rebuild them.

When we tried to introduce the ultraviolet lights to create the full effect of black-light theatre, new problems arose. The performers couldn't understand that they were supposed to be invisible. They loved watching the effect, but when it came time for them to go on stage, they would run in front of the piano, cutting it off from view with their black-clad bodies.

As for the musical aspect of the number, Ann spent forever trying to teach them to move in time with the music — with little success. The performers on the musical notes were forever jostling, nudging each other, and fighting for position. And their rhythm was so bad that we might as well have been playing a slow waltz.

In the middle of this chaos, I was trying to do everything at once: help to manipulate the Liberace puppet; talk to the performers; fix broken or damaged props; and plead with David Garrick to book the Famous People Players at the CNE in August.

After almost a week of frantic phone calls, he agreed to my proposal, but there was a catch. I also had to perform, in my own puppet show — sixteen times a day.

Delighted with the news, I decided to push my luck and try to get Liberace himself to come and see the show. But every call I made to Seymour Heller was unsuccessful. A coolly polite secretary would ask my name, put me on hold for almost five minutes, and return to tell me that Mr. Heller was in conference. There was never a response to my letters.

The performers were thrilled about going to the CNE, but their enthusiasm wasn't translating itself into theatrical excellence. No matter how often I showed them how to hold their props, they would make the same mistake, again and again. It was a constant battle to achieve the simplest results.

All that kept us going was the understanding we had reached on Day One: We would somehow destroy the label "mentally retarded." None of us realized how great an effort would be required, but we were determined to succeed.

And then there were the parents. Nonstop phone calls; nonstop questions. Why is my kid at work until 7 P.M.? Why are you yelling at them? What's all this nonsense about Liberace? And the worst one of all: Aren't you pushing these kids around for your own purposes? Aren't you exploiting them?

I was very aggressive in my answers. As far as I was concerned, what happened between me and the performers at work was our concern, not their parents' business. "Look, Mrs. So-and-so," I would say. "I don't have your social insurance number in my files; I have your son's. And he works for me. If he has a complaint, he comes and talks to me about it."

As for the issue of exploitation, it made me furious. "If anyone should be complaining," I told one mother, "it should be me. What makes you think I should have to put up with your daughter's behavior? That's exploitation, too!"

Once in a while, the complaints would reach Dr. Roeher's office and I'd be called in to account for my methods. I was no less aggressive with him than with the parents. "Why is it all right for them to scream and yell because they're 'retarded' but it's exploitation when I do it because I'm 'normal'?" I demanded. "Let me tell you, the Famous People Players are going to make a major breakthrough. We're going to get rid of those labels: 'retarded,' 'normal.' And we're going to do it *together*, because it's what we *all* want."

Dr. Roeher just smiled, as if to say: What do you do with such a bulldog? He sent me back to the rehearsal room, and I'm sure he heard the din resume at an even higher frequency than before.

Amidst all this activity, my wedding day was approaching. Mom came to the office three or four times to fit me for my dress. And very frustrating fittings they must have been: two minutes of fitting and an hour of trying to get Greg to bring the piano bench in right side up. It was hard to stay still while manipulating a puppet with one hand and showing Larry how to keep the candelabrum from drooping in his hands with the other.

When my wedding day finally arrived — June 22, 1974 — I'm surprised I didn't have my jeans on under my dress! The day after the wedding, I was back at work, still trying to whip the show into shape — all three minutes of it. The Liberace puppet was still without direction. The head went north, the arms went south, and the legs went east and west. Tom was still shaking his candelabrum like a rattle, Greg was still bringing the piano bench in upside-down, and Frank was still bypassing center stage with the piano.

One day Daphne threw an awful fit after I corrected her for holding her musical note sideways. She shrieked for almost an hour, and I finally went to the office and called her parents to come and get her. She never returned and thus became the first performer to leave the company. I refused to sit around second-guessing myself about what had happened. We had a show to rehearse, and we had to go on.

In July, when the performers got their first paychecks, I decided to throw a celebration party at my place. I made chicken tetrazzini; Keith and Mike brought homemade wine; Larry brought beer. Everyone was dressed to the nines. Irene even gave up her slacks for the day and looked lovely in her summer dress. I handed out the checks as if they were Oscars. "Now I'm a man," Larry said when he got his, "and I'm going to marry Sandra." We all cheered, but as it turned out, they never followed through on the announcement.

Occasionally, the staff of the Canadian Association for the Mentally Retarded would come upstairs to the lecture room and watch our rehearsals, always cheering and clapping heartily. I strongly objected to this: "Why are you applauding when the show is so bad?" I demanded. "It would be much more help if you booed them."

"Oh, no, we couldn't do *that*," said one of the social workers. "That would make them unhappy."

A few weeks later, when we did the show for the parents, it was the same attitude: they gave a standing ovation for what I knew was a mediocre performance. To make matters worse, most of the parents described the show as a nice break from the sheltered workshop to which the kids would surely be returning come September. But three of the parents were different. They saw that we had a long-term goal in mind, and they spoke of Famous People Players as an ongoing project. These three were Mrs. Kozak, Greg's mother, Mrs. Pritchard, Frank's mom, and Mrs. Edwards, Keith's mom. They also offered practical help, such as driving a group of the kids to the CNE when our shows began.

With their support, I finally had the courage to go back to the association staff and ask them to watch another rehearsal, this time with a critical eye. They protested again, but I insisted: "These kids have to find out what a real audience is like — talking during the performance; booing and jeering if the show is bad. That's the only way they'll learn how things really work in the theatre."

Dr. Roeher and his staff finally agreed. They chatted all the way through the number, and the boos, catcalls, and insulting remarks echoed through the rehearsal room. Suddenly, Irene threw off her hood, leaped from the stage, and shouted at the staff: "You bunch of idiots! Why don't you applaud?"

"You're not going to be able do that at the CNE," I told Irene, pulling her back toward the stage. "If you jump off the stage and yell at the audience, they *are* going to treat you like a 'retard.' You don't have to act like that; you can act like a professional, which means doing your show, not fighting with your audience."

Irene climbed back on stage, and the show went on, to the accompaniment of more boos and catcalls, which, I must say, were entirely deserved.

But this willingness to keep trying was in itself a sign of progress — one of the few I could see — and the performers' determination to improve was growing. They were always lined up at the door when Ann and I arrived in the morning, and it was always a contest to see who would leave latest.

Ready or not, the CNE show was getting closer. A few days before we were to open, I got some good news and some bad news. My doctor gave me the good news — I was pregnant! — and I heard the bad news on the radio at home. The Toronto Transit Commission had gone on strike. All the parents started calling, saying the project was obviously over, since the performers wouldn't be able to get to the Exhibition.

"No, it's not the end of the project," I said for the umpteenth time. "Here's what we're going to do. The players who can't get a lift to the CNE are going to stay with Bernard and me."

The parents agreed, and one of them, Mrs. Kozak, offered to drive the four performers who lived in her area. The other six would live with me for three weeks.

There remained only the small matter of letting Bernard in on the news that we would be hosting six house guests in our two-bedroom apartment. "Now, when Bernard comes in, don't tell him right away that you're going to be living here," I told the players, who were now gathered in the living room. They all nodded.

A few minutes later, Bernard came home from work. "Hey, guess what, Bernard!" Frank piped up. "We're all living with you for three weeks." Furious, Bernard turned on his heel and walked out of the apartment. But a few minutes later he was back — and promptly organized everyone to work on dinner.

The strike continued throughout the Exhibition, and it was a miracle that we all got to the CNE grounds each day. Some of us hitchhiked; others got a ride with Mom, who came into Toronto from Hamilton each day; and Mrs. Kozak took care of the others. The transit strike was a major difficulty, but it also gave the performers the chance to learn skills to which they had never been exposed. They learned to budget their money (we all kicked in for food), do their laundry, wash dishes, and use a vacuum cleaner. And, for the first time, they began to develop self-confidence. I particularly remember the change in Irene. She took responsibility for many of the chores in the apartment, stopped wearing men's clothes, and even scolded the rest of us if we were late leaving for the CNE.

But getting from Point A to Point B wasn't the biggest headache of our CNE appearances. The show was. On our first day, we got to our site to find that the black flats (used to darken the stage so its outlines aren't picked up by the ultraviolet light) were too big for the stage. In a frenzy, I rushed to the CNE carpentry shop. "Please, please, you've got to help us!" I wept to the chief carpenter. "Our show begins at one and our flats are too big!"

Two carpenters came over, shaking their heads at the sight of the Famous People Players, yelling and laughing like hyenas. They built new flats for us, and even helped us paint them. We were finished just before show time.

The first show was a disaster. As usual, Greg's piano bench came in upside-down; the piano once again lost a leg; the musical notes were several beats off the music; and Larry persisted in talking nonstop throughout the show. "Do I look 'normal,' Diane?" he asked as he waited in the wings.

"Yes, Larry, but don't talk in the wings," I said, coughing violently at the scent of what was evidently a full bottle of after-shave lotion.

A minute later, he was back: "How am I doing, Diane? Am I doing okay?"

"Larry, when you're doing something wrong, I'll tell you. *Don't* talk in the wings!"

As the number ended — to a smattering of half-hearted applause — I raced to the other end of the midway to do my own puppet show; then dashed back for the next Famous People Players show. All day long I ran back and forth, fixed props, encouraged the performers, and, finally, as the end of the day approached, I collapsed in one of the audience seats and closed my eyes in utter exhaustion.

"Diane?" I opened one eye. It was Mike, holding hands with a beautiful blonde girl. "Diane, this is Nancy, my girlfriend," he said. "She wants to be in the show."

We needed someone to do a musical note, so I hired Nancy. She learned the part very quickly; unfortunately, she was also quick to lose her temper. During one show, she even threw a fit on stage. She had apparently been bumped by one of the other musical notes. It took Ann and me almost an hour to calm her.

In the first week, the performances showed no signs of improvement. Sometimes the audiences applauded anyway; sometimes they booed; and sometimes we played to an empty house. But the parents thought their children were just great. And so did the media: The Famous People Players were terrific — considering they were mentally retarded. I was grateful for the attention, but I still believed we could accomplish much more.

By the second week, the performances were slowly starting to get better, and I was beginning to see a glimmer of the magic I had imagined in my mind: gleaming piano, cavorting candelabrum, and somersaulting Liberace, all glowing three-dimensional animated figures in the dark. Then, during our last show one day, I went backstage to look for a missing prop — and saw Alice on the floor having sex with another performer. I ignored them until after the show, then took Alice aside and told her — for the hundredth time, it seemed — that sexual activity on the job was completely unacceptable.

"Well, I didn't miss any of my cues," she said defiantly.

"That's not the point," I said. "You can't have sex during a show."

We argued it back and forth, our voices getting louder, but the discussion was going nowhere. I told Alice she was fired. The male performer was told off in no uncertain terms, but I didn't fire him. Until then, he had always obeyed company rules, whereas Alice had been warned many times. In retrospect, I think I'd do the same thing today, except that it probably would have been more fair to let them both go.

The only positive side to the experience was the way the other performers rallied. They all said they were ready to work harder to compensate for the smaller cast. And Sandra, who almost never spoke up unless she was asked a question, approached me and said, "I'll do the other musical note, Diane." For Sandra, this was a giant step, the birth of an initiative which hasn't failed her since. She's always there.

Alice's fate, and the perils of making decisions that can affect people's lives, came back to haunt me. One day, during our last week at the CNE, we arrived to find a policeman waiting for me. Alice had been missing for ten days. Horrified, and certain it was all my fault, I broke into tears and told the cop that I had fired her. Maybe this was the reason she had run away. We canceled the remaining shows, and I went to the police station to wait for news. While I was there, I learned that Alice's mother had filed the missing-person report only that morning. My guilt turned to anger. She had been missing *nine days* before her mother saw fit to report her disappearance!

Moments later, Mrs. Robins, Alice's mother, arrived at the station. "You don't take your responsibility very seriously!" she accused.

"Well, what about your sense of responsibility?" I fired back. "You didn't even bother looking for Alice until she was missing for nine days!" Just then a policeman brought Alice into the room. Her hair was filthy and tangled; her clothes were in tatters; her eyes had a glazed look; and she was trying to flirt with the policeman who had brought her to the station. Without a word, her mother took her by the arm and led her out to a waiting car.

Years later we were on a streetcar, coming back from a show. A ravaged-looking bleached-blonde woman in a tight dress was staring at us. "Hi, Greg. Hi, Diane," she said — and we suddenly realized it was Alice. What a sad sight she was, and how I wished I could have prevented it. She got off the streetcar at Yonge Street, and as we watched her lean against a building in the unmistakable posture of a prostitute, we were all close to tears.

Our last day at the CNE was a difficult one. All the parents were there, and I was thrilled when Mrs. Kozak and Mrs. Pritchard gave me a silver charm bracelet with miniatures of a piano and a piano bench. But we found out the same day that Irene's father and Larry's mother had decided not to allow their children to continue in Famous People Players.

In fact, I myself was unsure how the company would continue. Our grant money was gone. The association office could no longer accommodate us. And Ann had decided to go to university. As we packed away the last of the props, I wondered how I could keep the dream alive. Not only had I lost four company members, the staff, and the rehearsal space, but the remaining seven performers were going back to the Haney Centre for the school year.

I didn't know what to expect when I asked those seven performers if they wanted to meet at my apartment every day after school. "It won't be like at the association," I said, "with rehearsals and everything. It'll be more like a club. We can talk, and listen to the Liberace record, and maybe come up with some ideas. What do you say?"

"Yeah, for sure!" yelled Greg, and the others echoed his enthusiasm, crowding around me with arms outstretched for a big hug. I couldn't hold back the tears of happiness and relief. The dream was no longer mine alone and that was our strength.

Our informal get-togethers went on for weeks. The performers watched TV while I made phone calls, trying to find some support for continuing the project. In the early evening we played the Liberace recording and talked excitedly about the great numbers we would create to accompany the music. One of our favorites was "The Impossible Dream," which to us was a symbol, a theme song.

It's lucky we had each other, because the results of my phone calls weren't encouraging. All the institutional barriers were up again as they had been the winter before. Even the people from whom we had received letters of support now sounded noncommittal. I particularly recall a conversation with Dr. Ron Christie, who headed the Metro Toronto Association for the Mentally Retarded. "The only thing that's standing in our way is that we don't have any funding," I said. "Otherwise, we could perform anywhere. The St. Lawrence Centre, for example."

"Diane, I feel what you're doing is wonderful and commendable," he said. "But you just can't view this project of yours as permanent. These people need a workshop environment and long-term training at The Red Foster Employment Training Centre. What you've given them is a summer experience I'm sure they'll always remember. I think you should leave it at that."

I thanked him politely, but inside I was boiling with anger. Summer experience, eh? We'd see about that.

I stared at the phone for a few minutes, then dialed the

business office of the St. Lawrence Centre. After all, I had told Dr. Christie we could perform there, and that's exactly what we were going to do. I found out that the theatre rented for $300.00 for one night. "Fine," I said, without hesitation at what seemed a huge amount of money. "I want to book it for the Famous People Players."

I never even considered that I might be jumping the gun by renting a theatre before I had a company. My mind was too full of ideas to consider caution. Besides, the very act of booking the theatre was an impetus to carry through with the event. The possibilities were endless. We could invite Liberace to come and see the puppet of himself. We could make the show a fund-raising event, have a reception, and charge five dollars for tickets. We could send out invitations signed by a well-known Toronto personality so we would get a big audience.

A well-known personality . . . . Why not Garrick from the Canadian National Exhibition? He had been delighted with the Famous People Players' shows. I called his office and, to my surprise, got through to him immediately. He said he'd be happy to sign the invitations. "As long as I can keep one myself," he added.

Utterly elated, I rushed into the living room and told the players we were going to perform in the Town Hall of the St. Lawrence Centre for the Arts in the winter. "And I'm inviting Liberace, too," I said. "I'm writing to his manager this evening, and I'm sure he won't be able to ignore us this time." Everyone cheered.

Only two small problems remained to be solved: How would we get the money to pay for the theatre and the postage for all those invitations, and where would we find a place to rehearse?

I tackled the financial issue that very evening when Bernard got home from work. "Bernard, I think we're going to have to make an investment in the future of Famous People Players," I said, and explained what I had in mind.

"What do you mean, 'we'? Who's this 'we'?"

"You and me, Bernard."

"Oh no you don't. We just paid fifty dollars to the association for that new rug after you guys got paint all over it. And what about the salary you didn't take all summer?"

"Bernard, this is important! We have to keep the company going, don't you see?"

Bernard reluctantly agreed. We took our modest savings, which were supposed to go toward a down payment on a house, and used the money to help bail out Famous People Players.

I immediately started looking for a new home for the company that we could afford. As soon as I began pursuing a goal, other things started to happen. One day, while I was out looking at prospective rehearsal halls, Sybil Powell, who had helped me get the grant for the summer, left a message suggesting I apply for a grant from the Local Initiatives Program, which provided funds for up to six months. I applied immediately, hoping we could make it through the two to three months' wait for a decision on our application.

There was also some bad news: a letter from Liberace's manager in Las Vegas. "I received your most interesting announcement," Seymour Heller wrote, "and, as personal manager to Liberace, please advise me exactly what this is about. It sounds to me as if someone has put together a play or some sort of performance which might be termed 'spoof.' "

He also sent a copy of his letter to the St. Lawrence Centre, whose staff anxiously called me to find out if the company planned anything slanderous. Luckily, they were appeased after I described the "Aruba Liberace" number we had performed at the Exhibition. Mr. Heller, however, was not similarly mollified. Although my second letter assured him we were not planning any gags — just a tribute to Liberace — his response was brief: "Liberace will not be available."

Another impasse. I didn't give up my ambition to get Liberace to one of our shows; I just put it on hold for a while and resumed my search for rehearsal space. At the beginning of October, I found it: the basement of a church in the west end of Toronto. The basement was dark and cold, but the stage was even bigger than the one at the Exhibition. And the best part was the rent. The minister, Reverend Crighton, asked for only fifty dollars a month, although he warned me that the rent would double if we got our grant.

The very next day, the Famous People Players were back in rehearsal. We had a depleted cast, *very* limited funds, one staff member (me) and a repertoire consisting of one imperfectly staged three-minute number, "Aruba Liberace." But these considerable limitations didn't curb our enthusiasm or our determination to put together a show that would make even the most demanding audience sit up and take notice.

Just as they had during the summer, the performers usually waited for me outside the church when I arrived in the morning and frequently asked if we could stay for the evening. School was abandoned, and their excitement about the project was so intense that even the parents who had been concerned about their children's preference for a struggling black-light theatre company to a school like the Haney Centre accepted the situation and slowly began to acknowledge the positive effects of Famous People Players. Frank's mother even called to say how happy she was that her son was taking an interest in something again.

Despite everyone's enthusiasm, rehearsals were slow going: There were still problems with "Aruba Liberace," even though we had been practicing it for almost four months. We spent so much time working the kinks out of that number that the other pieces I had planned were still just ideas. There was "Impossible Dream" with a finale that featured dozens of glittering, multicolored stars; "Me and My Shadow," which would couple the Liberace puppet with a black-clad performer wearing a white top hat and shoes and carrying a white cane; and "Boogie-Woogie" with a squadron of army ants, spiders, ladybugs, and worms wriggling to the fast-paced chorus. Even if the performers had been ready to start learning these numbers, the company didn't have enough money to buy the materials and paints for the props we would need.

On a shoestring, Mom designed and built some new props for "Aruba." She always managed to find time to help, even though she still had a full-time job in Hamilton. There were even eight letters spelling out Liberace's name in the "Aruba" number — but there were times I wished I had never thought of them. It seemed impossible to teach the performers to keep the letters in sequence. Inevitably, a fight broke out, usually started by Nancy, whose temper flared up frequently. She threw down her *A* and viciously kicked the others' letters out of their hands, or she stood up on the black boxes, mumbling curses at everyone. If I turned up the music, she screamed at the top of her lungs and knocked over props, furniture, and anything breakable, as Reverend Crighton peered anxiously into the room.

I decided we should have a meeting every day in the lunchroom across from the rehearsal hall. Maybe we could solve some of the problems by talking about them. The discussions were great — all the performers aired their gripes and spoke about their problems — but the resolutions vanished into thin air when we went back to work. Most days, only about half an hour was devoted to rehearsal. The rest of the time was spent fighting or talking about why we shouldn't be fighting.

Almost broke, besieged by difficulties, barely able to limp through one number, The Famous People Players, in the late fall of 1974, was a far cry from the trend-setting triumph I had imagined a year before. Yet we would not give up.

At the end of October, Mike and some of the other performers started talking to me about a buddy of theirs, Renato Marulli, whom they were trying to convince to come to the church basement. "Why doesn't he want to come?" I asked. "We could really use another performer."

"He's got that — what do you call it? — where you're born with something wrong with your face," said Mike.

"Birth defect?"

"Yeah, and he doesn't want people to see him, and his mother's really strict about him going out."

"Well, it can't be that bad," I said. "Ask him again."

Mike did ask Renato again. Finally, he agreed to come to the church. At first he stood in front of the open door, watching Mom repainting props. After a few minutes he crept through the door and stood in the shadows. After more than an hour he walked right into the rehearsal room. "Hi, Renato!" shouted Mike, and I looked over at him. I've got to admit that the first glimpse was a shock. His head was enlarged; his entire face was covered with thick red and purple blotches; and his eyes were distorted by the thickest glasses I'd ever seen.

Dupuy, I scolded myself, don't you dare judge by appearances. I approached him, smiling. "Your friends have been talking about you for weeks, Renato," I said. "I'm really glad to meet you."

"How do you do, Mrs. Dupuy," Renato said in a soft, pleasant voice. (All the other performers called me Diane.)

"Would you like to be part of Famous People Players, Renato?" I saw him glance over at the prop table. "You're interested in building props?"

"Oh yes. I like making things."

"Do you want to perform on the stage, too?" Renato shook his head emphatically; even when I explained that he wouldn't be seen under black light, he refused. Instead, he worked on the props, and I've never seen anyone other than Mom work so hard. Even the smallest musical note was subjected to the closest attention, and when there weren't any props to repair or paint, he diligently answered the phone and took messages. Before the week was out, Renato was everyone's favorite person — and I was no exception.

One day Renato came to me with tears in his eyes. "Mrs. Dupuy, my mother doesn't want me coming here anymore."

"Why not?"

"She doesn't like me being outside the house too much."

I immediately went to the Marulli home and tried to explain what Famous People Players was all about, but Mrs. Marulli understood no English and I had only a few words of Italian, despite my heritage. So it was Mom to the rescue. After an hour's conversation and several cups of espresso, Mrs. Marulli was charmed into allowing her son to be part of the company.

But there were problems with some of the others. Keith was starting to lose his temper; his shy nature was disappearing. My doctor, who also acted as our company physician, said he thought Keith's outbursts might have to do with his affection for me. Now that my pregnancy was starting to show, he was forced to acknowledge that I was with someone else. One day Keith's temper flared into a rage. He lifted a heavy sandbag and heaved it at me, missing me by inches. I ran into the bathroom as Renato, whose gentle nature altered if I was threatened, chased him out of the room. I finally ventured out, trembling. "You go home now, Mrs. Dupuy," Renato said. I didn't protest and gave everyone the day off.

I felt very weak as I entered the apartment, and suddenly my legs went out from under me. I was alone: Bernard was in France, where his sister was gravely ill. But I managed to get to the phone to call Dr. Turner, who came right over and told me to stay in bed until further notice. "If you start having cramps, you go straight to the hospital," he ordered.

Rehearsals stopped, and the performers became my personal nursing team. They all sat in the bedroom with me, brought me drinks and meals (I'll never forget Mike's horrible eggplant!), and talked endlessly with me about the baby — planning showers, choosing from potential schools, even deciding on appropriate careers. One morning, early in December, I felt the cramps Dr. Turner had described. Bernard was coming home that day, but he hadn't yet arrived, so Mike took me to Wellesley Hospital. I had only been there a few hours when Bernard arrived, and he was with me when I lost the baby. It was a boy.

Bernard cried with me, held my hand tightly, and whispered: "We'll have another baby. I promise."

All the performers came to see me, and Renato, who had never in his life used public transportation, took the bus and the subway to the hospital, asked directions to my room, and walked in holding an enormous plant. "I'm so sorry about the baby, Mrs. Dupuy," he said. I looked up at him, astounded at the courage it must have taken for him to overcome his fear of public places — the stares, grimaces, and insults he had endured — just so he could visit me and offer me some comfort.

It was at this time that I began to understand more deeply the nature of the performers: the remarkable intuitiveness that drew them to my side just when I needed them most; the very simple but very real steps they took to sustain and comfort me when I was in trouble. Generalities are problematic at best, but one characteristic seemed to link the players together: They were more interested in taking action than in analyzing — or even identifying — their reactions. If I had asked Renato, for example, what enabled him to come to visit me in the hospital that day, he probably would have said, "I don't know, Mrs. Dupuy." It was more important that he came.

A few weeks later, we got a pre-Christmas present. The grant came through. It was for $40,000, which gave the performers $110.00 a week and enabled them to get off their pensions, with the proviso that they would be reinstated after the money was gone. As project leader, I got $140.00 a week, but I decided to use my salary for company phone bills and materials for props.

Finally, we were able to hire new staff: Christine Wyck, a dancer who had worked at Black Box Theatre; Dan Reiner, the first male staff member in the company; and Leigh Alexander. Christine was a wonderful performer. Leigh conducted exercises to improve rhythm and co-ordination. And Dan, also a good performer (he did the head and body of the Liberace puppet), was a great influence on the guys in the company — especially our newest performer, Peter Maxwell, and Frank and Keith, who sometimes had trouble talking to a female boss.

I was finally free to direct and stage the production. I already had a clear idea of the sequence. "Aruba" would lead into "Me and My Shadow," with Christine doing the duet with the Liberace puppet. Then, a Barbra Streisand number, "The Way

We Were," with dancing violins accompanying the Streisand puppet. "Boogie-Woogie" would follow, and the last number would be "Impossible Dream."

But with new ideas came new problems. Tom came in one day with a great idea for a number that would feature two long fluorescent ribbons, swirling and curling to the melody of "The Homecoming." I was delighted with his initiative, and said his idea would be part of the show, but the praise went straight to his head. He didn't want to work on anything but *his* number. When I tried to show him the transition from "Aruba" to "The Way We Were" — all he had to do was put down his musical note and pick up his violin — he stopped listening and wandered off. Only when I hinted that he might lose his solo did he reluctantly start to learn the transition.

Then there was the matter of the players' paychecks. I began getting worried phone calls from some of the parents, who wanted to know on Monday why their sons and daughters hadn't been paid on Friday. "Keith *was* paid, Mrs. Edwards," I said.

"He's got no money, Diane," she said. "What do you suppose happened?"

"I don't know, but I'm going to find out." I stomped into the rehearsal room. "Keith, where did you go on Saturday?"

"To the arcade," he replied without a twinge of guilt. He had spent all day and all evening playing pinball and then returned Sunday for another twenty games or so. And it turned out many of the others were spending all their money the weekend they were paid. Greg, for example, favored the strip joints. I pointed out the benefits of saving money: Tom was going to buy a new bed with built-in drawers; Nancy had just acquired a stylish new outfit; Renato planned to buy a new armchair for his mother. But it was clear that I would have to spend many Mondays on this subject before I got any results with the others.

Sometimes the feeling that we were all a family — through thick and thin — seemed to be evaporating. Frank, who was on the outs with Keith, started hanging around with Greg, which annoyed Keith, who picked on Peter. Tom and Greg argued endlessly about how to synchronize their movements of one of the army ants in "Boogie-Woogie." No matter what they decided, the unfortunate insect's arms and legs went in opposite directions. Half the company wasn't talking to the other half, and I was at my wits' end.

One morning, a few weeks before our show at the St. Lawrence Centre, I came to the rehearsal hall feeling particularly frustrated. I had just received a letter from Seymour Heller rejecting my latest effort to get Liberace to come to our show. As I approached the stage, I saw that one of the black-light tubes was broken — and those tubes were considerably more expensive than light bulbs!

"I want to know how this happened," I said.

Silence.

"Look, you've got five minutes to tell me who broke this tube."

"What happens to the person who did it?" asked Greg.

"They're fired," I said, and, grabbing my coat, I stalked out of the church.

A few minutes later, as I was cooling my anger in the frosty winter air, they all came trooping out and approached me. "You're going to have to fire all of us," Mike said defiantly.

"We're not gonna tell on anybody," added Frank to a chorus of "Yeah!" from the others.

Tears sprang to my eyes as I watched them banding together with such loyalty. It was an instant lesson about what it means to act like a family. "C'mon," I said. "Let's go have a pizza, and afterward we'll all chip in and buy a new black-light tube."

"A pizza for breakfast?" shouted Peter. "All right!"

Our rehearsals went much better after that incident. But as our show at the St. Lawrence Centre approached, we still had only a six-minute show: "Aruba," "The Way We Were," and "Impossible Dream." The other numbers just weren't ready. I tried hard not to think about the reaction of our invited audience to an evening at a top Toronto theatre consisting of a six-minute show, a 20-minute speech, and a glass of wine and a piece of cheese afterward.

Our minishow started out great. I could hear the audience gasp as the piano came flying out of the wings, followed by the bench (upside-down or not, it was amazing to see an inanimate object dance and whirl on its own!), and the bejeweled figure of Liberace. And they howled with laughter to see Liberace play the piano with his toes as he bounded across the keys. But somewhere between the end of "Aruba" and the beginning of "The Way We Were," one of the performers decided to leave the stage.

Peter sat in the audience through the rest of the show, then clambered back on stage to join the others in their bows. Ignoring their furious glares (he had completely thrown off their movements), he bellowed, "You guys were great!" It was loud enough to hear on Front Street; the audience tittered nervously, and I buried my face in my hands.

"Why did you do that, Peter?" I asked after the reception.

"I heard all the applause."

"So?"

"So I thought, 'This show must be great!' "

"Uh . . . yeah?"

"So I wanted to see it," he explained. "You're doing a great job."

I took a deep breath. "Peter, I'd like you to promise me something," I said very carefully. "Next time, stay on stage till the end of the show. That's what performers do." But there wasn't to be a next time. Shortly afterward, Peter decided to leave the company.

This was an extremely vulnerable time in the life of the company — in terms of both morale and artistry. We had barely been able to keep Famous People Players alive, and, even after securing a "real" concert hall for a performance, the show itself had been a fiasco. Nor did I have any idea when — or if — our next show would take place. We had no prospects at all for the future.

Breakthrough in Las Vegas

FEBRUARY 1975 - OCTOBER 1975

In early February, I found out that the Ontario Association for the Mentally Retarded held a gala luncheon once a year in April. I called one of their officials, Helen Honickman, and asked her if she had planned the entertainment for the event.

"No, not yet," she said.

"Well, how about the Famous People Players?"

She hesitated at first, but I argued, cajoled, and finally promised her Liberace as guest of honor. Helen agreed.

The fact that Seymour Heller, Liberace's manager, had said no seven or eight times didn't deter me. I picked up the phone and called his Los Angeles office. A supercilious receptionist answered the phone: "Whom shall I say is calling, please?"

"This is Mrs. Bradshaw of the Prime Minister's Office calling from Ottawa," I said, equally smug.

A few seconds later, Seymour Heller was on the line. "Yes, Mrs. Bradshaw," he said deferentially. "How may I help you?"

"Well, as you may know, Mr. Heller, I work closely with the Prime Minister. Now Mr. Trudeau has had occasion in recent weeks to see a life-size puppet of your client, Liberace, but he can't recall exactly where he saw it, as his travels have been extensive. He seemed to feel that your office might have additional information about it, and he would like to arrange for the puppet to perform at his residence, 24 Sussex Drive."

"It seems to me I've heard something about this before," Mr. Heller said. "Why don't you let me get back to you?"

"Unfortunately, I must return to the House of Commons immediately; you'll have to let me call you back. You see, we have a troublesome situation just now with an impending postal strike."

"Oh . . . . Well, just remind Mr. Trudeau that Liberace discovered Barbra Streisand."

I hung up the phone and raced back to rehearsal. Tom was still having trouble with his violin in "The Way We Were," and the army ants in "Boogie-Woogie" still weren't in sync. In fact, the number was almost as bad as it had been a month before. Mom and Renato were buried under a mountain of work: a new glittering red velvet costume for the Liberace puppet, a new wooden piano, and a new candelabra. To top it all off, Reverend Crighton was starting to grumble about all the noise we were making (not to mention evidence, in the kitchen, of a large-scale spaghetti supper we had made one night).

After a few days of this pandemonium, I grabbed a spare five minutes and got on the phone to Mr. Heller again, this time posing as a rich society lady from Forest Hill who wanted to hire Liberace — "the puppet, not the real Liberace," I giggled — for a country club party.

A week later, I made another phone call to Hollywood, this time pretending to be an organizer of the luncheon. "The Famous People Players will be performing with their wonderful Liberace puppet, and it would be fabulous if Liberace could attend. The mayor will be there, and the Prime Minister, Mr. Trudeau, who is a big fan of the — "

"I'll have to get back to you," he said.

The tennis game between Seymour Heller and me went on for weeks. But one day in March — just after I found out I was pregnant again — I got a call from Mr. Heller. "I've spoken with Liberace about your group's performance, Mrs. Dupuy," he said. (I held my breath.) "And I'm happy to tell you that he will be attending the luncheon on April 10."

I tore into the rehearsal hall, screaming, "Liberace's coming to our show! He's really going to be there!" Everyone jumped off the stage, cheering and hugging and clinging to one another.

At last, the day of the luncheon arrived. I went to meet Liberace at the Royal York Hotel, where he was staying all week; he was performing at the nearby O'Keefe Centre. I hadn't had an inkling, when I made my outrageous request, that our performance happened to coincide with his own engagement in Toronto. When Liberace emerged from behind the elevator doors, it was like watching a sunrise: He wore a denim outfit literally covered with jewels, and his rings just about took my breath away. As the car rolled onto the highway, I thought to myself: In just a few minutes, our dream will come true. The Famous People Players will be performing for Liberace.

The banquet room was packed, but I finally picked out Judi, Ann, and Mom in the audience, leaning forward expectantly. I prayed silently as the lights went down and the music came up. And I watched a miracle unfold. Months of hard work and stubborn faith came together before my eyes.

It looked like someone had taken a page out of a fairy-tale picture book, waved a wand, and brought the illustrations to life, setting them in motion against a backdrop of pure, velvety black. And these fairy-tale figures all moved precisely, perfectly through their miniature tableaux — thanks to the invisible performers. No one made a single mistake: Greg got the piano bench right side up; Frank brought the piano bench directly to center stage; all the letters came out in order. Everything was perfect. I kept looking over at Liberace. He wept over "The Way We Were," roared with laughter at the wriggling bugs in "Boogie-Woogie," and cried again as the glimmering stars signaled the end of "Impossible Dream."

It was over. The performers pulled off their black hoods and got a standing ovation, and Liberace suddenly jumped up and went over to the microphone. "I've never seen anything so wonderful," he said, "and I want these performers to come to Las Vegas and be part of my show!" Another thunderous burst of applause accompanied him back to his seat. As soon as he was seated, the performers came toward him one by one, each of them presenting him with a rose.

Only then did he seem to realize that most of them were retarded — I could tell by the look of amazement on his face — and he promptly returned to the microphone. "It's not because of who you are that makes people laugh or cry," he said. "It's because you're truly talented performers." To hear these words from the man who had been our inspiration through all these months of struggle and chaos was better than winning a million dollars.

We savored our triumph, but only for one day. Now, there was a new deadline to meet: a private performance in Hamilton the following week for Liberace, Seymour Heller, and several members of Liberace's company. Seymour had set up the show to give his client's troupe an idea of the act that would be joining the Vegas show.

Suddenly, while we were still high on our success, two staff members quit without notice. Dan announced that he didn't feel part of the company and walked out before I could even discuss his concerns with him. And Leigh left because of my speech at the luncheon. "It never occurred to you to thank any of us, or the parents, or anyone else who helped make the show possible," she said angrily. "That was really selfish." It was true: I hadn't thanked anyone except Liberace — not even my mother. After Leigh left, I sent her a dozen roses. She phoned to thank me but added that the flowers didn't make up for the way I had hurt her. "I'm sorry, Diane," she said, "but I'll never work for you again."

We desperately needed someone to do the head and body of the Liberace puppet for our performance in Hamilton. I phoned a friend, Ron Dick.

"I'd love to help, but I've got an exam coming up," he said.

"What if I get the exam moved?"

"Well, I'd come and be in your show. But they won't move the exam."

I got on the phone to Ron's professor and talked him into

postponing Ron's exam for one week, and Ron started rehearsing the next morning. At first he could hardly hold the puppet, but he worked nonstop, sometimes practicing until almost midnight. The morning of the show, he took his exam, and when he joined us at Hamilton Place, I could tell by his smile that he had passed.

We even added one new number to the show in Hamilton: Tom's "Homecoming" routine with the ribbons. Once again, the show went off without a hitch.

After the show, Mr. Heller quickly became "Seymour"; the performers got to know Liberace's musicians; and we all talked about working together in Las Vegas in September. The only sad part was that Renato was not allowed to join us, not even in Hamilton. His mother allowed him to be part of the company, but she drew the line at out-of-town trips.

Then it was back to the church basement to rehearse for Vegas. We had months to prepare for the trip, but we all knew how painfully slow our progress was, and we weren't taking any chances. After all, this was our big break, our "impossible dream" come true. But it was also a hard grind: two shows a night for three weeks was a whole different ball game from our one-shot appearances to date. We had to be ready because there would be no second chance.

In June, when our grant ran out, Sybil Powell came to the rescue again with a second Opportunities for Youth grant. And there was more good news: Ann accepted my invitation to come back to the company and Mom decided to give up her job in Hamilton and work full time on props. She repaired each prop and rebuilt several that were damaged beyond repair. She was also wonderful with Renato, taking him under her wing and teaching him the many techniques she used in design and painting. But it wasn't always easy for mother and daughter to work together. I rarely complimented her on her work and frequently blew my cool when she made any suggestions about the way I directed the company. "You're pushing too hard," she often said — and I would start hollering.

"I'm not treating these performers like basket cases!" I

shouted one time. "They're professionals, and that means hard work!" I suppose I should have been used to suggestions that I was driving these poor little retarded kids much too hard, but such comments continued to infuriate me, no matter who made them. If nothing much is expected of a person — retarded or not — then nothing much is likely to be achieved. And I was as focused on the performers' potential for success as a racehorse is on the finish line. Still, though, I had no business yelling at my mother that way, she just raised her eyes to the ceiling and sighed, as she does to this day.

In July — now five months pregnant — I had to fly to Lake Tahoe on one day's notice to discuss the forthcoming show with Liberace. As soon as one of the stewardesses saw my stomach, I was treated like royalty during the entire flight. And the treatment continued in Tahoe: a gourmet dinner and great seats for Liberace's show.

And then to work. After the show, I met Ray Arnett, Liberace's producer, choreographer, and stage manager. He showed me the backstage area and described the stage at the Las Vegas Hilton where we would be performing. He also told me that the performers would have to be able to move quickly when entering and exiting, because of the many cast and scene changes in the show. "Do you think you can train your cast to get on and off fast?"

"Oh yes," I said, trying to sound more confident than I felt.

Then Seymour explained that the background of the performers wouldn't be publicized. If we weren't working out, we would be sent home. The Liberace organization didn't want to be seen as the villain, pulling the plug on a group of handicapped young people. This arrangement was fine with me: the Famous People Players would be judged on the basis of their performances.

After Seymour spoke with me, it was Liberace's turn. "Now, first of all, I want you to call me Lee," he said. "All my friends do."

"Oh, of course," I said, delighted.

"There are just a few things, Diane. What numbers are you planning to do?"

"Just the ones we did for you, Lee."

"Don't you think you could use one more?"

"Uh . . . let me see." I thought furiously. "Oh, I know. We could do 'Viva Las Vegas' with an Elvis Presley puppet!"

"That's perfect," he said. "Now, I loved the way you spelled out my name, but I think the letters should be bigger, and instead of the puppet coming out after the letters, I'd like to come out." We worked out the timing: The players would have a six-second blackout before Lee made his trademark entrance — in the back seat of a huge, luxurious convertible.

Finally, Lee told me I should have understudies who could jump in and do any part if someone were ill. Famous People Players was being paid about $10,000 a week, but we had to cover airfares, prop shipments, and now, additional salaries. I wasn't complaining though, especially when Ray told me I was booked on a flight to Los Angeles, where the world-famous Bob Baker Marionette Productions was about to start building brand-new life-size puppets of Liberace, Streisand, and Elvis — all courtesy of the Liberace show.

When I got back to Toronto, rehearsals moved into overdrive. While Mom and Renato labored over new costumes and props, the performers struggled with the new transitions. Again and again they raced to stage left trying to meet the six-second deadline for their exit after the letters sequence. But it took almost a week to reduce the time from 12 to 11 seconds — and how they would ever bring it down to six seconds was beyond me. It was the same old problem: Nancy pushed Keith, Keith pushed Frank, and everyone ended up in a tangle of bodies somewhere between centre stage and the wings. It was clear to me, after more than a year of working with these performers, that the frustration of constant repetition was not something that would go away. Like the performers themselves, I had to accept this reality and develop some patience.

Staff crises were another disturbing constant. Just a few days after we celebrated the arrival of our new puppets from Los Angeles, Christine told me she couldn't go to Las Vegas and was leaving the company. "But how can you leave now?" I wailed in complete shock. "We've just got a new top hat, cane and shoes for you to do 'Me And My Shadow.' And Las Vegas — it'll be so great!"

"I'd love to go," said Christine, almost in tears. "But Mark won't let me, and you know how he is, Diane. Maybe I can come back after the trip; I don't know." Mark was Christine's ultra-possessive fiancé, and I knew there would be no talking him out of his stubborn stance. We threw a little surprise party for Christine — just a cake and a few small gifts — and then she was gone. We were all heartbroken, and I remember one of the performers hanging the old top hat, cane, and shoes over the stage with her name under them and a sign: DO NOT TOUCH — FOREVER.

There was no one in the company who could dance well enough to replace Christine, so I decided to hold auditions for the understudies right away. That is, I asked Judi to audition the applicants. She wasn't officially part of the company, but her administrative judgment was excellent. We picked two guys and a girl, all excellent professional dancers. They seemed enthusiastic about Famous People Players, but I couldn't help noticing that they were more excited about performing in Las Vegas than being part of the company. Ignoring my misgivings, I went ahead and hired them.

And we kept on working on our technical problems. The new number, "Viva Las Vegas," was presenting the most difficulty. For three people to synchronize Elvis's swiveling hips, sliding feet, guitar-strumming fingers, and tilting head was an exercise in frustration. And aside from the Elvis puppet, there were plenty of other complications in the number. The sheer number of props, for example: several sets of dice, huge dollar signs, roulette wheels, and a slot machine. The wheels were made of foam and got so damaged that Mom and Renato made a new set out of cardboard — but they split apart. So we went to wood, even though the wheels were much heavier.

In no time, it seemed, the departure date for Las Vegas was upon us — and so was yet another company crisis. Once again, Mrs. Marulli forbade Renato to go out of town, and once again Mom's pleas, in her most eloquent Italian, were in vain. Renato and I sat on the front steps of the church to wait for my taxi, keeping each other quiet company. I was leaving a day early to make sure everything was ready for the company's arrival. "Well, Mrs. Dupuy," he finally said, fighting back tears, "I *did* get to meet Liberace." We hugged, briefly; then the taxi honked its horn and I had to go.

After I checked into the imposing Las Vegas Hilton, I rushed to the backstage area of the lavish entertainment room, terrified that our props had somehow not been delivered; to my great relief, they were all there and nothing was broken.

That evening Bill Cosby was performing, so I saw his show and decided to go backstage afterward. I approached him, saying, "I loved your show, Mr. Cosby, and I'm not sure if you remember me, but . . ."

"You look really familiar," he said, scratching his head perplexedly.

"I met you a few years ago in Toronto," I said. "You saw my show and talked to me about black-light theatre."

"Oh yes, now I remember. Did you ever look into black-light theatre?"

"Yes, I did, and you know what? I have a black-light company now, and we're opening here in two days with the Liberace show."

"That's great!" he said, genuinely happy. "I hope you have every success."

The next morning, I looked out the window and saw the huge marquee had an addition to the LIBERACE sign that had been there alone the day before — FAMOUS PEOPLE PLAYERS.

When the company arrived, we faced our first crisis before we even got out of the lobby. I wanted to sign the hotel registration cards for the performers who couldn't write. But the desk clerk insisted that everyone sign individually. I couldn't explain that some of the performers' backgrounds were to remain a secret, and it took about two hours of coaching and coaxing before everyone signed in and headed to the elevator. That left the performers about fifteen minutes to change into their black jumpsuits and get back downstairs for rehearsal.

We had to wait almost two hours for Liberace. When he finally appeared, Ray Arnett blasted him for being late and demanded that he apologize to all the performers and stagehands. I thought Lee would blow his stack, but instead he was utterly contrite. "I'm so sorry, Ray," he said. "Please forgive me, Diane . . . ." I was impressed. Lee was a big enough star to get away with being temperamental, but I was just starting to learn that the biggest stars are also those who take professionalism most seriously.

Ray asked us to do our opening number, and the performers got all the way through the sequence. But after the six-second blackout, they were still on stage. "Try it again," said Ray. The same thing happened; Ray turned to me: "Didn't you rehearse this in Canada?"

"Yes, we did, but we can't seem to do it any faster." (I was sure we were going to be sent home in disgrace.)

"Let me teach you a little lesson about how to direct a group of people, Diane," he said, and he turned to Vince Cardell, Liberace's protégé, who performed in the show as well as driving the convertible that brought Lee on stage. "Vince, start up the car and bring it on stage, okay?"

The performers ran through the number again, and, as the blackout began, they heard the car coming toward them. You never saw a group of people get offstage so fast! "Five seconds," said Ray. "Little dose of reality; that's all they needed."

After the rehearsal was over, the understudies headed to the pool, leaving the rest of us milling around in the lobby. Everyone went upstairs, and I went out to the pool to speak to the understudies.

"When you were hired, I made it clear that part of the job involved spending time with all the performers," I said, keeping my voice low. "Instead, you're sticking together in a little clique."

"We were just having a quick swim," they protested.

"That's not the point," I said. "The point is that we do things together. We're all a team. A family."

They made all the right apologetic noises, but I wasn't convinced. As I walked back to the lobby, I found myself wishing I had never hired them.

Finally, it was curtain time. The letter sequence was fine, but after the blackout, I covered my eyes in horror to see Frank wrapped around a curtain as Liberace's car came on stage. Suddenly, a hand reached around the curtain, grabbed Frank, and hauled him into the wings. Then the old problem with the Elvis puppet resurfaced: The hands went one way; the legs the other. I started crying — obviously, we had bombed — and when I got to the dressing room, I yelled out each mistake, never even telling the performers what they had done well. I just couldn't get Seymour's warning out of my mind: If the show doesn't work, the company goes home. I also felt that if these performers were going to develop, they had to reach for excellence, not settle for mediocrity.

But apparently my assessment was a minority of one. A few minutes later, there was a knock at the door; there stood Ginger Rogers, eager to congratulate the performers. There was a stampede to approach her and get her autograph. No sooner had she left than Bo Ayars, Liberace's conductor, arrived with his praise — and an offer to rescue Frank from his entanglement with the curtain *every* night. "When there's a blackout, Frank, just hit the dirt and get behind the black boxes, and I'll be there behind the curtain to pull you through." (That's exactly what happened during the entire three weeks!)

Finally, Lee arrived, beaming. "That was terrific!" he exclaimed. "By the way, I know there weren't supposed to be any bows, but why don't you take a short one anyway? Right after you come out with the letters; and if they aren't in the right order, I can do a funny bit and correct them." We were all thrilled, and I thought maybe the show wasn't quite as bad as I had imagined.

The next day's reviews were glowing. Our first reviews! Syndicated columnist Forrest Duke, "The Duke of Las Vegas," wrote:

> The company of 11 inspired and gifted young people is sure to be listed among Lee's most illustrious discoveries. Working in black light the Players present life-size performing puppets . . . huge, brilliantly colored letters spelling out the showman's name, a heart, musical notes and little creatures floating and cavorting in mid-air. The Famous People Players' captivating act is an ideal complement for Liberace . . . .

And even the frequently tough *Variety* had nothing but praise for us:

> Octet opens the show with funny anthropomorphic figures shaped in letters to spell out Liberace's name, dancing around and on a ghostly white grand piano . . . .
>
> Group does leave off Liberace long enough to include a shot at Barbra Streisand and another toward Elvis Presley, complete with dancing designs moving around the central figures. Players' last depiction of Liberace takes his usual boogie-woogie sesh from the repertoire and places it imaginatively with the group. They have fun with the rhythms, bringing forth still more odd characters to bounce around the piano. Altogether the Players are a strong addition to the Liberace show and could be showcased exceedingly well in other environments.

I raced upstairs with the papers to read them to the performers.

"They all liked us, Diane!" exulted Greg.

"Boy, this show-business stuff is fun," added Frank. "I just hit the dirt and get behind the black boxes, like Bo said."

"What's 'other environments,' Diane?" asked Sandra.

"That means you could do shows in lots of other places — all over the world — *but only if you get the roulette wheels going in the same direction, Sandra, and Elvis's arms and legs, Mike, and everybody on your transitions!*"

They all looked at me, crestfallen. "Oh, all right; all right. You were good last night. But you can be better. You can be perfect!" Everyone cheered.

Later in the morning, Lee called me and asked if we could change our opening number to "Viva Las Vegas" and perform the letters sequence and "Aruba" later in the show. "Sure. That's no problem," I agreed. As soon as I put the phone down, I called all the performers to the dressing room. We weren't allowed to rehearse on the stage, but we had to practice somewhere: As we had learned in the church basement, transitions were the most demanding part of a show. It took all day, but we somehow managed to learn them all.

The shows were much smoother on the second night. There were mistakes, but they were probably only visible to me — I knew every move in every number. Nevertheless, when the performers came into my dressing room, it was to my recitation of every error in the show. Later on, when I was back in my room, Mom knocked on the door. "Diane, I've got to tell you that you're being much too hard on these people," she said.

"Hard? They have to know when they've made mistakes."

"Yes, but do you have to be so tough?"

"Mom, this is a *professional* theatre company, and if they're going to make it as professionals, they have to learn the reality of the business."

"Well, I think you're going about it in the wrong way. If I were you . . ."

"Mom, I don't want your opinion!" She walked out without a word and flew home the following day. We eventually made up, but neither of us changed our opinions. Mom continued to argue for a gentler approach, and I continued to insist that performers push hard to achieve higher standards.

As the days went on, the performances steadily improved, and I was delighted. But I can't say the same for the performers' offstage activities. Tom, probably unhappy with the understudies' continued indifference to him and the other performers, suddenly went solitary on us: He went to the dressing room alone, back to his room alone, and even sat alone at a table in the coffee shop. Squabbles began to break out; the understudies continued to keep to themselves; and a mood of instability spread. One time, I asked everyone to use the stairs instead of the elevator to get backstage. "But Liberace uses the elevator," said Keith. "We can use the elevator, too."

"No, you do not use the elevator; you use the stairs. What if the elevator breaks down?"

"Liberace uses the elevator," the others chorused.

"Well, you don't! Use the stairs, and that's final!" My tone of voice produced the desired effect: silence.

The elevator episode was over, but there was another incident the next day. And the next. Ray Arnett and I had become friends during the first few days of our stay. One evening, just before the show, he found me alone in the dressing room, staring into space. "What's the trouble, Dora Doom?" he asked cheerfully.

I had to laugh at the nickname. "Ray, I want my company to work together like a family."

"Don't worry about it so much, Dora," he said. "Give it time. It'll happen."

For a few days there were no incidents. Then trouble struck again. Keith became lost in one of the corridors and wandered up and down until a hotel employee found him. Dick Lane, the entertainment director of the hotel, was informed. He promptly called me — it was the first I'd heard about it — and told me in no uncertain terms that a repeat performance would not be appreciated.

A few hours later, Ron called my room to tell me that Keith had ordered a case of Heineken sent up to the room they shared. "I tried to talk him out of it, but he just blew sky-high and started punching the wall . . . ."

"I'll be right there."

Up in their room, I managed to persuade Keith to cancel the order. "You don't even *like* beer, Keith," I reminded him.

"Besides, you don't have the money," Ron added.

"Wait a second," I said. "What happened to all that money your parents gave you?" Mr. and Mrs. Edwards had given Keith $800.00 before we left, which was far too much money to give him.

"I played some games in the casino." When I referred to the discussion we had had about the casino being off limits to hotel employees, he shrugged and agreed with me that he had made a mistake. "I won't do it again," he promised. But I knew it was only because he was broke that he would keep this promise.

The very next night my phone rang again. It was Mike. "Tom's down in the lobby, and he's wearing his pajamas and he's crying."

Oh no. Now what? I struggled into my clothes and headed downstairs, to find Tom still in tears. "It's okay," I told the flustered hotel clerk, who was standing a little to the side as if afraid to get too close. "He's fine now, and I don't think we have to mention this to anyone." She nodded numbly and slowly walked back to the counter.

"Tom, tell me what happened," I said when we got back to his room.

"I heard a funny noise in the bathroom and I went to see what it was, but I couldn't get in the bathroom because the door was locked, so I said, 'Hello? Is anybody there?' But nobody answered me and I got scared. So I looked under the crack in the door and I saw some green underwear on the floor. Then I looked in the keyhole and I saw two people having sex."

The two people turned out to be two of the understudies. I didn't fire them on the spot (I would if it happened today), but I certainly told them plainly how I felt about their behavior: "I really don't give a damn what you do on your own time, but when you're working for this company, you just do without sex for three weeks. These people need your support, which you have not given them once. They don't need to see you screwing in the bathroom." I slammed the door of the room and headed downstairs to find a quiet place.

In the entertainment room, I stared at the stage and wondered what was tearing us apart. Was it the pressure of being here? Was it the understudies? Was it me?

"Who's that with the long face?" It was Ray. "Oh, it's Dora. What's the tragedy this time, Dora?"

"I don't know, Ray," I said. "I just want to keep the company together, and things keep falling apart. The normal people won't hang around with the retarded people and feelings are hurt. Everybody is acting up. Then I'm wondering if I'm doing the right thing . . . ."

"Everybody who's director of a company wonders if they're doing the right thing," he said, "and I'll tell you, the only right thing to do is what you decide is right."

"Well, there are a few people in particular whom I'd be very happy to lose."

"Dora, you've got people working for you who aren't good for the company," Ray said, and I could tell he was talking about the understudies. "But there's nothing you can do about it now. Just wait until you get home and don't renew their contracts. Meanwhile, try to think about the good things — like the great job your company is doing on stage."

"Is it really great?"

"Yes, it is. And I don't use that word a lot." Ray's vote of confidence helped me weather the storm, and boosted the performers' spirits when I passed it on to them. I was learning, too, to temper my criticism with praise.

The third week in Las Vegas was the best. Except for the

continued indifference of the understudies to everyone else in the company, we had no problems. And the performers' relationships with Lee were wonderful. In fact, there was an exchange between him and Frank one night that I can't recall without smiling.

Lee was getting ready for the show and chatting with me when Frank walked into the dressing room. "You're a pretty popular guy, Liberace," he said, fixing Lee with a determined stare.

"I like to think so; thank you, Frank."

"I'm telling ya, Liberace, you're pretty popular," Frank repeated, plunking himself down in an armchair as if preparing to settle the matter for posterity. "You know that couple?"

"What couple?"

"*You* know. Every night you tell the audience there's a couple who just got married, and she's 68 and he's 72, and it's the second time around for both of them." What Liberace said on stage was that a couple had requested their favorite song, "It's Impossible," to be played early in the evening, because they couldn't stay out late. It's questionable if these lovebirds ever really existed!

"Oh, yeah, *that* couple," said Lee, winking at me.

"Yeah, they come every night. For both shows . . . . You're a pretty popular guy!"

That night, as Lee sat down to play the song, Frank was right there in the wings, watching him like a hawk. When Lee announced "It's Impossible," Frank piped up: "I knew it! They're here again tonight!"

After the show, Frank was waiting for Lee as he came offstage. "I'm telling ya, Liberace, you sure are one popular guy."

"Thank you, Frank," he said. "Now tell me one thing. What happens if I'm not popular?"

"That couple stops coming to your show!"

It wasn't just Frank. Lee was constantly chatting with the performers, and they loved the attention — except once. Toward the end of a show, Lee was standing in the convertible, smoking and talking to the stagehands. He noticed Nancy clutching her letter and looking very serious. "How do you like Las Vegas, Nancy?" Silence. "Are you enjoying working for me?" Silence. "Are you happy?" Deafening silence.

After he took his bow, Lee came over to me and said wistfully, "I don't think they like me anymore."

I opened my mouth to protest, but Nancy was faster. "Liberace! How unprofessional to talk in the wings! You might miss a cue!" He laughed for a good five minutes.

Three nights later, he *did* miss a cue while talking in the wings. After the show, Nancy came over to him, gloating. "See?"

"Yes, I do see, Nancy," he said, utterly in earnest, "and I'll never let it happen again."

After the last show, Lee threw a farewell party for us and made a surprise announcement — he wanted us back in February.

By the time we were on the plane, I was thinking again about all the turmoil the company had endured during the past three weeks. I was getting ready to plunge into my Dora Doom persona when I noticed, in the seats opposite, Keith and Nancy chatting quietly with Greg. They were all sitting ramrod-straight; their voices were calm and articulate. They had a look of self-confidence and pride that I'd never seen before. I looked around at the others, and it was the same. Even Sandra was deep in conversation with — of all people — one of the understudies. I glanced back to the seats across from me just in time to see Keith offer his coffee creamer to Nancy. "Are you sure you don't want it?" she asked.

"Oh, no; go ahead," Keith replied politely.

My eyes filled with tears. It may seem strange that such a simple exchange would elicit such a strong reaction, but I had spent more than a year trying to stop bitter fights that could erupt over nothing more serious than a coffee creamer. To see Keith and Nancy treating each other with respect was very moving to me.

bove: *Mary Gioberti and Stanley Thornton on their dding day.*

Right: *Diane Dupuy at Loretto Academy.*

Leonard Warren, Guido Gioberti and Stanley Thornton at a party for Leonard Warren at the Gioberti home.

Diane Dupuy, Liberace and some of the players, Las Vegas, 1975.

Above: *Celebratory dinner, Las Vegas.*

Below: *The marquee for the Las Vegas performance.*

Above: *Anne Murray and friends.*

Right: *The director.*

Above: ***Carnival of the Animals*** *puppets with Gorden Pinsent.*

Left: *Kenny Rogers puppet.*

Right: ***Scheherazade*** *puppets and their handlers.*

Mary C. Thornton, Diane's mother, working behind the scenes.

(AP/WIDE WORLD PHOTOS)

iberace, the man and the puppet, and friends.

Brooke Adams, star of **Special People**, *and the Famous People Players company.*

ooke Adams and Benny D'Onofrio in a scene from **Special People.**

bove: *Albert Gentili, Maureen McTeer and Renato Marulli.*

eft: *The company on their Chinese tour, 1982.*

The Famous People Players open in **A Little Like Magic** at the Lyceum theatre on Broadway, 198

(CANAPRESS)

bove: *Joanne Woodward and Paul Newman pose with the cast at the Lyceum.*

elow: *Sandy Duncan lends her moral support.*

Diane Dupuy and the cast of the Famous People Players.

A Company of Professionals

NOVEMBER 1975 - DECEMBER 1978

It suddenly hit me that we were now a professional company, and increasingly treated as such by the entertainment industry. Liberace and the show in Vegas had helped us open doors: We had bookings and a new respect. And that meant tight schedules, new numbers to expand our show, increased costs, and more performers. I could see the tip of the iceberg of responsibility: I was elated and terrified, both for the company and for myself.

The sense of a change in our status permeated the company. Back in Toronto, we all threw ourselves into rehearsals with more seriousness than ever before. There was a new energy and cohesiveness which seemed to arise to meet the increasing demands on us. "We have to rehearse," became the most-used phrase of Famous People Players — and it was coming from the performers as often as from me.

The performers' parents, too, were becoming more appreciative of the company's accomplishments. They even threw a surprise shower for me, which was a great morale booster — and ensured that I would never have to buy diapers for the baby I expected in December. It must have been a sign because, soon afterward, Jeannine decided to come on stage, in her own good time — a month early.

At the doctor's urging, I sang "Aruba Liberace" during the delivery to ease the pain. And when the performers arrived to visit me and Jeannine at the hospital, we decided on the spot to do another benefit, charging only $2.00 a ticket this time so we could get a bigger audience. Our confidence was growing along with our expertise. While I was still in the hospital, I got on the phone and booked the St. Lawrence Centre again, then sent the performers to pick up the bag of tickets, which we sorted out on my bedside table.

No sooner did they set out to start selling than the phone rang. "It's Lorraine Thomson calling; I'm the story researcher of 'Front Page Challenge.' I read the great review of the Famous People Players in *Variety*, and we'd like to feature you on the show."

I was delighted. "Front Page Challenge" was one of the most popular shows on television. "Of course," I said. "I'd love to be on the show."

"Can I reach you at this number later to discuss the details?"

"Well, not really. You see, this is Women's College Hospital, and I was just in here having a baby!" Lorraine cracked up, and I just managed to slip in my home phone number between her chortles.

A few days after I went home, I was invited to appear on another TV show, "In Good Company." My television appearances were a welcome sign of our growing recognition, and, as the date of our St. Lawrence Centre benefit approached, it was heartening to see that the company was becoming ever more disciplined and professional. Tom was making great progress with his difficult transitions: A few days before the benefit, we did a run-through, and he was perfect. At the end of "Ribbons," he climbed onto a black box, made his ribbons "disappear" behind it (both box and black-clad performer are invisible under ultraviolet light), reached behind the box for his violin, and, at the end of "The Way We Were," walked calmly to stage right to pick up his spider for "Boogie-Woogie."

Great, I thought. We're all set. But I had temporarily forgotten what can happen when you grow too confident. Tom blocked everyone's entrance in every number, and, by the time

"Boogie-Woogie" started, disaster was imminent. The other performers, frustrated, started to push him, shouting, "The ladybugs come on before your stupid spider!" Tom pushed back and finally succeeded in toppling the makeshift black flat. The others collapsed on top of each other — assorted insects hitting the deck — and Tom proudly raised his spider as the black-light stand toppled with a resounding crash. As I shrank back further in the wings, Victor Polley, the general manager of the theatre, patiently righted the flat and stand. And all this in front of an audience of three hundred people!

We were so embarrassed that we waited until we were sure the audience had left before we ventured out to the lobby, and no one spoke to Tom for the rest of the day. Luckily, the second and third shows were much better. Audiences sought us out backstage — and even asked for autographs — telling us again and again how mind-boggling it was to see fantasy creatures and famous characters come alive in the dark. And we were also pleased with the $2,000 we took in — without any advertising except for the posters the performers put up all over town.

As 1976 began, we were all in high gear, getting ready for our second trip to Las Vegas. I decided we would bring the props as baggage, saving ourselves $2,000 in shipping costs and giving Mom and Renato more time to finish repairing and repainting them. I made it clear to our new understudies that they would be required to spend time with the performers. And there would be a new young addition to the company: Jeannine Dupuy was coming along. But not Renato. His mother once again forbade him to take the trip.

At the airport, everyone was up. All the performers formed a line at Customs as their parents looked on proudly. "Where are you going?" the official asked Greg, brushing aside Mrs. Kozak's offer to speak for her son.

"Las Vegas," Greg said.

"What is the purpose of your trip?"

"Perform with Liberace."

"Liberace?" He looked questioningly at Mrs. Kozak, but she just smiled and said nothing. So he continued: "What's in the box?"

"Spider."

He looked worried. "Madam," he said to Mrs. Kozak, "would you kindly explain to me what's going on here?" She opened the box and showed him that it was a puppet of a spider.

One by one, the company filed through, with candelabras, letters, worms, army ants, dice, ribbons, and finally the piano, which Renato had brought out to the airport. We all said goodbye and moved on to the Immigration counter. Then came a crisis so immediate and potentially disastrous that I still shake my head in disbelief. There was no record of work permits for us, and we were told we couldn't board the plane.

"But our show is opening in Las Vegas tonight!" I wailed.

"Look, lady," the Immigration officer said, "I don't care if your show is opening in New York, Hollywood, and Las Vegas all on the same night. You don't get on that flight without your work permits in order."

Somehow, I gathered my wits. We had forty-five minutes until the next flight — the last flight — to Vegas, and we had to get on that plane. What to do? The telephone has always been one of my best friends, so I dialed the operator and asked her to put me through to the White House. "I'd like to speak to the President," I said.

"Just a moment, please." Could it be that easy?

I got a secretary who listened patiently to my tale of woe and then put me on hold for five minutes. Another secretary came on the line, and I explained yet again that the Famous People Players were stranded at the Toronto airport and that a major breakthrough in the field of mental retardation would be blocked if we didn't get our work permits. She asked for the number of the pay phone: "Someone will be calling you back after we look into the situation."

We must have checked out all right. A short time later, the pay phone rang, and a woman identified herself as a special assistant to President Jimmy Carter. "Now, what we're going to do is call the Immigration office in the Toronto airport and have you cleared through the President's office," she said.

A few minutes later — barely in time to make our flight — we were cleared by Immigration. "You sure have some important friends," the officer told me, shaking his head in disbelief. "I've never seen anyone put through Immigration by request of the White House!"

Looking back on it I see that getting over that hurdle was a sign of good things to come. And I have to say I'm still proud of myself for the way I dealt with it. I don't know where I got the gall — but a part of me knew we'd come too far to be stopped in our tracks.

Our second appearance in Vegas was enthusiastically received by the audiences, which included celebrities we held in awe. People like Robert Wagner and Natalie Wood lavished praise on the company. Ann-Margret was performing at the Hilton, and when she saw us in the audience, she amazed us by saying, "We have a very talented group here with us, and I hope you'll go and see them perform — the Famous People Players!" We all took a bow and felt like a million bucks.

Lee was warmer than ever in his relationships with the performers, but I'm afraid that on this trip he played favorites: His first choice was Jeannine. At dinner, he always wanted to hold her on his lap and feed her while he ate. But one night the inevitable happened: Jeannine doused his stunning red brocade costume. His smile didn't dim a bit. "It was the 'Dancing Waters' in my show that did it to you, Jeannine!" he laughed, handing the baby to me and making a quick exit.

Another star who took an interest in Famous People Players was Tony Orlando, who was about to open at the Riviera. He came to see our show and was so enthusiastic and friendly when he visited us backstage that we decided to pay him a return call. Our shows were at the same time, so the company couldn't see his act, but we went to the Riviera between shows and spent a few hours in his dressing room, talking and filling up on the soft drinks and potato chips he ordered. Tony had a sister who was retarded, so he was fascinated by what we were trying to accomplish. "You look so much like me that I might ask you to double for me some night!" he told a delighted Mike. As I watched him chatting animatedly with the performers, I had a brainstorm.

"I'm going to do a puppet of you," I told him.

That evening, I started to rough out a sequence based on his hit song "Tie a Yellow Ribbon." Between shows, I gathered the performers in our dressing room and we started to rehearse. There would be dozens of yellow ribbons all over the stage, and three giant oak trees in the center. At the end, the center tree would split open to reveal the puppet of Tony, dressed in prison stripes and on his way home to find the girl he had left behind. We all used our imagination, and had a lot of fun acting out the story.

About a week later, Tony came to our show again. When Lee saw him in the audience, he lost no time introducing him. "The Famous People Players tell me they're going to do a Tony Orlando puppet," Lee said, adding impishly, "and I've got to tell you, Tony, I think you'd make a great puppet!" Tony burst into helpless laughter.

Maybe it was because everything was going so well on this second trip to Las Vegas that my mind started seeking out ways to stir things up; maybe it was because I wanted our audiences to know just how far this company had come, but I got the idea that we should announce to the audience that some of the performers were mentally retarded. This idea went totally against the views of the Hilton management and Liberace's organization, who said the performers' backgrounds should not be publicized. It was also a total about-face for me: I had always believed that the Famous People Players would earn their applause on the merits of our performances.

At my bidding, Tom, Mike, and Nancy went to Lee's dressing room after the first show. They looked doubtful — Mike even asked, "Are you sure, Diane?" — but when I insisted, they asked him if he would tell the audience that there were retarded performers in the company. Lee protested strongly, agreeing only when they insisted. "You know I could never say no to you, Nancy," he said. Before the second show started, Lee made the fateful announcement, adding that he was "so proud of what these people have been able to accomplish." As I watched from the wings, I could tell from the strain in his voice that Lee wished he had never agreed to say anything. And I began to realize what a terrible mistake I had made.

The performers were so upset — Tom, Mike, and Nancy included — that they wouldn't speak to me; Mom just shook her head sadly, and I ran up to my room in tears. There, waiting for me, was a letter from Lee's conductor, Bo Ayars, saying that Famous People Players was a professional company that didn't deserve to be put through such a humiliating ordeal. About an hour later, Lee called to tell me that the manager of the Hilton was very distressed about the announcement.

There were no recriminations, from Lee or anyone else, and the performers started talking to me by the end of the next day, but I couldn't let the matter slide. It had been a painful lesson: I had started the company with the goal of developing performers who were so good that they would never again be labeled "retarded." Yet this time, I had been the one sticking the label on them. I promised the entire company that I would never come up with such an idea again. And I never have. What amazes me now is that Lee and the Hilton let me have my way — letting me learn through my own mistakes. And more amazing is that the company trusted me enough to go along with my decision — and then forgave my mistake so readily. It was a lesson in love and trust I'll never forget.

A few days later, as our Las Vegas engagement was drawing to a close, Lee called me into his dressing room between shows and invited the Famous People Players to join a tour his company was planning in the spring and summer of 1977: Montreal, Ottawa, Hamilton, Toronto, and Lake Tahoe. We were all thrilled.

When we returned home in March of 1976 I was to begin

preparing for our first major tour. Now we had a better idea of the difficulties this would involve — not just months of rehearsing and learning new numbers for the show, but the business side of being professionals. Raising money would mean holding more benefits. We had found out they worked for us. By now I could anticipate some of the problems that were sure to arise, and I was also learning that opportunities and difficulties go hand in hand.

Still, I was thrown for a loop when, a week later, Reverend Crighton came to see me, looking somewhat embarrassed. He appreciated the difficulties of our work, he said, but members of his congregation were complaining about the noise in the basement. We would have to find another place to rehearse. I held off telling the performers the bad news and went back to work. Later that afternoon, I got a call from a representative of Goodwill services: The organization was holding its international delegate assembly in Toronto in June. Would we be the entertainment? After he watched a run-through the next morning, he told me he was very impressed and asked how much we would charge.

"The thing is, we're looking for rehearsal space at the moment," I said, explaining our predicament.

"I have a suggestion," he said. "There's a large space sitting empty in the Goodwill building. Suppose we gave it to you, rent-free, in exchange for the show?"

I couldn't believe my ears, but I didn't want to risk asking him if he was sure — he might reconsider — so I said yes as coolly as possible. The instant he left, I made my face look as gloomy as possible (which isn't hard for me!) and told everyone that we were being kicked out of the church basement. There was a chorus of groans and boos.

"But we've got a new place!" I shrieked. "And it's free!" The groans promptly turned to cheers.

That afternoon, Mike, Renato, Mom, and I went to look at our new home: a long, narrow space — like a bowling alley — with rooms for prop storage and an office. There wasn't a stage, but that was okay. We could do without one. On the other hand, we would have to put up flats. "No, wait. We'll just paint the walls black," I said. And the four of us stayed all night to get the job done.

With the move came other changes. I went to see Ron, who had told me after the Vegas show he was leaving because he needed something new, and asked him to reconsider. "We miss you," I said. "The performers adore you, and I need someone who can work well with them. I know we've had our differences in the past, but won't you consider coming back?" I was surprised at my own diplomatic tone, and even more surprised when he said yes. A few days later, Christine returned, promising to come on the Liberace tour and even laying down the law to her fiancé when he tried to change her mind.

Just before we moved, the Haney Centre told me one of its students had asked repeatedly to join Famous People Players. We welcomed a new performer: Benny D'Onofrio, a short, chubby kid with a round, friendly face and a wonderful smile that endeared him to everyone in the company.

Moving day was a much more emotional experience than I had expected. After the last prop had been loaded onto a borrowed truck, I stood in the deserted basement, remembering. We used to imagine this room painted in bright colors, with fresh curtains and paintings on the walls. In our daydreams, it even belonged to us. We got ourselves into incredible scrapes here — like the time Renato and I repainted the musical notes and got paint all over the outside wall. (When I visited the church recently, there was still green fluorescent paint on the wall, despite our cleanup efforts!) We had the most remarkable encounters in this basement — like the one with Ken Bell, a wonderful photographer who took some promotional shots for the company's first trip to Vegas. He arrived during a rehearsal, exclaiming, "It's a miracle!" I thought he was talking about the show, but he continued, "I was an altar boy in this church." Ken refused to charge us for the photos and went on to become one of the company's closest friends.

But now we were leaving. And we would find that the transition was a crucial one as we headed into a period of intense expansion which would place enormous demands on our personal and professional stamina.

One of the first phone calls I got at Goodwill was from Richard Owen, the production stage manager of the Hamilton Philharmonic Orchestra. He and Boris Brott, the conductor, had been discussing Famous People Players and wondered if we had ever considered performing numbers that didn't feature famous people.

"Like what?" I asked.

"Have you ever heard of Saint-Saëns' *Carnival of the Animals*?" he asked. I hadn't, so he suggested I listen to the recording and call Boris if I had any ideas. The music was so strong, so varied, that images flew through my head. "March of the Lion" conjured a huge, furry beast surrounded by tiny chicks, grooming him and combing his mane while struggling to keep control of a huge comb, a giant nail file, and an enormous hairbrush. "Hens and Cocks" would have the same chicks reunited with their mothers, who chase the enormous lion off the stage. Meanwhile one of the roosters claims the lion's royal crown. "The Dying Swan" would be tragic: a lovely, graceful swan slowly sinking to the ground. "Aquarium" would be filled with fish of every color of the rainbow, and "Fossils" would feature giant dinosaur skeletons, their bones struck like the xylophones in the music.

As I listened to *Carnival* again, I knew it would be the most ambitious project we had ever undertaken: a theme piece with fourteen numbers that would require perfect transitions and a lot of variation in style. Boris Brott loved the idea and promptly asked the company to premiere *Carnival* at Hamilton Place with his orchestra in January 1977.

Other than our appearances with Liberace in Las Vegas, where Lee's band had accompanied our numbers, we had always used recorded music for our shows, and the opportunity to perform to the accompaniment of a full orchestra represented an exciting challenge.

But before we could even start staging *Carnival*, there was a show coming up fast at the Goodwill conference. As we settled into our new home and started to rehearse, we began to meet some of the staff, who were wonderful people. Not only did they come to watch us rehearse and encourage our efforts, but they also offered practical help. When I mentioned our ongoing need for financial support, they offered to prepare tax receipts for any of our donors, since Famous People Players didn't yet have a charitable status.

The Goodwill show went very well (we were becoming old hands at single performances) and afterward the organizers introduced us to Lieutenant-Governor Pauline McGibbon. Her Honor was the ideal representative of the Queen: a regal lady with a crown of shining hair, a radiant smile, and an air of grace and dignity. Her response to our show left us speechless: "It's a living miracle." She helped us get our first grant from the Ontario Arts Council; she became our honorary patron, and, most of all, she gave us her friendship, which we're honored to still have today.

We now had several projects under way — the Tony Orlando sequence and a new Barbra Streisand number as well as *Carnival of the Animals*. The prop room had become quite the operation, turning out dozens of birds, oak trees, butterflies, dinosaur bones, lions, ribbons, and fish. To help with the prop-building, we hired a man named Fred Kay. Mom found him through — of all sources — the Santa Claus Parade committee. He proved to be indispensable. Without him, Mom and Renato couldn't have built all those props on schedule.

The morale in the company was very high as we approached the spring of 1976. We all felt that Famous People Players was our family, not just a place where we worked. Ann and Ron were particularly good with the other performers, working tremendously hard to help them learn new parts and behaving with great sensitivity toward them. But, as always, there were a few problem areas. Benny, for example, spent his first two weeks with the company sitting on the floor, staring at the others as they rehearsed, and refusing to utter a word. "Benny, what would you like to do?" I finally asked him. He pointed to the two butterflies that had just come out of the prop room for the Streisand number "Evergreen."

"Fine," I said. "Why don't you try them out?" But Benny couldn't even move the butterflies, much less make them sway or swoop. I showed him; Christine showed him; Ann showed him — but it was no use. I began to wonder whether we could even take him to Hamilton Place in January, and taking him with us on the tour seemed a very distant possibility.

Then there was Nancy. During our second Vegas appearance, she had been fine, but as the pace of rehearsals heated up so did she. One afternoon, in a fury over my criticism of the way she held her ribbon in the Tony Orlando number, she pulled the phone out of the wall, yanked the toilet tank from the floor, and threw it across the room. I got to her just as she was pulling down a bookcase in my office, and I slapped her across the face to make her stop. She burst into tears and fled from the building. Later, Mrs. Lawrence called me, furious — she said she would sue — but a few minutes later the mother called me back in tears.

"I was so upset, Diane," she wept. "I can't live this life of hell anymore; she smashes everything in the house, and I just don't know what to do." I comforted her as best I could, and the next day I found a psychiatrist for Nancy at Surrey Place. She was great with Nancy, and the drugs she prescribed stopped her tantrums; unfortunately, Nancy became listless and indifferent as a result. After a few weeks, she went off the drugs, and, for a little while, everything was fine.

When we started rehearsing *Carnival*, I was beginning to realize that I could incorporate the performers' personalities into the numbers. For example, Tom, who was always bumping into everyone on stage, had to be the first hen coming after the lion. Christine, who was a natural comedian, became the quivering legs of the dying swan. (We tried to do the number seriously, but we fell down laughing every time we saw this bird dying on stage. So we redesigned the swan as an ungainly comic figure with skinny legs, accompanied by two silly-looking little cygnets.) And all the performers had improved so much that they could work in pairs on a puppet without any help from Ann, Ron, or Christine.

In the summer, I found out I was pregnant again; and by the time I was starting to show, I decided to ask Renato to pick me up and come to work with me on the subway every day — partly to get him out of the house more, and partly to help me carry Jeannine. Everyone on the subway stared at us, and when we got to work, Renato complained: "I just can't take it, Mrs. Dupuy." But I insisted. One day, I asked him to watch Jeannine in the waiting room at the salon while I had my hair done. As I was leaving, the stylist asked me if Renato was my husband, and I said yes. Outside, he asked me how I could embarrass him that way: "Did you see how she was looking at me? She looked sick, Mrs. Dupuy."

"Well, I don't care, Renato. I'm proud of you," I told him, "and these people are just going to have to get used to it."

A few days later, I asked Renato to come with me to Eaton's to find a carriage for two babies. I bought a highchair as well, and we decided to take them with us on the subway. By the time we got off, rush hour was in full swing; Renato got up the escalator first, as I pushed the carriage onto the bottom rung. Suddenly, the escalator stopped, and a man about halfway up shouted: "Get that goddamned carriage off the escalator, you dumb bitch!"

Renato plunked the highchair down. "You shut your mouth!" he shouted down. "And you apologize to this lady right now or I'm waiting for you up here." Silence descended on the crowd as the man glanced at Renato and hurriedly mumbled an apology. Back at the apartment, I begged Renato never to do anything like that again, but he just shook his head sadly. "I'm sorry, Mrs. Dupuy, but I just couldn't take it, him talking like that. I respect you like my mother, Mrs. Dupuy, and I just couldn't take it."

Renato's more frequent contacts with the world outside his home — although initially shocking — began to have a very positive effect. Very gradually, he learned to ignore the stares and the remarks, and today he doesn't even notice them.

Late 1976 brought more pleasant surprises. One was financial: an anonymous donation, the magnitude of which made us gasp. The cheque was for $20,000. The only source was John Armstrong, the public relations man who had mailed us the cheque, so I called and thanked him. "Don't thank me," he said. "Thank . . . whoever it was." And he stubbornly refused to tell me the name of our incredibly generous benefactor.

One night, I got a call from a man who said he was coming to Toronto to direct a movie called *Emily, Emily*, which was about the father of a girl who is retarded. "I'm looking for several retarded young people to perform in the movie, and the Haney Centre gave me your name," he said. "My name is Marc Daniels."

The atmosphere was electric by the time Mr. Daniels arrived at Goodwill the next day. Everybody was angling for a part in the movie: There was talk of Hollywood, and the Academy Awards. It was all I could do to get the rehearsal started. Finally, the director picked Mike and Nancy, who made every attempt not to let out a whoop of victory — and failed. "We'll need them for about two weeks," he said, "and they'll be paid, of course." The days that followed were full of exciting stories about the shoot as Mike and Nancy wafted into the afternoon rehearsals after their mornings on the set.

"We had breakfast with John and James today, and they were telling us all about the movies they've made, and then we were in a scene with John . . ." said Mike.

"I was in a scene with James," bragged Nancy. "He's cute!"

"And we were telling John and Marc all about Famous People Players!" Mike said.

John? James? It finally came out: John Forsythe and James Farentino. And Marc Daniels was no ordinary director. His credits included "Star Trek," "Gunsmoke," and my all-time favorite, "I Love Lucy." We all saw the finished product, and cheered loudly whenever Mike or Nancy appeared on the screen.

Before we went to Hamilton Place, I decided we should try out *Carnival* somewhere small. A university in Lennoxville, Quebec, invited us, and we rented a bus for the trip. *Carnival* was a big hit, and immediately after the show we struck the stage and drove all night to be in Hamilton by the next morning so we could prepare for the show that evening. Everyone was dead-tired, and the truck carrying the props was two hours late. But Boris was incredibly understanding. He was the kind of professional who would have found a way to put on the show even if we had never arrived.

At the end of our rehearsal, Boris said, "It's wonderful, but . . ."

"But what?"

"Well, you just go through the numbers, one after the other."

"Yeah, we do . . ." I was a bit confused.

"But what about the Ogden Nash verses?"

"Who's Ogden Nash?" I asked, totally unaware that he had written an entire series of verses based on Saint-Saëns' *Carnival of the Animals.* Boris offered to narrate the verses, and I delightedly agreed.

The audience cheered and laughed all the way through *Carnival*, and, for me, it was amazing to see the numbers in a theatre instead of a narrow room; to watch, dazzled, as the performers conjured the pompous golden lion, the flying red donkeys with green wings, the elephant swinging from a bar, and the amorous kangaroos. As I watched the glimmering, open-mouthed fish gliding sinuously through a "sea" of black, I realized all our hours of practice to perfect the precise bob and weave of the fish — right down to the flick of their tails — was worth it. I was very proud of the company, and Boris was very proud of us. "That's the best *Carnival* I've ever seen," he said. "You should do more long pieces."

Sorcerer's Apprentice sprang to mind. The exciting music, by Paul Dukas, was full of variety and color. And I knew the performers would love the story. But Boris was hesitant: "I think it might be a little too ambitious. What about something simpler, like *Peter and the Wolf*?" The music was terrific, but I thought the story had been performed too many times in other theatrical settings, so we left our future plans on hold for the time being. Still, the idea of doing *Sorcerer's Apprentice* lingered in the back of my mind.

In early 1977 another organization gave us a big boost: the Ontario Association for the Mentally Retarded, through the recommendation of Henry Botchford and Helen Honickman made it possible for us to go from week to week, month to month without panicking about money. They recommended to their board of directors that Famous People Players be put on the association payroll. At the end of each year, we would repay the money — without interest.

Then, one morning in early March, there was yet another surprise. I went into labor; early again, and once again a breech birth. The first thing I said when the baby was born was, "Can you get me a Big Mac?"

"Don't you want to see your little girl?" asked a nurse.

"Of course I do!" I shouted. "Where is she? Give her to me!" and into my arms was placed a little ugly duckling who has grown into a beauty.

Joanne was less than a month old when we headed out on our tour, but along with me and Mom, she and Jeannine had an entire busload of willing baby sitters.

At Place des Arts, as in Las Vegas, there were no rehearsals — a run-through is expensive because of stagehands and crew — so we had to go on cold. The first night, we had a problem; Benny still couldn't move his butterflies in the Streisand number. (It probably wouldn't have mattered even if we had rehearsed; Benny still couldn't have learned that part.) Lee and Seymour suggested I send Benny home. "The young man just isn't working out," Lee said as kindly as possible. "This work just isn't for everyone."

But I wasn't ready to give up on Benny just yet. "Let's just wait until Ottawa, and then we'll see."

But Benny didn't improve. He couldn't manipulate the props and wouldn't talk about the problem. Even Ron and Ann, with whom he had a good relationship, couldn't get through to him. He seemed so frightened of me most of the time that he frequently wouldn't look at me, let alone talk to me.

On opening night in the National Arts Centre in Ottawa, Benny didn't show up for his part. He just sat in the dressing room and moped. After the show, I ran into the dressing room, shouted, "You're fired!" and raced into the girls' dressing room, where I burst into tears. A few minutes later, one of the performers came in and said Benny wanted to see me. He was all alone in the other room when I got there.

"I want you to give me another chance," he said, starting to cry.

"But, Benny, why do you want another chance when I yelled at you and fired you?"

Suddenly, the words just poured from him, as if he had been storing them up for years. "I know you yell at us because you want us to be good, and I want to be good and do my butterflies, and you've gotta give me one more chance, 'cos my parents are coming to the show in Toronto, and I wanta be in that show, and I want them to be proud of me and you too, Diane."

Now I was the one at a loss for words. Benny and I hugged each other, and I gave him yet another chance. The next night, he performed superbly: It was a complete transformation. The following night was a repeat performance — and from then on, Benny not only soared as a performer, but also opened up as a person.

The next stop on the tour was Toronto's O'Keefe Centre, where I had first met Liberace, making that fateful leap over the roped barrier. Being there made me think we should do something special at the luncheon for the troupe that Helen Honickman was organizing. I decided to present a series of awards, which have since become a company tradition. Greg won the first "Liberace Award" for most improved performer. He had gone from a klutz who couldn't bring a prop in right side up to a professional who could perform any part in our repertoire. Other awards went to people who had given us their support: Lorraine Thomson, who featured us on "Front Page Challenge"; Jack McAndrew, head of CBC-TV Variety, who planned to involved us in some shows; Helen Honickman; Seymour Heller; and Ray Arnett, who taught me how to direct. "In Hollywood, we have something called the Academy Awards," he said accepting his award. "But this is *my* Oscar."

In June, we flew to Lake Tahoe, the last leg of the tour. Coincidentally, Tony Orlando's show was just closing while ours was about to open, and he treated us to dinner and the show. At the end, he introduced us: "I'd like you to meet the mentally retarded citizens of our country." Tony meant well, but to begin with, we were citizens of another country. And when he referred to retardation, I understood even better why everyone had been so upset with me when I engineered that announcement of our background the year before. I tried to play down the incident as much as possible, just as my friends had done for me.

It was a little more difficult to play down my inauspicious return to the stage one night. Nancy was off her medication, and her temper flared up to such an extent that she couldn't perform. While Ann stayed with her, I got into a black jumpsuit and took her parts. After two years of working offstage, the darkness and isolation were a severe shock, but I managed, and I was so pleased with myself that I completely forgot about the blackout at the end of the Tony Orlando number. (The black light goes off and the performers have to scoot into the wings to avoid being seen.) Totally at a loss where to go, I froze. Mike and Tom had to push me toward the wings, where Christine and

Ron were waiting to pull me offstage — just as the white lights came on for Lee's entrance in the convertible. I'm sure the audience caught a glimpse of my feet as I was being dragged to safety.

"Why didn't you hit the dirt?" Frank demanded later, recalling his own similar experience during our first appearance in Las Vegas.

During our last week in Tahoe, I started to feel some misgivings about the relationship that was developing between Christine, who was still engaged, and Mike. They were beginning to keep to themselves: an unpleasant reminder of the factions that had emerged during our trip to Vegas. Then some of the other guys got talking about finding a "normal" girlfriend; while the girls, like Sandra, and especially Nancy — who had dated Mike — became insecure and jealous.

By the time we returned to Toronto at the end of June, I couldn't correct anything Mike was doing in rehearsal without Christine jumping in to defend him. I made the big mistake of talking to Christine. She was extremely defensive, denied she was showing favoritism, and insisted that she and Mike were "just friends." When I mentioned that they had been seen walking hand in hand, she told me to mind my own business.

Maybe it wasn't my business if Christine and Mike fell in love. But it was my business that the relationship was causing difficulties in the company. The other performers felt hurt and resentful because they didn't have similar relationships, and, as Tom said, because "those two never talk to us." I was also worried that Mike could lose all the ground he had gained in three years with Famous People Players if their relationship suddenly ended.

When Christine broke off her engagement and moved out of her family's house to an apartment — Mike and Renato helped her move — I discussed the situation with Mike's father. Mr. Ribeiro said he was delighted with the relationship, but I wondered if he was really delighted.

When Mike found out I had talked to his father, he was furious. "You're trying to break up me and Christine!" he shouted. "You can't do that!"

"We've been through too much for you to say that to me," I said. "I'm just worried about you, Mike. You've come a long way, and . . ."

"Yeah, and I'm gonna go a lot further, with Christine's help," he said. "She's even teaching me how to read."

"That's great," I said, "but she doesn't have the experience to do it. You should see a teacher at Surrey Place who specializes in teaching people with learning disabilities how to read. And if Christine cares about you as you say she does, then she'll agree." Mike did go to Surrey Place, where he made great progress. If it hadn't been for Christine, that never would have happened.

For a while, the tensions eased; but instinct told me it was only a matter of time before Mike and Christine drifted away from the company. The rifts had been too deep for a complete recovery. Nancy, for example, never spoke to either of them, which meant that the three of them couldn't work together on a puppet.

In the midst of the turmoil over Mike and Christine, two new performers arrived at Famous People Players: Andy Thomas and Richard Schneider, recommended to us by the Haney Centre. Both of them were extremely energetic and had a great aptitude for learning the techniques of black-light theatre. But while Andy slowed down occasionally, Richard seemed to be a perpetual motion machine. He ran to work; he ran to the bus; and he ran up the stairs of Goodwill so fast that he frequently crashed into the wall at the opposite end of the room. For Richard, a slow or lyrical number was out of the question — he just stood there, rocking back and forth at top speed until I'm sure even the puppet got dizzy. But he was terrific in numbers like "Viva Las Vegas."

Unfortunately, Richard also had a rather disturbing personal habit. While talking to me, he repeatedly looked down at his crotch and up at my face; up and down, over and over again. "Richard, don't do that!" I'd say for the zillionth time.

"I knowIknowIknow," he'd rattle, repeating the gesture.

Even more disturbing, Richard followed girls along the street and pestered them with personal remarks. He lived across the street from me, so I could often intervene, but the next day, he was right back at it again. All I could do was continue to talk to him and hope my advice would eventually sink in.

The company's professional stock kept rising throughout all our personal crises, and that made us certain we must be doing something right. In July 1977, Jack McAndrew asked us to be part of a CBC television special on the composer André Gagnon, featuring — along with Famous People Players — National Ballet of Canada star Karen Kain and Gagnon himself. Mom and Fred immediately started building a big platform for two pianos — one for the Gagnon puppet and one for the real Gagnon. Along the sides of the platform, which would rotate, they built oversized piano keys. And for a spectacular entrance, they made a huge sun, which would split open to reveal the two Gagnons locked in fierce competition at their respective keyboards.

Bernie Picard, the producer, was very impressed with the company during the filming. He was amazed, for example, that Andy and Richard had been with us such a short time. And Jack McAndrew spoke to me about the possibility of another special, based on our *Carnival of the Animals*, which Bernie would produce.

After the filming was over, we took the balloons with which we had surrounded the piano platform and released them into the wild blue yonder. "Let everything be all right for us," I wished as the balloons soared into the sky.

One day in early 1978, just after the special had aired, Renato came in to Goodwill early and found Keith in my office with a huge stack of silver coins piled up on my desk. "Where did you get these?" Renato asked.

"From my mother's drawer."

"Did you steal them?"

"Yeah," Keith said with a scowl. "So?"

Renato called me, and I came right over. "Keith, these are old coins and they're probably very valuable," I said. "You've got to take them home." Keith glared at me for a moment, then raised his fist and put it right through the wall. With that, he gathered up the coins and stomped out. I called his father, and the two of us found Keith in a pawnshop. He had just sold the coins for $15.00.

"Mr. Edwards," I said, "I can't keep Keith anymore. I just can't."

It was a heartbreaking decision — Keith had been with us since the beginning — but I had to do it. Sure, other performers, like Nancy, had outbursts of violence. But they didn't steal, and I wasn't willing to take the chance that a theft could be blamed on one of the performers.

Partly, I guess, to take my mind off what seemed a defeat, I threw myself into a new idea: to expand our André Gagnon sequence into a full-length show based on his music. It would be called "The Gifts of André Gagnon." We received an Ontario Arts Council grant as well as support from a number of corporations. What I most remember, however, is a donation made by a woman named Marion Patterson, who wrote to us from Markdale, a small town north of Toronto. She enclosed a cheque for $200.00, collected from the proceeds of her $2.50 chapbook, *Meditations from a Rocking Chair.* We sent her a thank-you note and a bouquet; the following year, she raised $600.00. "I am so happy to help you in this small way," she wrote.

John Forsythe (whom Mike and Nancy had mentioned so warmly during the filming of *Emily, Emily*) agreed to become our first celebrity guest narrator. And Marc Daniels also accepted my invitation to come and see the premiere in May of 1978 at Hamilton Place. The two of them were a sheer delight, not because they were famous, but because, despite their fame, they never condescended to anyone.

Boris Brott once again conducted the Hamilton Philharmonic for our performance, which began on a stage empty except for an ornate, polished church door surrounded by the iridescent blaze of stained-glass windows. The gift of music, a single musical note, appeared in the darkness, followed by the gift of love, a shining heart. Then the fun began: The Gagnon puppet, sitting at his keyboard on the rotating platform, sweated and swayed over a virtuoso piece while two clowns cavorted below. After the clowns? A fiddling contest between a huge rooster and a giant mouse, both in the requisite overalls and plaid. This number, "Concertino for Carignan," has become one of our most popular pieces.

Toward the end of the summer, we got a call from Tony Orlando's manager. Tony's group was in Vancouver and had lost its opening act. Could we join him in Calgary in three weeks? It was the shortest notice we had ever had for a show, but everyone was thrilled at the prospect of performing with Tony and seeing his reaction to the puppet of himself. The show was great, but what I best remember was the unusual finale. Tony's last number was the Beatles song "Hey Jude," and he asked the Famous People Players to accompany him in the final chorus. So what did Richard do? He walked upstage, directly in front of Tony, who returned the favor. Richard upstaged him a second time, and the two of them were almost at the footlights when the chorus finally ended. In a strange way, this outrageous "showmanship" was also proof of how far Famous People Players had come!

Back in Toronto, I saw that Mike and Christine's departure was imminent. They were keeping to themselves almost exclusively, and I got the distinct impression that Mike, with Christine's encouragement, thought he could do better than Famous People Players.

One day, Mike just left. He didn't even give us time to throw a farewell party for him. One day, he simply got up and walked out the door, shutting it gently as he vanished from our lives.

Christine had made it clear that she, too, wanted to leave. But I was tired of having people walk out the door on me, so I moved first. I told her that we didn't have enough funding for a staff person, but perhaps she could perform on a contractual basis in the future.

I must say that I missed them both a great deal: Christine had been a wonderful performer and Mike had been with us since Day One. For Renato, Mike's departure was particularly difficult. It destroyed their friendship, but, as it happened, Renato and I became much closer.

I realized, too, that I had developed a calmer acceptance of all the company's crises. There was only so much that the performers and I could do for each other. There was only so much that I could control.

Soon after Mike and Christine left, we found we had to move again. There just wasn't enough room at Goodwill for the mountain of props we had accumulated: three pianos and three oak trees, for example. It was hard to go, because Goodwill had been such a strong support system for us, but there was no choice. Mom found us the spacious second floor of a warehouse building in the west end of the city, and we quickly settled into our new home.

Challenges take many forms, and I soon received one to my own artistic integrity. My reaction showed that I might have become more accepting — but I was a long way from mellowing out!

Full of enthusiasm for our upcoming *Carnival* special for CBC-TV, I flew to Montreal to meet the woman in charge of prop designs. Pictures of them were enough to show me they were a disaster. They were absurdly elaborate: a lion bedecked with fleurs-de-lis; a rooster out of 17th-century France.

I went straight to producer Bernie Picard and exploded. "Leave the puppets the way they are! If you start putting costumes on the roosters, you don't see their legs move, and that's the funniest and most endearing part of the act! How do you even manipulate the puppets with all the costumes in the way?"

"Well, if you meet with the designer and work out some of these concerns . . ."

"I'm not going to start all over. I'm telling you from my experience with puppets that if you put too many goddamned clothes on them, you might as well do a fashion show!" And I burst into angry tears. "So you might as well cancel this special right now!"

I cried all the way home on the plane, but back in Toronto I found support from Jack McAndrew. When I showed him the photos of the proposed designs, he laughed so hard that his beard started quivering. "Don't worry," he said. "What I want to see on this special is what I saw in Hamilton. I'll straighten this out."

Another blessing in disguise, because the blowup put Mom — and her astounding talent for prop design — in charge. Once again she came to the rescue. And the props were magnificent. One process of which she was especially proud was a technique called flocking, which is rarely used today. Enamel paint is sprayed on an object while very fine lint — the same color as the paint — is sifted onto the paint through a sieve. The lint sticks to the paint, producing a velour effect that also hides the seams. The lint also causes asthma during production of the prop, but Mom didn't even think about that danger. "There's enough air in the room," she said, sifting more lint. The mice's faces and hands, the pink elephant's trunk, the cuckoo bird, the ballerina mouse's face and hands, and the two concert pianists (a boy and a girl) all got flocked. The effect was stunning.

All the props had to be made in six weeks. The night before we were to leave for Montreal, Mom still wasn't quite finished with the elephant's yards and yards of ballet skirt. She was so tired that she couldn't see anymore, and we all came in — Mrs. Lawrence and Mrs. Kozak included — and sat there until the wee hours, finishing the elephant while Mom slept.

The CBC studio in Montreal looked like something out of Hollywood: a massive set; a massive crew. Our narrator, Gordon Pinsent, obediently struggled into a penguin suit to make like the ringmaster, and the sight of Gordon gave Bernie another idea: a giant penguin puppet to "conduct" the Montreal Symphony Orchestra. (The real conductor was Charles Dutoit.) Mom made a penguin suit, and awed everyone with the quality and speed of her work. Ann got into the suit and was lifted ten feet in the air by a crane so she could "conduct" the orchestra. Ann was in the air for two hours, and when she finally took the suit off, it was as if she had been in a downpour; that's how much she was sweating. But she never complained.

Bernie and I were communicating a bit better, but we still had our differences. He insisted on redesigning one of the numbers to feature a rooster and a hooker instead of a rooster and chickens. I responded to this idea by throwing the nearest object (a coffeepot) at him, but a few hours later Jack was on the phone to me. "We have a rule: No throwing dishes at your producer," he said. I let him have his hooker, but even he admitted afterward that it had been the worst number in the show.

One of my favorite memories of taping the special is my walk on Mount Royal with Gordon Pinsent: we talked and talked and got into a fierce snowball fight. "This is what I miss about the way the theatre used to be," he said. "It was fun. Now it's all business. I wish there were more fun times like this."

I felt a little shiver that had nothing to do with the cold. Suddenly, I wondered if our group would ever feel this kind of disillusionment. On the set, Gordon was extraordinarily professional, and he was remarkably sensitive to the performers. I'll always remember how he threw his arms around Nancy and did a little soft-shoe routine to make her laugh when he saw one of her temper tantrums on the horizon. And we were all delighted when he told us he hoped we would work together again.

The TV special was a feather in our cap, and we were always glad to gain more experience, but there was something missing: the tension of live theatre. We were looking forward to getting back on the boards.

A Growing Circle of Friends

JANUARY 1979 – APRIL 1980

Alone in the office one morning, I sank into a deep pit of depression. *Another* round of resignations had just rocked the company, and I just couldn't be philosophical about it anymore: We had lost seven people in as many months. It was like a virus, I thought, and I couldn't identify the cause. I felt guilty. Maybe I had done something terribly wrong. Maybe I should just pull the plug on the company myself. In the past year, three of the original performers — Keith, Mike, and Christine — had left us. The second earthquake was about to hit us — all at once.

First, it was Tom. He wouldn't tell me why he was quitting. During our conversation, he did manage to ask me three times whether he would get his farewell party, and I wonder if his decision to leave had anything to do with being the guest of honor at a party. I tried to change his mind, but he stubbornly shook his head and asked me once again about the party. To give Tom the benefit of the doubt, maybe it was his time to move on; at any rate, he did get his party, at the Chinese restaurant where we went whenever someone was leaving.

We would be regulars at that restaurant before long: The next guest of honor was Frank, who said he wanted to get a job cleaning windows on the CN Tower, then opted for a sheltered workshop. "Frank, why don't you stay a little longer and see how it goes," I almost pleaded.

"No, I gotta say I can't take it. I'm quitting."

A few days later, Ann came to me with a long face, and said she appreciated how fed up I must be with people quitting. "Oh, no," I said. "Not you, Ann. Not again." But I couldn't even yell at her for giving me notice a third time; I sat and listened numbly as Ann explained how important it was for her to finally get her degree. It didn't surprise me, somehow, that Ron was next in line.

Before I left for the night, Ron knocked on my door. "Look, I'm not going to leave you this way," he said. "I think I should phase myself out gradually and help train the person who replaces me so there won't be so much of a shock for the performers." I was so touched by his thoughtfulness that I couldn't even say anything. And his difficulty in leaving the company — setting aside what had become such an important part of his life — to move on to other things, gave me a new perspective on the departure of staff and performers. It reminded me that Famous People Players had been conceived as a stepping stone, not a dead end. The company was old enough now that of course there would be changes in personnel. Somehow this had to be prepared for, and people who were ready to move on should be encouraged and assisted.

Then the phone rang.

"Her Honor would be pleased to have the members of Famous People Players attend a reception in the Lieutenant-Governor's chambers at the Provincial Legislature," the elegant voice said. "A formal invitation will be following shortly, for February 15, 1979."

"We . . . we . . ." I stammered. (He probably thought I was French!) "We would be deeply honored."

I raced out into the rehearsal room and screamed: "We're invited to a reception with Pauline McGibbon! That's like going to see the Queen!" Everyone was awestruck. When Greg went home, he told his mother that the Queen wanted to meet the Famous People Players!

And there was more good news. I was able to get a grant from the Canada Works program to employ three young people in the company. A friend of mine, Father Tom McKillop, who founded the Youth Corps, recommended a man named Warren Quinn. Warren came in for a job interview, and I can't say I was very impressed with this big, bearded, hippie-ish guy who clumped into my office. But because Father Tom said he was good, I went along with his suggestion. It was the best advice I ever followed. With help from Ron, Warren established a great relationship with the performers, who quickly responded to his sympathetic ear and helpful ways.

The other two new staff members were Wendy Miller, who was recommended to me by a teacher friend, and the company's first administrator, Frances Harding. But Frances almost didn't make it past the job interview. "I'll have to see if this is the sort of job I really want," she told me, nonchalantly running a hand through her hair. I didn't like her attitude; after all, who was interviewing whom? But Judi, who was also in the office during the interview, talked me into hiring her. Frances proved to be a great administrator, and one of the few people who could get away with bossing *me* around! "Hey, Diane, get over here," and she'd motion me over with a jerk of her thumb. "Go on upstairs and tell them to fix that pipe; it's leaking on my head, and I'm not going to take it." Meekly, I'd obey.

Ron stayed on as a performer long enough for us to do a show at the Royal York Hotel in early February. Ann's resignation also proved to be a qualified one: She agreed to perform with us on a contract basis for that show and in the future. The Royal York show marked the debut of our Anne Murray puppet. "Everything Old Is New Again" was the accompanying song, which had a great deal of personal significance for us, as it seemed to echo our situation as a company. The number was difficult to stage: Anne Murray's performing style is to stand still and just sing, while Liberace and Elvis used much more physical movement. The challenge was to convey her elegance and simplicity without making her look stiff. But to judge from the standing ovation we got at the end of the show, we met that challenge.

Soon afterward came Pauline McGibbon's reception, which was nothing like what we had imagined. Pauline — and that's what she insisted we call her after Greg addressed her as "Your Majesty" — made the formality of the imposing reception room shrink to the dimensions of a cozy parlor. Being with Pauline was like being with the grandmother who always has a plate of warm cookies waiting for you — but Pauline had more in store for us than cookies. As I followed Nancy's pointing finger down the red-carpeted hallway, I was shocked to see Anne Murray coming toward us. We stood there, staring, as she went over to the microphone that Pauline had discreetly placed in the corner of the room.

"You know, this year has really been good to me," she said, and everyone laughed because Anne had just won a Grammy Award for her song "You Needed Me." She continued: "I was reminded of the way I felt when I was starting out; how I wished there had been someone there for me. Now I want to be here for you, so to celebrate 'You Needed Me,' we need you. We need the Famous People Players."

She then called me to the microphone and presented me with a check for $10,000, which I later had enlarged, framed, and placed directly across from my desk so I would always remember Anne's generosity and Pauline's kindness in planning this wonderful surprise for us.

With this impetus — both financial and emotional — I was more determined than ever to attempt a black-light production of *Sorcerer's Apprentice.* The idea had been simmering for more than a year; now, my mind exploded into imagery. I had seen Walt Disney's *Fantasia* when I was three, so only the feeling of the piece remained in my memory. But the recollection was enough to make me realize how tough it would be to emulate or surpass the magic of the Disney film. Also *Sorcerer's Apprentice* had never been attempted on stage. I decided not to even try to go Disney one better. We would do the production our way. And when I noticed an ad in the paper for a special screening of *Fantasia*, I deliberately stayed away so I wouldn't be more influenced by it than I already was.

Everything about creating *Sorcerer's Apprentice* was a high. The story invited a fast-paced, action-packed adventure surrounding the mishaps of a magician's apprentice who gets into terrible trouble when the boss goes out of town one day. The lad steals his master's magic wand and starts making all sorts of things appear and vanish. He turns the sorcerer's ugly pet vulture into a broom; conjures up kaleidoscopes and twirling ribbons; captures falling comets; illuminates dozens of stars; and sends himself soaring on a trip to the moon. But the boy's dabblings in magic get out of control. The moon turns into a canoe which sends him tumbling down a wild river. The broom starts multiplying into a floor-sweeping army. The boy plunges into a terrifying underwater world of swordfish, octopi, and sharks. And the boy and broom, each on a splendid charger, face each other on the field of battle. Finally, the sorcerer returns, puts everything back to normal, and gives his apprentice a well-deserved spanking.

Once we began rehearsing the show, we couldn't stop. By this point, we had already decided to premiere it at the St. Lawrence Centre in June. We rented a theatre in a high school so that we could get a better sense of the production by rehearsing it on a stage, and we often stayed till late at night. Unlike *Carnival of the Animals*, with its breaks between numbers for narration of the Ogden Nash verses, *Sorcerer* was nonstop, breakneck action. The number required an enormous amount of co-operation among the performers. Warren was great at encouraging them to work together, and Wendy was a terrific performer whom they followed by example.

The rehearsals were going so well that I should have known some calamity was lurking in the background. One night, or rather at three o'clock one morning, the phone rang. "We have your son here," a police officer said.

"My son?"

"Yes, your son, Richard Schneider . . . ."

Richard had been charged with intimidation and common assault. "Richard, you've really screwed up," I said as he stared up at me like a puppy who's been caught sampling the filet mignon. "How could you?"

"IknowIknowIknow, Diane. I made a mistake . . . ."

"What happened?"

"I was on the subway coming home from work and I was really being good, Diane. I wasn't looking at my crotch or anything, I really wasn't, and this girl smiled at me, so I smiled back, and then she really smiled. So I followed her when she got off the subway because I could tell she really liked me. So she got to her house and I went up the stairs. But she slammed the door in my face, so I bashed the door and said bad words . . . ."

"What bad words?"

"Oh, Diane, they were really bad."

"Tell me anyway."

"I said, 'You f —— bitch, I'm gonna screw your little pants off!' So she called the police, and they took me to 999 Queen (the Queen Street Mental Health Centre) and they made me take some tests because they thought I was crazy. But I'm not crazy. So they took me to the police station and asked for my mother's phone number. But I didn't want them to call her, because she would've killed me. So I gave them your number."

Richard stayed at our apartment for the night because I really was afraid his mother would hurt him. I had seen her chasing him down the street with a broom, beating him so badly that he was covered with bruises. I would talk to her myself the next day, when I had sorted everything out.

In the morning, our company lawyer told me that the girl had pressed charges against Richard and he would have to go to court. "Diane, I strongly advise you to let this kid go," he said. "If anything like this should ever happen again . . ."

"No, I'm going to keep him," I said. "I feel he's learned his lesson, and I don't want to give up on him." This decision may seem contradictory. Just a year before, I had fired Keith over the theft of his mother's silver coins — a less serious incident than Richard's harassment of the girl on the subway. But Richard had been with the company a much shorter time, and I felt we had more of a chance to help him learn to overcome his problems. Apparently, the court agreed. Richard wasn't sent to jail, but he was ordered to take treatment at Surrey Place Centre — something I had been trying to convince him to do voluntarily for months. At work, I began to discover that Richard was much more stable if he was constantly kept busy carrying props, hauling boxes, and doing chores. This way, his attention was less inclined to wander to other areas of interest. Luckily, there wasn't any shortage of extra work for him to do.

I thought that for the premiere of *Sorcerer's Apprentice* it would be great to have as guest of honor someone who had worked on the original production of *Fantasia.* I wrote to Disney Productions, and they suggested James Macdonald, a sound effects expert who had created the voice of Mickey Mouse.

I went to California and had lunch with James Macdonald, one of the most elegant, distinguished-looking gentlemen I had ever seen in my life. He was delighted at my interest in his work, and we hit it off immediately. After lunch, he took me to the sound studio and showed me how he created various sound effects: lions, waterfalls, and even birdcalls. Not only did he agree to be our guest of honor for the premiere; he even agreed to perform some sound effects for the show.

The financial crunch was even tighter than usual because we were determined to do *Sorcerer's Apprentice* right. But money always seemed to come from somewhere. We were renting the bigger of the two theatres at the St. Lawrence Centre and planning to hire our own orchestra.

As usual, I needn't have worried quite so much. Solutions appeared. When I mentioned to David Miller, principal cellist with the Hamilton Philharmonic, that we were looking for an orchestra for the premiere, he said he'd love to conduct it.

"I didn't know you could conduct, David."

"Oh yes, and I can get you a terrific orchestra. Nothing but the best." David's ensemble even included members of the Canadian Brass.

And financial support did pour in. There was both direct funding, from corporations and individuals, and help from businesses that donated materials and services. For the first time, some of these donors could get tax receipts from us rather than from Goodwill or any other organization — a small point, perhaps, but a signal of our growing self-sufficiency. We had just incorporated and formed a board of directors, which included only people with an active connection to the company. One of our first members was Ed Kozak, Greg's father.

One generous donor didn't get her tax receipt because we lost touch with her. She called me one morning, introducing herself as Christie Cass, and told me she had a child who is mentally handicapped. "I've been reading about your company, and I wondered if I could come and visit you someday." Mrs. Cass did come to the warehouse to see us. She was a lovely woman who could have doubled for Anne Murray. After quietly watching us rehearse *Sorcerer's Apprentice,* she left, only to return the next day with a cheque for $5,000 — our orchestra's fee.

We needed a narrator for our show at the St. Lawrence Centre, because as well as premiering *Sorcerer's Apprentice,* we were doing *Carnival of the Animals* and a tribute to Anne Murray. I called Marc Daniels and asked him for suggestions. "I know who you can ask," Marc said, a mischievous tone creeping into his voice, "but I don't know if you've ever heard of this man. His name is Lorne Greene."

"*Lorne Greene?* Of course I know who Lorne Greene is. I grew up on 'Bonanza'!"

"So did I," Marc said impishly. "I directed it." Lorne promptly agreed to be our narrator (I'm sure Marc's recommendation made the difference) and I arranged to have airfare and accommodation donated for him, as well as for Marc and Jimmy Macdonald.

Throughout this period we kept getting boosts of confidence in the form of recognition from the most surprising sources. In the midst of preparations for our premiere, I got a letter from Bud Van Orden, who represented the U.S. president's Committee on the Employment of the Handicapped. He was inviting the Famous People Players to perform at the Washington Hilton Hotel in May. What an honor! We were all thrilled. I remembered how President Carter's office had helped us get out of that awful jam at the airport in 1976, when our work permits for Vegas weren't ready.

Ken Bell suggested inviting Celia Franca, founder of the National Ballet of Canada, to narrate *Carnival of the Animals* in Washington. (Ken was a founding member of the ballet company, as well as its official photographer.)

There was only one missing element: a stage manager. Frances recommended a friend of hers, Cathy Camp, who quickly made such a strong connection with the performers that I asked her to join the company.

The show went very well, and Celia was a superb narrator. But what most sticks in my memory of the evening is the image of a young man who was particularly taken with the performance and demonstrated his enthusiasm in a very moving way. Circling the audience in a wheelchair after the show, the man, who had no legs and only one arm, collected a huge cloth bag full of money in exchange for some buttons he was selling. His eyes brimming, he presented the bag to me. "Thank you," he said, "for bringing so much magic into our lives."

A few days after we got back to Toronto, we received a wonderful letter from Mr. Van Orden in Washington: "From the standing ovation following your performance and the many people who spoke to you, I am sure that you are well aware of the feelings of satisfaction and enjoyment we all share."

What a high point for us all! So of course the shoe had to drop. Shortly after the show in Washington, we gave a performance in London, Ontario, and everything — but everything —

went wrong from beginning to end. First, we were booked into an arena that seated thousands — but there were no more than 300 people in the audience. Then, the show was a disaster. The only person I felt sorry for was poor Celia Franca, doing her best to narrate as the performers turned *Carnival of the Animals* into a complete zoo. They stood in front of trees, bumped into each other, dropped their props. One of them — it turned out to be Andy — fell down at center stage and started crying. Everyone missed cues, including Warren and Wendy. By the time they struggled to the end of the show, half the audience had gone home.

I was grimly silent all the way back to Toronto, but the next day I let my troupe have it. I decided the discussion couldn't take place in the warehouse with the upstairs tenants. Instead, I marched everyone over to nearby Varsity Stadium and howled at them for a full hour. "And you're nothing but a bunch of 'retards'!" I concluded.

Andy started crying again, and I rushed up to him, furiously waving a finger in his face. "If I ever see you cry like that again," I shouted, "I'm gonna take those tears and put them in a bucket, and then I'm gonna take your face and shove it in the bucket till you drown!"

"And as for you — " and I turned on Richard, who was staring down at his crotch "— if you ever do that again, I'm gonna get a saw from the prop room and you'll never have anything to stare at again! Do you get my drift?!"

"Yes, Diane," he said.

"Now, let's get *back to work*!"

To my amazement, the tongue-lashing worked. Andy stopped crying, and Richard stopped staring at himself (most of the time, at least), while the rehearsals went better and better. It was a reminder to everyone, myself included, that although we'd come so far, we still had to work at it. A real flop gives meaning to the old show business cliché about being only as good as your last performance. In a way, that show in London *had* been good for us: We all learned not to be complacent.

The premiere of *Sorcerer's Apprentice* in Toronto was a triumph, not only as a performance but as an outpouring of confidence in and support for the company and what it represented, artistically and humanly. Ron and Ann returned just to perform in the show. Lorne Greene, who had memorized the Ogden Nash verses for *Carnival of the Animals*, brought them alive with his rich, expressive voice. Jimmy Macdonald, whom I introduced as "an American legend," demonstrated the accuracy of that word with his uncanny reproductions of the sounds of birds and beasts. Anne Murray was there to cheer for her puppet. Television producer Allan Thicke came, bringing Valerie Harper, who told us that she'd seen us perform in Las Vegas the year before and loved both shows. And in the audience were all our old friends: Gordon Pinsent, Jack McAndrew, Pauline McGibbon. We presented awards to Pauline and Anne. And Nancy won the Liberace Award as the most improved performer. It was a delight to see her standing straight and tall on stage, so proud that Pauline was watching her from the audience.

The reaction to *Sorcerer's Apprentice*? The critics couldn't find enough praise for it. Here's what *The Globe and Mail* had to say:

> The Sorcerer's Apprentice who thinks he can outdo his master was a perfect reproduction of his animated self. And animation is really what this black-light show is all about — animation that doesn't rely on celluloid tricks, or on complex systems of strings and pulleys. Getting his magic incantations mixed up, the Apprentice ends up being beaten by disembodied hands wielding brooms, paddling on the crescent of a moon, encountering barracudas and stars and capricious wash-buckets. The choreography, timing, costumes and puppets were all excellent.

A few weeks later, the company was returning from a small

out-of-town show. Everyone was exhausted, and while we were unloading the truck, Wendy picked up a very heavy box. She couldn't handle it, and it fell, breaking her foot. Sadly, this meant her leaving the company. It would be months before her ankle healed completely, and we just couldn't wait for her that long. We all felt terrible, because Wendy was a good, energetic performer who fit in very well.

After Wendy left, Cathy started taking on some of her parts. Just as she'd shown a great ability to quickly adapt to the company in Washington, she demonstrated the same capacity in rehearsals.

Throughout the summer, some of the former company members, and others who now participated on an occasional basis, came back to the warehouse to visit and encourage us. Ron and Ann dropped in frequently; Tom came in with his girlfriend and told me he had a job interview the next day to clean windows at the CN Tower. Frank arrived one day to watch a rehearsal. At the end, before I even had a chance to get up and tell everyone what needed correcting, he was right in there with his considered opinion. "Guys, I gotta tell you, that stinks," he said. "The Toronto Maple Leafs are better than you guys." Our very own theatre critic!

I was surprised and very pleased to see this loyalty — especially on the part of Tom and Frank. I knew now that members would come and go and the extent of some people's involvement would change. But always there would be a growing circle of friends. This was our future. I could hardly believe I'd been so devastated by the resignations, so afraid to face the future.

That November, we had a couple of firsts: our first shows in Western Canada (Calgary and Edmonton), booked through the Great West Entertainment, a theatre promotion company, and — hallelujah! — Renato's first out-of-town trip with the company to which he'd given so much for five years. Mom finally talked Mrs. Marulli into it. Renato was beside himself with excitement. I was shocked when he called me at 6 A.M. the day we were supposed to leave, telling me he wasn't coming. "But why, Renato?" was all I could say.

"I just can't."

"You have to, Renato. You're a professional performer," I said, "and you've been talking about this trip for weeks."

"I know, Mrs. Dupuy, but I can't."

"Why?" Dead silence. I could hear him breathing. "Renato?"

"Oh, my God, I've had a stroke!" he screamed. "I can't go to Calgary!"

"Now, just a second, Renato," I said. "Feel your arms and legs. Are they okay?"

"No. I can't move."

"Look, Renato, don't worry about your stroke," I said. "We'll come and get you in a taxi and carry you onto the plane if necessary."

"I can't go, Mrs. Dupuy."

"We'll be there in a half-hour." And when we got to Renato's street, there he was, pacing furiously outside his house!

Our growing tradition of help from friends sustained us wonderfully once again. Lorne Greene graciously agreed to come from Los Angeles to narrate the shows. Steve Hyde of "Front Page Challenge" donated his services as stage manager; friends sold advance tickets by phone. And Wally Neil of Goodwill Services stepped into the breech and did the part of the broom in *Sorcerer's Apprentice* (even though he'd never performed before) because Ann was unable to come.

In Calgary, the company performed *Sorcerer's Apprentice* (with Wally absolutely superb as the broom), *Carnival of the Animals*, and a few Famous People numbers. Lorne Greene was so good with the audience — with his ad-libbing and storytelling — that he stretched the evening into a two-hour show. Without him, it would barely have been an hour. He even told jokes about me: "Do you know what Diane Dupuy is like?" he asked, and the audience was transfixed by his deep, serious voice. "I'll tell you what she's like. Do you see this?" And he pointed down at the stage as the spotlight followed his finger: Nothing was there. "Don't you see it?" Everyone peered at the stage: Nothing. "Well, this is what Madame Dupuy worries about." They broke up.

After the show, I went flying backstage to tell the performers about all the mistakes they had made; when I finished the long list, Lorne called me into his dressing room privately. "Diane, I want you to listen to what I have to say," he intoned in the voice of doom he had made famous. "Don't you ever scold a performer right after a show. The audience had a great time, the performers got a standing ovation, and you're the only one who knows there were mistakes in the show. So why not let them go to the reception and have a good time and tell them about the problems the next day?"

That shut me up, and I thought a lot about what Lorne had said.

Immediately after our western trip, we were off to Las Vegas to take part in a benefit performance for Liberace's scholarship fund for young artists. (We had become regular troupers!) Ken Bell came with us and so did Frank Jones, a feature writer for *The Toronto Star* who was doing an article on the Famous People Players. He saw all our warts during the road trip, and I was terrified at what he might say in his article. But it was wonderful. Frank talked about our trials and tribulations in a very sensitive way, and he understood why our difficulties devastated me so much: I wanted the Famous People Players to be great.

And so did one of our friends who, unbeknownst to me, had opened the biggest door we'd ever had the opportunity to walk through: Radio City Music Hall. That fabulous theatrical institution was sending two choreographers and its musical director to Toronto to see our show, thanks to Jimmy Macdonald, who'd praised us to Bob Jani, Radio City's president and the creative consultant to Disneyland.

Toronto's Ryerson Theatre generously donated its stage for our audition, and we performed *Sorcerer*, *Carnival* and some

Famous People numbers while the Radio City staff sat in the empty theatre, applauding and laughing.

A few days later, one of the choreographers called and asked if we could combine some of the Famous People numbers so that, for example, Presley and Streisand would be on the stage at the same time.

"I'm afraid not," I said. "You would have to spend two years training people to do two Famous People puppets on stage at the same time. It's a very difficult technique — each puppet takes three people to manipulate — and for them to co-ordinate with three others would take years."

"Don't worry," he said, "we'll get back to you."

This sounded like the typical show-biz brush-off, so I tried not to get my hopes up, but a few days later, Bob Jani called and offered us a contract to do *Sorcerer's Apprentice* at Radio City Music Hall for five weeks in March and April of 1980. The entire company was turning cartwheels (and Greg actually executed one). This was the big time!

It took a few days for the euphoria to wear off. We suddenly realized that if this was our greatest opportunity, it was also our biggest challenge. We had only a few months to prepare for it. That meant working like never before.

Mom and I flew to New York because the choreographers wanted us to see the stage and get an idea what redesigning and restaging of our show would be necessary to adjust to it. Radio City Music Hall isn't a normal theatre, they warned us — and they weren't kidding. It was like a football field, with more than 6,000 seats. I was terrified! We needed to make all the props bigger, and the staging had to be completely reworked. A performance would have to be nothing short of spectacular in a place like this.

And, of course, we needed more staff. A Toronto high school teacher I knew recommended an older student named Ida Colallilo. During the interview with Ida, Frances and I went on and on about everything being integrated and sharing duties like cleaning the bathroom, running errands, and helping performers not just with their parts but with personal hygiene and table manners.

"Well, I know the fork goes on the left and the knife on the right, and which spoon to use for soup," Ida suddenly put in.

I wasn't yet familiar with Ida's wry sense of humor — nor she with my expectations. She looked startled when I asked her to pick up a broom — she thought I wanted her to sweep the floor — but when I showed her the movements of the broom in *Sorcerer's Apprentice* she got right into it, even though she was wearing a tight skirt. Such spunk was a big point in her favor.

"What do you think?" I asked Frances after Ida had left.

"Well, I think anyone who would come in wearing a straight skirt, not expecting to have to audition, and then goes ahead and does the broom is a good sport. I like this girl, and I think you should hire her." It was a smart decision. Ida proved herself invaluable in the office and on stage. Her tough spirit helped her adapt well to the company.

We needed a big rehearsal space to get used to the cavernous Radio City stage, so we rented what was called the Ice House, a part of Toronto's Harbourfront development. It wasn't as big as the Music Hall, but it would do. Learning transitions on a bigger stage was the greatest challenge. For the performers to cover these distances while shifting props — from a ribbon to a broom to a swordfish in a matter of minutes — was incredibly demanding. And I didn't make it any easier when I decided everyone should learn someone else's part in case anyone got sick. But this time everyone gave their utmost to prepare the show. We all knew what was at stake. And the efforts were so prodigious as to be sometimes humorous, such as watching Warren race around the stage, going from the sorcerer to the bird to the broom to the bucket.

When we left for New York, in March of 1980, we were as ready as we could be. All the performers were in their new uniforms: white jeans and black-and-white T-shirts, donated by Levi-Strauss. For once, our work permits were in order, and there were great rooms waiting for us at the Mayflower Hotel.

At Radio City, we were sharing the bill with the Vienna Boys Choir, a magician, The Rockettes, and the singing group that performs "I Love New York." Technical rehearsals started the day after our arrival: We were expected to be at the theatre at 8 A.M., even though our run-through wasn't scheduled until nine. Nine o'clock came and went, and we still weren't called. Ten o'clock. Eleven. When lunchtime came, we were afraid to go out because we thought we might miss something, so Warren brought in some sandwiches and we went back to waiting.

It had to be 10 P.M. when we were finally called. The waiting had got to everyone, and the rehearsal was awful: I ran on stage screaming, "This banner is drooping!" and "This bucket is upside-down!" Everyone was terrified, and I was sure we would all be fired, but there was nothing but praise from Elman Anderson, the musical director. "You sat there all day and never complained, and you performed like a true group of professionals," he said. "Don't you worry about the mistakes. Everything's going to be fine, and we all wish you the best of luck."

But I was sure our luck had run out during the first show. I cried all the way through it because I saw every little mistake and was convinced that *now* we would certainly be fired. Slip-ups in rehearsal were one thing, but this was a performance: I shuddered to think what the stage manager must have been thinking. He was a tough professional. He had delayed the opening of the magician until his act was ready, and I fully expected the same fate for Famous People Players. But when I went backstage all the house staff and the ushers were gathered around Greg, Sandra, and the others, congratulating them enthusiastically.

Still, we didn't hear anything from the stage manager. When the second show was over and the audience gone, we were finally told we could leave. We hoped that no news was good news.

That's the way it was at Radio City. The rules were strict: You never went anywhere until the stage manager or one of his assistants said so, and if your call was for 2 P.M., you were in big trouble if you turned up at 2:01. As for the Famous People Players, we didn't even take any bows, and there was no mention in the program of the performers' background, the idea being that nothing would then detract from the magic of black-light theatre. These were decisions I completely supported, but it continued to bother me that the stage manager at the Radio City Music Hall had said nothing about the quality of the show. We did get good reviews in the newspapers: *The New York Times* called us "a nice little novelty act that features black light and giant puppets . . . the inspiration, of course, is Walt Disney's 'Fantasia.' " And the *New York Daily News* said we were ". . . an inventive set of puppeteers who do a delightful animation of 'The Sorcerer's Apprentice.' "

Fortified by the kudos, I screwed up enough courage to approach the stage manager and ask him how we were doing.

"Fine," he said.

"But do you think the show is good?"

"Listen," he said, "you'd know about it soon enough if it wasn't."

So we accepted the tough regime and also had some fun. One night, I treated everyone to dinner at Mamma Leone's, the famous Broadway restaurant. The food was classic Italian — even Mom was impressed — and the many carafes of wine on the table kept the conversation and laughter flowing. Andy and Greg had bought T-shirts saying, I TOOK A BITE OF THE BIG APPLE, which seemed to set the mood for all of us.

But our schedule didn't allow much time for being tourists. We did two shows a day, six days a week, with only one day off to explore the city. We took full advantage of the limited time and even got into the rhythm of New York. Our walk quickened and we became more aware of where we were going instead of just meandering along the streets. Cathy and Ida took all the girls shopping at Macy's and Saks Fifth Avenue, and Nancy, who usually wore pants, appeared one night at dinner in a designer dress she'd bought on sale. She looked sensational! When it came time for the Easter Parade, we all went with everyone decked out in new outfits, Ida and Mom in big picture hats.

One day, we got a call at the hotel from ABC-TV public-affairs program "Good Morning America," which wanted to produce an item on Famous People Players. We were delighted at the prospect of being filmed at Radio City Music Hall, but this was not to be. Union rules meant that filming in the theatre was too expensive. Instead, the show's staff and crew flew to Toronto later, filming us in rehearsal and performance. The documentary was hosted by Tom Sullivan, who composed the music for *Fame* and was the subject of the film *If You Could See What I Hear.* We all fell in love with Tom, a very kind, compassionate man who took to the performers instantly and became a fast friend of the company.

Being at the Music Hall made me think big; just being in New York made the adrenalin flow. One day, when I was on the phone to Marc Daniels, telling him about our successes, the conversation turned to the future. "What other big symphonic pieces do you know besides *Sorcerer's Apprentice*?"

"Well, there's *Scheherazade,*" he offered. "The music is great — it's by Rimsky-Korsakov — and the story is beautiful. I think you and the performers would love it."

That afternoon, I went out and bought a tape of *Scheherazade*, and for the next few days I sat in the big, empty theatre between shows, listening to the glorious music and letting pictures fill my mind.

In a palace, the princess Scheherazade lies sleeping. The Sultan enters, drags her from her bed and throws her to the floor: Her execution is at hand. But as the gleaming sword descends, Scheherazade cries: "Wait! Listen first to my story, then slay me if you will."

He stays his blow and is drawn into the tale, and as they leave the chamber, the great palace windows soar upward. The story comes to life . . . .

Camels appear, snake charmers crouch over their baskets, and Sinbad the Sailor swaggers into the marketplace, holding a lamp which releases a genie and a dazzling array of jewels and gold treasures. But when the treasure lies gleaming on the ground, the lamp releases its horrors: snakes, each more slimy, gruesome — deadly — than the next. Yet Sinbad slays them all, and when the battle is done, he clasps the magic lamp and the rich treasures, bearing them to the harbor where his ship awaits.

The sea is cruel tonight. A monstrous purple wind god descends, borne by blinding bolts of lightning and deafening thunder: Sinbad's ship is doomed. But wait! The god of the sea is here to save him and his ship, whose prow — an angel — carries him to the heavens as the . . .

. . . palace windows slowly reappear. Scheherazade waits for the Sultan's sentence. "You are spared," he tells her, "but I must hear such a tale each night, until a thousand and one nights are burned into dawn."

I could see the whole number so clearly that I knew it would work. Excitedly, I cornered the Radio City set designer and poured out my idea. He said it sounded wonderful, and, as proof of his enthusiasm, he came to me the next day with a set of drawings that matched my description of the story. "Here's a little present for you," he said, "and I hope you can bring it to life."

The whole company got caught up in the excitement of a new creation, and we even started blocking out the production in our dressing room. Ida was the genie, Cathy was Sinbad, Warren was the Sultan, Renato was the king of the snakes, and he and Benny were the ship. Everyone else played sea gods, camels, snakes, palm trees. At one point, Mom threw up her hands and said: "How do you expect me to build all those palm trees? And all those gargoyles and sea gods!" But I could tell her imagination was captured by *Scheherazade.* This would be our most ambitious undertaking to date. Here we were at Radio City Music Hall, something we couldn't even have imagined two years before. Where better to start planning our next escapade? It seemed there was no barrier to our dreams.

Leaving New York in April was sad. After our last show, all

the other Music Hall performers came to our dressing room, along with some of the staff. The Vienna Boys Choir sang "Auld Lang Syne" for us, and we all hugged, cried, and vowed we would somehow see each other again. After the others had left, I told everyone in the company how proud I was of them. Great things had happened here: Benny had blossomed into a conversationalist; Renato had walked up Times Square and Fifth Avenue without letting the stares or cruel remarks bother him; and Nancy hadn't lost her temper once during our entire stay.

On our way out of the theatre, one of the stagehands called after me. "Diane, hold on a second," he said. "I just wanted to tell you this. I think you guys are good enough for Broadway."

"You've got to be kidding," I said.

"No, I really mean it," he insisted. "You should do it."

As we walked along Avenue of the Americas, I glanced back at the illuminated marquees advertising the latest Broadway shows. "We're going to be up there someday," I told the performers. "Just you wait and see."

The Road to China

MAY 1980 – NOVEMBER 1982

After Radio City, there seemed no separating the dreams and Famous People Players' performances. Each was an aspect of the other, and both were becoming more intense, more grandiose.

Staging *Scheherazade* had so gripped everyone's imagination that we began rehearsing it right away. It was so complicated to perform and required such elaborate props that we were looking almost a year down the road before premiering it. At the same time we were preparing for a three-night show at the St. Lawrence Centre in June 1980.

In the midst of this, another dream surfaced in my mind: The Famous People Players would perform in China. As always, I immediately shared my enthusiasm with the company. They repaid it in kind, and going to China became a plan just waiting to be implemented. Everything we did from then on became part of the preparation. We carried this enthusiasm to the St. Lawrence Centre in June.

The performance at St. Lawrence Centre was a triumphant homecoming for us after Radio City. Opening night was a gala evening in the presence of the Lieutenant-Governor. Broadcaster Alex Trebek narrated *Carnival* and Pauline McGibbon presented the awards: Imperial Oil and Xerox got awards for their contributions to us in previous years, and so did Marion Patterson. Although smaller in dollar terms, her contribution was no less significant. For each of the poetry books she had sold over the years, all the proceeds went to us. Marion was willing to share everything with us because she believed in us.

The performances — and I held my breath as usual — were consistently good, and we unveiled a new number that had them rolling in the aisles. Cathy Camp, dancing to "The Stripper," peeled off an ornate fluorescent costume until, clad only in her black jumpsuit, she "vanished."

"The Stripper" proved to be a favorite of *Globe and Mail* critic Rick Groen, who called it "charmingly risque . . . a bump-and-grind routine featuring a heart-poundingly realistic stripper. The dancer tosses off her flowing attire with the elan of a nubile burlesque queen until, after a final flick of her supple wrist, she bares all and reveals nothing — having shrunk discreetly into the black light."

In the audience the second night was a young woman, Debbie Lim, who came to the show with her mother. She had seen Famous People Players on television and was obsessed with the idea of joining the company. After the show, she shyly approached Jimmy Macdonald — who had agreed to perform his wonderful sound effects for us again — and patiently waited until he had finished signing autographs. Then she asked him if he could introduce her to me.

"Sure!" said Jimmy, and brought her over to me. "This is Debbie, and she's a friend of mine, so I want you to be extra nice to her." Debbie and I talked briefly, and I liked her at once: She was very well mannered, charming, and articulate, and she also impressed me as someone who had already learned what I was trying to teach the performers — that a handicap can be overcome. Though she had a sight impairment, she carried herself with a great deal of self-confidence. I was immediately reminded of my own impulsive determination to meet Liberace under very similar circumstances. In her own, much more polite way, Debbie showed the same determination to seize the fateful moment. When I asked her to join the company, she looked as if she'd just awoken on Christmas morning.

Our reputation had grown so much that we were now booked for our first cross-Canada tour in August 1980. We were playing Charlottetown, Prince Edward Island, and Glace Bay, Nova Scotia. Then we would go west to Brandon and Winnipeg, Manitoba, and Red Deer, Lethbridge, Calgary, and Edmonton, Alberta.

We chartered a bus for the tour. Warren, Richard and Renato traveled in a truck with the props. "We're roadies!" Richard crowed. It was a unique feeling moving from town to town, rising with the sun and struggling, late at night, to load the truck after the show.

On the eastern part of the tour, the CTV network's public affairs program "W-5" was filming a segment on us, so the crew and reporter Jim Reed came along with us. I felt very strongly that anyone coming on tour with us should become part of the family. And Jim was great about getting involved, even when we put him on the spot by asking him to narrate *Carnival* for us in Glace Bay.

In Glace Bay we learned a lot about Maritimes hospitality — and going with the flow. At 7:55 P.M., with the show due to start in five minutes, the stagehands still hadn't set up. "Don't worry," one of them said. "No one's going to show up until at least eight thirty or nine." He was right. And from curtain on, everything was great. We had never had such an enthusiastic audience. They reacted immediately to the dramatic quality of black light (I thought of the rugged coastline we'd seen on our drive). And when their own "Snowbird," Anne Murray, appeared — glowing on the dark stage — there was a deafening roar of approval. After the show there were more than twenty-five people backstage clamoring to help us load the props.

This same warm lesson in appreciation continued on the western leg of our tour. In Lethbridge, we had an audience of three, fifteen minutes before curtain time, and were feeling pretty down in the dumps. "Maybe we should cancel," Warren said.

I almost agreed with him, but then I remembered a story Seymour Heller had told me about one show early in Liberace's career. Five people showed up, but Seymour told Lee he had to perform anyway. "They thought enough of you to come out," Seymour said, "and they deserve the best."

"So that's what we'll do," I told Warren. "We'll give these three people the best damn show they've ever seen." But, to our surprise, people suddenly started streaming into the theatre just as were about to start, and they gave us one of the best damn shows *we'd* ever seen — cheering and applauding with enthusiasm you rarely get from a big-city audience, even though it arrives early.

Back in Toronto, we started rehearsing for *Scheherazade* in earnest. As the props piled up — with nine-foot camels and 18-foot palm trees that had to be doubled over twice to fit in the room — it became clear that we were running out of space again.

Warren couldn't wear his sorcerer hat when we rehearsed *Sorcerer's Apprentice.* We had to take the camels' heads off when we were practising *Scheherazade.* All around us were piled props from the André Gagnon production, the *Carnival* special, the Famous People numbers, and our current shows. There wasn't any room left for the people.

In September 1980, we all started looking around for a new home. It was Warren who finally found an entire floor of a warehouse building for rent, not far from where we were, in the west end of Toronto. The place had to be scrubbed from top to bottom and fumigated before we moved in. When we arrived, the whole place was full of birds flapping around the ceiling. They had come in through a giant fan outside the window — and they still fly in occasionally.

Shortly after we moved, we got another new performer, Debbie Rossen. When a new performer joins the company, we usually start by asking him or her to do things like deliver letters, go to the store, or pick up a package from the post office. The idea is to show new people that there's more to Famous People

Players than spotlights and applause. Everyone is responsible for his or her props; everyone shares in the work of loading and unloading the truck; and everyone is expected to help with menial tasks such as running errands and cleaning the building.

One morning Ida asked Debbie to deliver a check to the bank. Sandra had already taken her there three times, so we thought she would be familiar with the route. When Ida asked, "Are you sure you know how to get there?" Debbie confidently said yes. At 6 P.M. there was still no sign of Debbie. I decided to call Mrs. Rossen, who immediately came to the office to wait with us. She was very pleasant to us, but I could tell she was worried sick. I was also concerned, but I had a sneaking suspicion what might happen next.

Sure enough, a few minutes later the Toronto Transit Commission office was on the phone to me. Debbie had been found riding round and round on the subway, and someone from their office was on the way to our building with her.

"What were you doing on the subway all this time?" I demanded when Debbie was dropped off at the office.

"I was sitting there."

"Why?"

"I got lost." (Where had I heard this before?)

"Well, if you're lost, you have to get directions."

"But there were all these names going by so fast, and I didn't know what to do."

"You have to tell someone that you're lost and ask them how to get there!"

Debbie started crying, but, to my surprise, her mother didn't intervene; she just sat there quietly until the tears subsided. Then, very calmly, Mrs. Rossen asked if we would give Debbie another chance.

"Yes, we will," I said, and I'm glad we did. Not only did Debbie learn how to travel on the subway, she also became an excellent performer and a valued member of Famous People Players.

My faith in the other Debbie — Debbie Lim — was also justified. She worked extremely hard to learn the black-light technique, which was particularly difficult for her because she is blind in one eye and almost blind in the other. Even with thick glasses she can barely see. And since the black hood a performer wears in black-light performance impairs even 20/20 vision, getting around the stage was doubly hard for Debbie.

Scheherazade was to premiere in June 1981, so by the new year rehearsals intensified. There were dozens of complicated transitions for the performers to learn and a lot of work still to do on the props. For once, however, the financial pressures were less. The Canadian Organizing Committee of International Year of the Disabled was backing the production as well as other performances we were planning and there was a great deal of corporate assistance.

As spring approached, and the performers started to shed their big coats and baggy sweaters, I noticed that Sandra was starting to put on a lot of weight. I spoke to her about it several times, and even wrote a note to her mother. But she kept on packing in the french fries and piling on the pounds. And her personal hygiene was slipping, too. I decided to take direct action: One afternoon, when rehearsals were over, I called her into my office. "Sandra," I said, "how would you like to look like a fashion model for the premiere of *Scheherazade*?"

She gazed down at her protruding stomach and spreading hips. "Me?" She looked utterly incredulous.

"Yes, you," I said. "But there's something you have to do first."

"What?"

"You have to move in with me for three months, go on a diet, and do lots of exercise, and . . ."

"Oh, no!"

"Well, you can forget about looking like a model, then."

There was a long pause. Then Sandra looked up at me with a new expression of hope. "Will I look like Brooke Shields?"

"No, you'll look like Sexy Ciccone," I said, and she blushed happily. At my place, we went to work on the transformation, starting with diet, exercise, and a daily hygiene program every afternoon after work.

I was amazed to find that Sandra didn't know how to wash herself properly. I'd find her standing up in a tub full of bubblebath — she was afraid of the water — and scooping up little handfuls of foam to dab onto a square centimeter of arm or leg. "Sandra, that won't work," I said. "You have to really scrub," and I showed her with a washcloth. It took weeks before she actually immersed herself in the water without being told!

As for the diet and exercise program, I decided it would be more of an incentive for Sandra if we both got involved (at the same time, I could keep an eye on her french fry addiction!). I'm happy to say that by the end of the three months — with dieting and a daily fitness routine of twenty laps in the pool, a half mile around the track, and fifty sit-ups — we both looked absolutely stunning. On her last day with us, I treated Sandra to a permanent and hair coloring, and when she looked at herself in the mirror, her hair shining and her body svelte in tight jeans and a clinging sweater, she blurted out: "I'm beautiful!" And so she was.

As busy as we were, my creative impulses wouldn't leave me alone — nor would the world outside. The company began working on two new puppets that spring — Frank Sinatra and Liza Minnelli — and I began blocking out another extravaganza based on all our favorite outer-space imagery from *Superman*, *Star Trek*, and, of course, *Star Wars*.

One morning in early May, while I was in the midst of breaking up a miniature "star war" between the spaceships wielded by Benny and another performer, Ida called me to the phone. It was my friend Father Tom McKillop, the founder of the Youth Corps, who had recommended Warren Quinn to me. "It's an emergency, baby," he said. (That's the way he always talks; he's a very hip priest!) "Just say yes."

"Say yes to what, Father Tom?"

"Just say yes, baby, for 7 A.M. on Saturday."

"Okay, but . . ."

"Great! You're doing a performance for me at a prison, and the truck will be there on Saturday morning to pick up the props."

"You've got to be kidding! We can't get ready that fast!"

"Oh, please don't let me down, baby," he pleaded. "These are people who need to be touched by your magic, and I can't reach them. You've got to come." He must have known I couldn't say no to that!

The prison was just outside Toronto, and I have to be honest — we were all very apprehensive because we had never been in such an environment before. The physical look of the place was extremely intimidating: the automatic gates which closed behind us as we entered the grounds; the drab grey of the walls inside; the clanging bars; and the awful feeling of being trapped, which persisted even though we knew we would be getting out in a few hours.

In the prison auditorium, there was none of the banter that usually accompanies our setup. We quietly got the stage ready, and just as we were finishing, a loud bell rang and the prisoners started filing into the room. They loved the show; the final applause seemed endless.

Afterward, they were so eager to talk to us that we spent all day there, and, just as we were getting ready to leave, a number of the inmates asked if I could come back to help them produce a play or learn to become stage managers. They were desperate for something that would bring creativity into their lives. On the way back to Toronto, I told Father Tom how much I wanted to work with these prisoners, and I tried, over several months, to get something organized. But I couldn't co-ordinate a return visit with the shows we had coming up in the summer.

After the prison show, I was in a very distracted state: A million thoughts scattered in all directions. After a particularly long day of rehearsals for *Scheherazade*, I stayed late at work, sitting alone in the empty rehearsal room with the radio on, trying to clear my mind. The second song that came on was "Send In the Clowns" by Stephen Sondheim, and, as I listened to the haunting melody, I started to block out a number.

The image I saw was a lonely old clown, on the road but going nowhere. The poignancy of the number (our prison performance was still fresh in everyone's mind) captured the entire company's imagination. We started rehearsing it immediately while Mom designed the props. But we ran into a snag — literally — with the clown's clothesline-cum-tightrope: It kept getting tangled into knots. Everytime we untied it, the thing tangled into a knot again. "Why don't you just leave it like that?" suggested Benny. "It looks sort of sad like that. Just like the clown."

I was astounded by his insight; it was too obvious for me to see. The big knot in the clothesline was a perfect symbol of the clown's pathos — it gave a new dimension to the number. And this young man was labeled retarded! I remembered reading that Albert Einstein had been considered retarded in high school because of his ineptness in mathematics. I thought of the prisoners we had entertained and how much ability lay wasted there.

Shortly before the gala premiere of *Scheherazade*, at the St. Lawrence Centre, Warren told me he would be leaving the company after the opening. I was heartbroken, but Warren was adamant about moving on to other interests, and by now I respected that kind of decision.

Scheherazade was a smash. I've never heard so many ooohs and aahs in response to a number. Pauline McGibbon was a superb narrator for *Carnival of the Animals*. Salome Bey sang "He Ain't Heavy . . . He's My Brother" in honor of Warren, while we showed slides of the company at work and on the road.

We had little time to rest on our laurels. We had a performance coming up at the National Arts Centre in Ottawa in October of 1981 as well as another western tour which would culminate in Vancouver in December. The Ottawa gala would have to be organized, and the person who immediately came to mind was Maureen McTeer, the wife of former Prime Minister Joe Clark (then the Opposition Leader in the House of Commons). I identified with her — an independent, outspoken person, a lawyer who still found time to be a wife and mother. As usual, I first decided what I wanted, then set out to get it. I kept my fingers crossed when I dialed Maureen's private number. Maureen took the call and said yes immediately; a woman after my own heart! The preparations couldn't have been put in more competent hands. Maureen formed a committee to sell tickets and organize the event itself, while IBM generously committed $15,000 to the gala and undertook to arrange the post-performance reception. Maureen cannily broke party lines for the committee, enlisting politicians' wives from all three parties. All the tickets were sold weeks before the show.

Our trip to Ottawa proved to be one of our most memorable experiences. We were met at the airport then taken on a tour of the Parliament Buildings, including a visit to the House of Commons during Question Period.

"No wonder they call it Question Period," Andy whispered to me. "They never get any answers." I almost had to dive under my seat to keep from laughing. But I must say, answers or no answers, it was great to see Joe Clark and Pierre Trudeau squaring off against each other.

In the evening, Maureen held a buffet dinner for the company at Stornoway, the official residence of the Opposition Leader. I couldn't believe how all the Liberals, Conservatives, and New Democrats who had just been at each other's throats in the House of Commons were enjoying each other's company just a few hours later.

The dinner set the tone for the whole evening. While the VIPs mingled, my two daughters and Maureen's daughter Catherine got to know each other by chasing each other up and down the stairs and around the house. The informality of it all put the performers at ease. Governor-General Ed Schreyer and his wife attended the gala and mingled with the crowd. Everyone who paid for a ticket was a VIP that night.

The trip left us all with a warm glow, along with a feeling of official respectability and acceptance that was different from but just as important as being able to say we'd performed at Radio City. And the icing on the cake was my appointment with the Chinese ambassador.

It struck me that Maureen would appreciate the company's dream of going to China and could perhaps help us realize it. I shared the idea with her and asked whether she knew how I could meet the Chinese ambassador to Canada. She promised to try to arrange it. He had seen our performance, was enthusiastic about the company, and graciously promised to write a letter of support for our idea of performing in China. My determination was now keener than ever.

Not long afterward, I got a letter from the B'nai B'rith of Metropolitan Toronto. I guess I wasn't paying a lot of attention and I thought I was being asked to nominate someone for the organization's Woman of the Year award. I had an appointment, so I headed out of the office, tossing the letter onto Cathy's desk, saying, "Think of someone to nominate, okay?"

When I got back, Cathy looked at me with a strange expression on her face. "What's the matter?" I asked.

"About that letter from the B'nai B'rith, Diane . . ."

"Oh yeah. Did you think of anyone we can nominate?"

"No, Diane, you don't understand. It's you who's receiving the award!"

I was thrilled. This award was from a group that did wonderful work, and I thought of the members as people who, like my mother, pick up the pieces when the rest of us fall apart. I was terribly nervous when I went to receive the award. I had never made an acceptance speech before, and the awards ceremony — a breakfast — was packed with people. The performers, our board of directors, and Peter Brophy of Xerox were there, but I was still scared. By the time I got up to the lectern I was shaking like a leaf. The only thing that made me feel calmer was looking at the performers and Mom in the front row; I just impulsively started talking to them, forgetting about my prepared speech.

"Greg, I want to thank you for teaching me the meaning of patience when you had that terrible migraine headache and kept smiling through it. I thought twice about complaining the next time I wasn't feeling well. And Nancy, I want to thank you for showing me something about self-control, because I lose my temper too, and sometimes I don't hide it as well as you do.

"Cathy, I want to thank your for standing by us through thick and thin, for being gracious to people who come up to you after a show and say, 'Isn't she a pretty girl even though she's retarded.' You don't mind if you're perceived as one of the other performers because you consider yourself part of them, and you're the kind of special person it takes to work with special people.

"Mom, I want to thank you so many times — for the swan and the lion you stayed up all night to build; for always being there to help us and cheer us on when we feel like giving up; for giving so much of yourself without so much as a thank you from me. Well, I thank you now, Mom, a hundred times.

"And to the wonderful people who honored me with this award, I want to say that it's really an award for a dream, an impossible dream we can all share and we can all attain."

It was an extraordinary feeling to be honored by people with such a powerful commitment to helping others, and of all the awards I've received subsequently — including the Order of Canada — this is the one I most treasure.

1981 was almost over when we left on our tour of British Columbia. While we were performing in Victoria, I spoke with the theatre manager, John Dyck, about our hopes of touring China. He introduced me to Richard Liu, vice-president of the Chinese-Canadian Friendship Association, and Richard came to our show that night. Afterward, he told me he thought Famous People Players would be perfect for China. There would be no language barrier with our performance. He offered to help in any way he could. Impulsive, as always, I offered to pay his way to China if he would pave the way for a tour and he agreed. This support, and the letter the Chinese ambassador had written, made me feel we were getting closer and closer to realizing our dream.

As we sat on the ferry from Victoria to Vancouver, I saw a huge rainbow, which seemed to follow us all the way into port. Call me superstitious, but I took it as an omen, a wonderful omen that we really would be going to China.

Jack Webster, British Columbia's legendary curmudgeon of broadcasting and a devoted supporter of the company, had paved the way to our Vancouver performance beautifully. He'd promoted us on his show for weeks, lent his name to a fund-raising letter, and arranged for our airfare and the rental of the theatre. As if this weren't enough, he'd agreed to narrate *Carnival of the Animals* in the show.

The occasion was in honor of Lieutenant-Governor Henry Bell-Irving; we premiered *Les Patineurs*, a Christmas fantasy inspired by the music of Meyerbeer's ballet of the same name. "*There's Santa!*" exulted the hundreds of children in the audience, and it was so easy to see the magic through their eyes: the huge, glittering Christmas tree surrounded by so many bright, beribboned boxes — some of them tantalizingly open, the toy trains and soldiers spilling out onto the floor. . . . Eeeek! A mouse! Playing hide-and-seek with Santa, disappearing near the tree and — oops! — there he is, poking his little pink nose out from behind a big easy chair into which Santa thankfully collapses as the room vanishes.

A light snow is falling and pine trees gleam in the darkness as the skaters glide. There's a tiny fawn, a pair of storks in earmuffs, a penguin wearing a toque (only I knew it was Benny!), a gorilla waving a hockey stick (that's Renato!) and an absolutely enormous giraffe that took four performers to keep aloft, and an elderly couple in a sleigh, floating eerily above the ice and gently wafting down to skate to the lilt of the romantic waltz.

This must be the king of Christmas trees! It soars endlessly upward. But there's no star! The elves are up to mischief: spinning across the floor on a giant shining top; galloping enormous candy canes around the tree. Look! They're into

Santa's hat, and who's in that boot clumping over the presents? Oh! A cannon! This'll be fun: One elf is in the cannon; the other lights the fuse and *bang*! Right to the top of the tree, where the Christmas elf turns into a shining, golden Christmas star.

And right on the final beat of music, too! It was a first: We'd been rehearsing this finale for months, without success. I stood with the rest of the audience and applauded proudly: What a way for Famous People Players to bring in the new year!

Better organization became a catch phrase in my mind in 1982. Our increasingly busy performance schedule, which placed greater pressure on the whole company, demanded it. In addition, our new productions were becoming ever more complex and required a new level of technical skill. It was becoming difficult to put a new company member into a black jumpsuit and hood immediately. We needed a way to train these new people in advance as well as a means to replace anyone who quit or was fired.

We decided to form an understudy school to prepare people for the demands of being a full performer. Ann, who had been with me at the start (she was now married to another Famous People Players veteran, Ron Dick), agreed to be the director for the school, which would begin later in the spring and operate two days a week. Ann promptly named it The Famous People Players Farm Team!

Throughout the spring, personal crises in the company illustrated that the understudy school, while not a solution to such difficulties, was essential to help us survive the loss of performers.

Cathy Camp was leaving the company. We were all very upset by the news, but Nancy took it the hardest. She had been very fond of Cathy. In the past, she had flown into monumental rages, but now she continually mumbled under her breath and accused people of looking at her strangely. It was starting to get unbearable to spend any time with her. Richard was also causing us problems again. He had been fine on the road, where we could keep an eye on him and give him enough work to burn up his vast quantities of excess energy. But as soon as he got home, it would be back to the old routine of terrorizing subway passengers and shoppers in the few malls that hadn't yet barred him.

A perennial difficulty we experienced in Famous People Players was coping with the problems of performers like Richard and Nancy, who had been experiencing difficulties with self-control since childhood — difficulties that had never been addressed by either their parents or their teachers.

And in the midst of all this turmoil, we were starting a new production — yes, another one! The classical pieces we had performed, like *Scheherazade* and *Les Patineurs*, were very popular with audiences, but it seemed to me that numbers like "Superman" were even more appealing, especially to younger audiences, influenced as they were by the excitement and the special effects of movies and television. So I decided to choose theme songs from some of the best-known James Bond movies and put them together in a sequence. "Live and Let Die" would feature a witch doctor doing a ritualistic dance; "You Only Live Twice" would have a lovely Oriental motif of cherry blossoms and giant waving butterflies; "For Your Eyes Only" would show an underwater scene with a submarine whose hatch opens to reveal scuba divers; "Nobody Does It Better" would have bikini-clad girls floating through the air while James Bond stood sipping his martini; and "Goldfinger" would star the fearsome Oddjob, who would decapitate a couple of statues and, as a finale, slice off his own head and spin it through the air.

As we began rehearsing the James Bond sequence, Richard Liu returned from China with great news. We were invited to the People's Republic for an extensive tour in October!

When the initial excitement died down and I began looking at some of the exhaustive questionnaires we were expected to answer, I quickly realized that Richard, who had been charged with a criminal offence, would not be able to go. I wanted him to stay with the company nevertheless, and I arranged for him to undergo therapy to make this possible.

In an attempt to add to Richard's workload — and curb his excess energy — I asked him to come to my place occasionally and do some chores. One evening, he saw me barefoot: He stood there, staring at my feet and suddenly got an erection. I backed away; he got down on all fours and crawled across the floor toward me, pleading, "Please, let me touch your feet."

I was terrified, but for some reason I didn't panic or scream. "Richard, come quick and see this, and then I'll let you touch my feet," I said cheerily, running past him and down the hall and flinging open the door. "Look who's here!"

As he ventured out the door and looked down the apartment corridor to see who was there, I slammed the door behind him and locked it. He started scratching at the door, begging again: "Let me touch your feet. . . . I want your feet. . . ." I raced to the phone and called Ida.

"Look," she said, "enough is enough. You've got to fire him."

Eventually, Richard gave up and went home. The next day, I called his psychiatrist and told her we couldn't keep Richard in the company any longer. Then I called him into my office and told him that it was time to get out into the working world, that he would have help finding a job, through an employment center, and that he could be placed in a group home through his social worker, who had worked with him for several years. I kept in touch with this social worker for years after Richard left the company, but it was usually bad news. He kept accosting women, anywhere and everywhere. The employment center didn't want him, and the few group homes willing to take him had to throw him out, usually after only a few days.

I had always thought Richard would flourish on a farm, where the physical work would tire him out, and by some happy coincidence, his mother and stepfather bought a farm near Toronto. He was active and happy at first, but he started going into Toronto occasionally, and harassed the female passengers so much that he was barred from the GO Train. A few months later, tragedy struck. Richard burned down the barn; his stepfather, devastated, died of a heart attack, and his mother took

Richard back to Toronto. There he ran rampant, even attacking a teacher in a life-skills program he was taking. "He was in desperate need of stability, care, and close supervision," the social worker told me, "but none of the group homes or centers he needed would take him. The problem for which he needed help was also the reason he was turned away. It was a real Catch-22 situation."

The social worker tried to place Richard in a special institution that offered a gymnasium, school, workshop, and cottage-style residences. There was a long waiting list, but Richard was finally transferred there. But who knows if he stayed?

What Richard and his family had to endure was tragic. For us, it was heartbreaking to spend years working with him only to watch him regress and deteriorate beyond our help. It happens too often.

Shortly after Richard left the company, in May of 1982, we got a new Famous People Player — and one of the first members of Ann's understudy school — Darlene Arsenault, a tall, attractive blonde (to whom Andy proposed on numerous occasions) with a pronounced shyness that once drove her cowering under a pile of props while rehearsing. Ann worked patiently with her on this problem, but I decided the best way for her to overcome it was the way Benny had learned: on the road. We had some shows coming up in Petrolia, Ontario, so we headed out with our newest performer, Darlene, and our new bus driver, Dave Balinsky, who soon became part of the family.

The people who met us in Petrolia were wonderful: As well as our performance fee and accommodation, they gave us a buffet that Fenton's would die for. One of the ladies, Marge, found out (from whom I don't know!) that Dave Balinsky loved pies, so she baked every imaginable kind: pumpkin, apple, cherry, lemon meringue. And she wouldn't let anyone touch them before Dave had the first piece. The only problem in the show was that Darlene didn't perform any of her parts. At intermission, I asked her what had happened.

"I don't know."

"Why didn't you do your parts?"

"I don't know."

"Well, where were you?"

"I don't know," she mumbled, and her tongue started poking out the corner of her mouth. Here we go again!

During the second half of the show, I stayed backstage to watch Darlene carefully during the James Bond sequence in which she was supposed to be wiggling some coral in the underwater sequence and holding one of the statues in "Goldfinger." Lo and behold, there she was in the wings, singing, "Goldfinger . . ." I explained to her that she had to perform her parts, not watch the show and sing the numbers. And I made up my mind to give her more parts later on. She wouldn't have time to stand in the wings and take in the spectacle, because she'd be too busy getting from stage right to stage left to pick up her next prop.

On the other hand, no time like the present. I gave Darlene two more parts to do the following evening, with only a few minutes of rehearsal. She was excellent in the performance.

Back in Toronto, we were having more and more problems with Nancy. One day, I asked her into my office and sat her down. "Nancy," I said, "maybe it's your time to leave the company. You seem to be getting tired of it."

"Oh no," she said. "I don't want to leave."

"Well, Nancy, you can't go around mumbling and threatening people all the time," I said. "If you have a problem, you have to talk about it. I think you should go back and have therapy." She agreed and began seeing a psychiatrist who met with me and Nancy's mother as well.

But as the weeks went on, so did her mumbling. One afternoon during rehearsals, I asked Nancy to shift her grip on the butterfly prop she was using in the James Bond sequence. "You have to hold it in both hands, Nancy," I said, "so it'll look more real."

She ignored me.

"Nancy, I want you to *hold that butterfly in both hands*!"

"*No*!"

The words came pouring out of my mouth. "You know, I'm getting really sick and tired of this! You seem to think I owe you, when the fact is that you owe me, too. You owe me the respect to get out there and perform your part and quit that mumbling which none of us can take. And there's only one thing I have to say to you right now: Get your coat on and get the hell out of here!" Nancy stared at me for a moment, stunned. Then she ran to the washroom, locked herself in, and burst into loud tears.

Sandra made a move to go after her, but I stopped her. "Let her cry if she wants to," I said. After almost an hour had passed, Nancy realized that no one was going to comfort her, so she unlocked the cubicle and came out. I was in my office; she knocked, came in, and said: "You were right. My time with the company is up." And she took her coat and left.

I continued to be involved in Nancy's therapy, and at one session with Nancy and her mother, the psychiatrist asked me to consider taking her back in the company if her problems were brought under control. "I don't think that would be a good idea," I said, though I was sorely tempted to agree. "Nancy's been with the company for eight years, and what she needs now is an entirely different environment." As it turned out, Nancy got a good job in a company that mainly employed Greek workers, so when she muttered imprecations under her breath, no one understood what she was talking about. Over the years, Nancy and I stayed in touch and spoke frequently over the phone; she still comes to some Famous People Players functions and is doing very well in her life.

As always, there was too much going on for me to afford the luxury of a long depression. We were approaching our tour of China, and I was still wondering if we were really going to get there. The enormity of the financial challenge was just beginning to penetrate. In their invitation, our Chinese hosts had told us that the company was the first of its kind to be invited to

China, and, as the first of our kind, we were finding monetary support very scarce. Luckily, Peter Brophy of Xerox came to our rescue by agreeing to head up a campaign to raise the $40,000 we needed for the trip. With his help, and that of John Black Aird, Pauline's successor as Lieutenant-Governor, we were able to get substantial support from the Ontario Ministry of Culture and Recreation, Xerox, and Famous Players Realty. The rest of the money came from our contacts and from T-shirt sales. And we also got a great break on transportation costs: CP Air donated the cost of shipping the props and gave us a group rate on our plane tickets.

The summer seemed to crawl by as we put the finishing touches on our plans for China. We wanted a sign that said CANADA AND CHINA; FRIENDSHIP FOREVER GREEN. Richard Liu translated the words into Chinese, which Mom painstakingly reproduced on a banner. Dr. Liu also translated the Ogden Nash verses into Chinese for his narration of *Carnival of the Animals* and arranged for the mayor of Victoria, British Columbia, to accompany us. The city of Suzhou, which we would be visiting, was to become the twin city of Victoria. A film crew would be traveling with us to shoot a documentary, for a pay-TV channel, and we were also taking a friend of mine, Judy Brake of CBC-TV (who helped out the film crew considerably) and the littlest Players, Jeannine and Joanne.

Besides *Carnival*, our program included *Scheherazade*, *Sorcerer's Apprentice*, and the Anne Murray puppet, accompanied at the piano by the Liberace puppet to the tune of "You Needed Me." A few days before we left, Anne Murray and her husband came to the rehearsal hall to wish her puppet and us good luck. "Look at this!" she joked. "The puppet gets to go to China, but what about me?" She delightedly agreed to my request for an autograph — on the cubicle door in the girls' washroom! "May I not be the last!" she wrote.

Our first stop was Vancouver, where Lieutenant-Governor Bell-Irving and his aides came out to the airport to wish us a pleasant journey. Then it was on to Hong Kong, where we had a two-day layover. We did all the expected tourist activities and loved them: afternoon tea at the posh Peninsula Hotel and a boat tour of Hong Kong harbor, where we marveled at the community thriving on the water.

As we got off the boat, we noticed a group of elderly men who looked so frail that a light breeze might have knocked them over. But as soon as they saw us coming, they sprang to life like teen-agers. Next thing we knew, we were all sitting aboard four rickshaws. Imagine four or five people on a rickshaw intended for three, at most, and these ancient, emaciated men wheeling us around the narrow streets as if they were on the straightaway at Indianapolis! The whole bunch of us started singing "Before the Parade Passes By" at the top of our lungs just as we reached the financial district. It was no wonder that dozens of passers-by stopped in their tracks to stare at this wild procession! At the end of the ride, when we took out our wallets to pay, the men just grabbed whole handfuls of cash from our hands and ran. We figured out later that we must have paid more than $150.00 for that rickshaw ride!

Finally, we were on board the small plane to mainland China — and I mean small. There was barely room for our group. The stewardesses handed out miniature key chains, and the same two songs kept playing on the sound system: "Jingle Bells" and "Red River Valley," both in Chinese. I can still hear the high, clear sopranos. We landed in Shanghai, and as I gazed out at the rows of soldiers on the tarmac, I thought to myself that despite the martial pomp, I had never seen such a peaceful scene. Everyone was smiling, and no one had the frustrated look of competitiveness I was so used to seeing in Toronto.

We met our interpreter, Lu — "He's gorgeous!" Sandra whispered to me — and got into a limousine festooned with doilies and frilly curtains that looked for all the world like Grandma's lace tablecloths. When we got to the hotel in Suzhou, there were hundreds of children outside, waving banners, holding plastic flowers, and chanting a welcome. Henry

Kissinger had been visiting China, so we thought this tribute was for him, and we looked around, hoping to catch a glimpse of him. But Lu said the welcome was for us!

In the hotel, Jeannine and Joanne suddenly disappeared. I panicked: "What's happened to my children?" I demanded of Lu.

"They have been taken to their room," he said.

"Oh, the children usually stay with me," I said. "They would make a terrible mess in the room by themselves."

"But, you see, in China we treat our children with respect, and as adults," Lu explained, "and so they behave accordingly."

I was skeptical, but when I got upstairs, the girls had already unpacked, hung up their clothes, and even lined up their shoes at the foot of their beds. I was amazed; I was even more startled when I discovered there were no locks on any of the doors — yet we never lost a thing during our entire stay. In fact, I accidentally left behind a lovely silk scroll I had bought in Suzhou, only to have it returned to me when we arrived in Wuxi, the next town on our itinerary.

That night there was a sixteen-course banquet in honor of our group. I would come to realize that a splendid — and endless — banquet was a matter of course for guests of China; by the end of the trip, I couldn't fit into the Oscar de la Renta suit I had bought especially for the trip! At that first magnificent feast, the appetizer alone was a work of art: vegetables, meats, and fish arranged in the shape of a rooster, perfect in every detail. At the end of the banquet, there were several speeches, and when it was my turn, I said, "I wonder if we could meet the chefs who gave us such a great performance tonight, because we only hope our performance will be nearly as good tomorrow night." And the whole kitchen staff came out, smiling with delight, to have their pictures taken with us.

I had heard that we would only be able to visit certain parts of the cities we were touring and that our interpreter and other officials would restrict our activities. The next morning, Renato and Darlene joined me in a walk through the "City of Flowers." The name was certainly appropriate. The blossoms were everywhere, and many of the streets — cobbled instead of paved — looked like a fairy tale come alive. We turned down one narrow lane in which the foliage was so lush that the tree branches met in the center of the road. Through the open door of one little house, I heard familiar voices. It was Jeannine and Joanne! I hadn't even been aware that they had left the hotel. Yet there they were in the house, being plied with breakfast by a lovely woman who was smiling and giggling at the girls as if they were her own.

"Look, Mommy; it's eggs in fish oil," said Joanne, ever the connoisseur. "Want some?" I took a nibble and gave a big grin as if the stuff were the greatest delicacy I had ever tasted; but when the woman handed me a bowl of noodles, my smile was genuine. They were delicious. We said goodbye with the universal sign language of a wave, and, on our way back, I thought, How truly unlike North America this is; a place where children can wander out into the street and be safe with anyone they meet.

Back at the hotel, Lu was ready to take us on our official tour of the city: gardens, gardens, and more gardens! But I never got tired of looking at them: There were flowers of every description, ornamental bushes and trees, and little rivers and ponds running under exquisite tiny bridges. One garden even had swans in its pond. Everywhere we went, we were followed by the delicate tinkle of bicycle bells and an endless series of polite but curious glances. "Why are they looking at us all the time?" asked Benny.

"They're trying to understand why you all look the same," said Lu.

"But, Lu," I said, "look at Renato with his big thick glasses, and Benny's short and fat, and Debbie's tiny, and Darlene's tall and blonde. How can you say we all look alike?"

"Well, you do!" he laughed.

A little farther along our route, we came to a footbridge Lu wanted us to see. "This is called Watergate Bridge," he said straight-faced.

"Watergate! There's a Watergate in Washington, but it isn't a bridge," I said, laughing. "It's a hotel. A very famous hotel."

"I know," said Lu still looking innocent. "But why do they make such a commotion over a hotel?" And he finally allowed himself a wry smile.

That evening a large group of factory workers came to the hall where we were performing and helped us set up the stage. I've never seen sets and flies go up so quickly and so accurately. Somehow, the bottom of Liberace's piano was lost in the prop shipment. Our Chinese assistants built a new one right on the spot while we watched in awe.

Backstage, before the show began, I talked to the performers while the TV crew filmed me. I read out congratulatory telegrams from Trudeau, Pauline McGibbon, Anne Murray, and many other well-wishers. Then I spoke to the company about the wonder of being in China. "Look how far you've come," I said, and Renato looked up proudly. "From your four walls to the Great Wall of China."

I was about to say more, but Lu suddenly started plucking at my sleeve. "Lu, we're filming something now," I whispering to him.

"In China," he said, "curtain goes up at seven thirty sharp!"

We obediently filed into the main room, and I promptly did a double take. There, in front of the curtain, was a table swathed in lace and laid for tea! Renato nudged me in the ribs and whispered, "Is this a show or a tea party?" I nudged him back sharply, trying to hold back the laughter. We filed up to the table and drank tea while the audience watched. I couldn't believe it!

Then came long speeches, and, at the end, Lu motioned me to the microphone. As I stared out at the crowd smiling at me with such goodwill, I felt a burst of emotion so strong that I had to take a deep breath before I spoke. "When I look at all of you," and Lu translated my words, "I think of my storybook back home which tells about a child who digs through the beach to China and sees the faces of all the Chinese people looking up at him and welcoming him. Today, I see those people looking at me." They all smiled and applauded and waved to me, holding their babies up to show me.

The performance went like a dream: The audience giggled, clapped, even came forward with their children to get a better look at the magic. It was amazing to see their strong reaction to the Anne Murray puppet, with its blonde hair, blue eyes, and husky voice, so unlike the delicate sopranos of the Chinese singers I had heard. It was enlightening to discover just how much people's reactions to theatre vary: This audience laughed resoundingly at the perils of the poor little apprentice sorcerer and sat in respectful silence through *Carnival of the Animals* — even breathing a collective sigh of sympathy at the death throes of the absurd and decidedly comic swan! And it was hilarious to watch Dr. Liu sitting at a little desk lit by an old-fashioned lamp which he would extinguish with the click of a chain after reading each Ogden Nash verse in Chinese. At intermission, a group of children from a school for the deaf performed songs and dances — they were fabulous — and at the end of the show, the applause was overwhelming.

The next day, we were taken on a tour of a factory, where the noise of the machinery was so loud I almost bolted from the room. "How can all these people be smiling with that noise?" I asked, and Lu told me they were all deaf. He said that in China, there was no such thing as a handicapped person: "Everyone's ability is put to good use." I thought that was a remarkably intelligent approach, and wished it were more prevalent in North America.

Later in the day, we visited the school for the deaf whose students had performed during our show. Jeannine and Joanne joined a class in a series of eye exercises designed to prevent nearsightedness. Then the performers and I worked with the children for about an hour, teaching them some of the movements from the "Aquarium" number in *Carnival of the Animals.* And finally, it was their turn to teach us. We all went out to the playground and joined them in a sequence of movements. The graceful gestures were so compelling that even Darlene joined in without any self-consciousness. It was an extraordinary experience: People from opposite ends of the globe; people whom society labels as handicapped, disabled, retarded; people partaking of a gift that many of us don't receive in a lifetime — a gift of love — shared in a silence more eloquent than poetry.

All the cities we visited gave us the same warm welcome: fabulous banquets, fascinating tours of factories and workshops for the handicapped; appreciative and lively audiences for our performances. Everywhere, the principles Lu had explained to me were put into practice. In Nanking, we toured a silkworm factory where blind workers whose hearing had developed more keenly as a result of their blindness held the worms to their ears to determine if the animal would produce good silk. After touring the assembly line, we were brought into another room, where about thirty of these workers performed beautiful symphonic music for us. And it was the same wherever we went: whatever their disability, we saw people who were in jobs that used their talents and gave them self-sufficiency. Just what we were working to achieve in Famous People Players.

We finally reached Beijing and the Forbidden City and were awed by the splendor of ages past, the massiveness of a place more impressive than any imaginary image of Chinese history. And, on our final day, the Great Wall of China. At last.

The wall is a gradual, continuous sweep of sheer rock. From our lofty perch, we could see trains, like toys in the distance, with tiny puffs of smoke wafting from their engines. The film crew was shooting as we carefully picked our way along the wall, holding the handrails. The other visitors, curious, came crowding around us, smiling and pointing. Suddenly, Benny broke into "O Sole Mio" — why, I don't know — and the crowd swelled, pushing closer and closer to get a glimpse of this unusual warbler. And on the ground below, the soldiers on guard at the Great Wall craned their necks to hear this Famous People Players serenade.

And then it was over and we were home — too abruptly. On the flight from Hong Kong, I kept thinking how much I wanted to return someday, to add whatever skills I had to the great work the Chinese were doing with the handicapped, to share with them the excitement of theatre, to learn from them. But we had another tour coming up fast, and my dreams of a new life in China quickly faded before the reality of our next performance.

"Special People"

NOVEMBER 1982 - DECEMBER 1984

When we returned from our tour of China, yet another staff member resigned. Great timing: We had another performance coming up in ten days and I was worried that there weren't enough performers to do the show smoothly. I stayed up all night trying to figure out what to do. At about five in the morning, with little sleep and no solution in sight, I drove to work, parked the car, and slowly walked to the front door. There stood Greg, snow billowing around him, his toque pulled down over his eyes. He looked like a little Christmas elf.

"Greg, what are you doing at work at this hour?"

"I was worried about you," he said. "I just wanted to come and help." But how had he known I was coming to the office? What kind of miracle was it that he was there just when I most needed someone?

I asked him, but he just shrugged, his eyes eloquent with understanding. He didn't need a lot of fancy words to show how much he cared. Seeing him in front of the building made all the difference.

Our show was a benefit organized by Father Tom McKillop for Pelletier Home (a residence which responds to the needs of adolescent girls with personal, social and family difficulties) and before the performance we all went to visit the house. As we sat in the tiny living room with the residents, Father Tom suddenly asked us a provocative question: "If you could change anything about yourselves, what would it be?"

"I'd get a new brain," Benny promptly answered.

"I'd find somebody who loved me," said Debbie Lim, "and the whole world would share in my love."

Tears started to flow down my cheeks; I was overcome by the courage it must have taken for my performers to speak out so candidly in a room full of strangers. It sounded like something out of *The Wizard of Oz* and, like the wizard, Father Tom told them they already had what they wished for, just by giving voice to their desires.

We did three fund-raising events for Pelletier Home over the next three years, giving the organization sufficient funds each time. The fact that the staff told us that our help made the difference between the house staying open or closing its doors was all the thanks we wanted.

January 1983 brought a lot of change, both to the company and my family. Bernard and I found our first home — where we still live — a lovely house halfway along a crescent road in west-end Toronto near one of the city's most beautiful and peaceful parks. The girls fell in love with the place, with its big basement recreation room and big, treed back yard. It was wonderful having all the space, after years in an apartment, and the house was a welcome retreat from all my pressures. Mom moved to an apartment nearby, and we spent Sundays together when we weren't touring.

We soon had our first guest at the Dupuy home: Andy Thomas, who was starting to develop a drinking problem. I thought something could be done if I had my eye on him constantly, and I knew he just wasn't getting this kind of attention at home. I no longer blamed the performers' parents for the troubles their sons and daughters were experiencing, since I had gained more appreciation of what they had to cope with year in and year out.

While he was living with us, Andy was forbidden to drink. And when he had dried out, there were other improvements: taking a bath every day; helping with the housecleaning; and, most of all, cooking. We soon discovered that Andy had a gift for livening up even the simplest dishes. I complimented him often, and so did the girls. "Who did the mashed potatoes?" Jeannine asked one night. "And what's in them?"

"I did them," Andy said. "I put in some cheese and milk and pepper."

"They're great, Andy," she said, passing her plate for more.

"Yeah, those are the best potatoes I've ever had," I said. "Why can't you learn to make potatoes like that, Bernard?" (And everyone laughed because Bernard is a great cook!)

Debbie Lim had developed into an excellent pianist after just a few lessons — she had a natural ear for music — and I wanted the others to have their own opportunity to develop a skill. Andy's affinity for cookery gave me the idea that he and some of the other performers would benefit from cooking lessons. But I had trouble getting them enrolled in a course. The argument was that they would slow down the rest of the class and wouldn't be able to follow the intricacies of the lessons.

We'll see about that, I said to myself, and proceeded to look for the very best cooking school in Toronto. The one recommended to me was the Beverley Burge School of Cooking. I enrolled the performers without mentioning anything about their background, but I sent Ida along to the twice-weekly classes to cover up for them. She would read the menus out loud to them and help them to measure. All of them, especially Andy, did very well in the course.

At their graduating dinner — a scrumptious Chicken Kiev — one of the chefs called me over, looking perplexed. "They've done very well," he said, "but we've never seen people quite like them." I explained that his star pupils were retarded. He seemed amazed — almost a bit miffed — and said if he'd known their background, he would have modified the course. Lucky thing, I thought. This way, they got the real course, not some watered-down version.

For more than a year, Marc Daniels had been talking to me about wanting to direct a movie about the Famous People Players. The company had met two other people interested in the project: a producer, Joseph Cates, and a screenwriter, Corey Blechman, who had come on tour with us. But we hadn't heard anything about the project in months. One day, Ida casually asked me if I thought the movie about Famous People Players would ever be made.

"I know exactly what's going to happen," I said. "One day we'll get a phone call saying the film crew will be here in a couple of weeks, and we'll have to drop all our engagements. That's the way things work in show business!" But I really wasn't expecting anything soon. The last I'd heard, Corey Blechman was reworking the script, while Marc Daniels and Joseph Cates were having trouble finding someone to play me.

Nevertheless, just a few days later I got a phone call from Marc, who said that he, Joseph, and the cast and crew would be arriving in Toronto in May to film our movie, which was eventually called *Special People*. Brooke Adams had been cast as yours truly: I had never heard of her, but several of the performers had seen her in the movie *Invasion of the Body Snatchers*, with Donald Sutherland, and said she was an excellent actress.

Before the filming started, I flew to Los Angeles to discuss details of the contract with CBS network staff. *Special People* was to be a two-hour movie special, but commercials would cut the running time considerably, so the script had to cover a lot of territory — from the formation of the company to our first appearance in Las Vegas — without going into the kind of detail that I would have liked. But I understood that television has its constraints, so I agreed.

In May, the movie crew descended on 301 Lansdowne. I noticed, the day they arrived, that Renato and Benny kept looking at Brooke Adams. "Do you want to meet her?" I asked.

"Yes," said Benny. "We want to see her roll her eyes like in the movie."

"Oh, that's just a special effect," I said as I brought them over to say hello to Brooke, who smiled delightedly when Renato asked her about the trick; she responded by spinning her eyes in their sockets. We were all stunned.

"How on earth did you do that?" I asked.

"Oh, that's a little trick I've been able to do since I was a kid," she said. "That's why I don't wear glasses, because I've always exercised my eyes." My mind went back to China and the exercises the children did with their eyes in the school for the deaf we had visited.

Brooke was a delightful person and developed an excellent rapport with the performers. Before the filming began — at another downtown location — Brooke spent almost a week following me around, watching me rehearse the company, and getting to know my style. And the other actors were equally likable: Ron James, who played Doug (a fictitious character who combined elements of several performers), Lesleh Donaldson, who played Robin Bates (vaguely based on Alice, the girl who became a hooker after leaving Famous People Players), and Susan Roman, a Canadian actress, who played Ann Laitin. Benny, Renato, Sandra, Greg, Andy, and Nancy, whom we invited back just to be in the movie, played themselves.

There were a few elements of the script that didn't exactly adhere to the facts. The Diane Dupuy character, at one point, threatened to lie down in front of Liberace's limo if he refused to see the company's show. I was capable of such a stunt, but I didn't do it! But there was an even greater departure from the real story. My character gave up on the company after the disastrous first show for parents' night — only to try again when the performers arrived at her door with a newspaper clipping announcing Liberace's imminent Toronto show. But when I mentioned any of this poetic licence, Marc told me that there just wasn't the time for a long explanation of our circumstances. The film had to move smoothly and quickly and capture the audience right from the start.

Another aspect of the filming that began to bother me was the feeling of being on display as Brooke and the others watched me direct the performers during rehearsals. Toward the end of her week of observation, I suggested that she just take over and direct them herself. "After all, you're trying to be me, so you should get involved," I told her. One day, I didn't come in to work at all, and when I arrived the next morning, Brooke had taken over very effectively. It was an odd feeling to watch her directing "Aruba Liberace" and "Impossible Dream" — like watching myself in another dimension. I felt like an outsider in my own rehearsal hall. And she screamed so *LOUD*! "I don't scream like that, do I?" I asked Greg later.

"Louder," he said, grinning. (Thanks a lot, Greggie!)

The performers loved playing themselves. Renato's performance was uncanny. As he moved through the prop room of the church basement set to re-create his first tentative, furtive foray into our topsy-turvy world of black light (and mayhem), it was as if I was seeing him again for the first time — this lonely outsider who quickly found a place in all our hearts. And the others were equally effective. Unlike trained actors, they didn't have to learn to conjure emotions. Theirs were always brimming near the surface, ready to be seen and touched.

For me, it was fascinating, and sometimes excruciating, to sit and watch. I kept questioning my own actions. Why doesn't she just quit when Nancy keeps throwing fits? Why doesn't she insist that Sandra keep clean or that Greg bring his piano bench on stage right side up? Why is she being so rough on these poor people? It was the first time I had ever seen myself objectively.

Also for the first time, I understood more about the bonds between myself and the performers. Sandra, for example, was so much like my grandmother — looked like her, moved like her, even had the same rough-edged voice. I saw how much Nancy and I were alike: the temper, the great need for attention and love. And I saw the performers — all of them — as guides who were in my life for a reason: to teach me, as much as I was teaching them. In their silent way, they showed me that there's more to life than you can discover with your brain.

For the last scene, we went back to Las Vegas, where the final shoot was done at the Hilton. It was an incredible sensation for us to relive those early moments of success, but, just as there had been difficulties with our first shows in Vegas, there was a problem with the scene. Marc had wanted the musical notes to emerge from the piano in "Impossible Dream," but the performers only knew how to make them appear around the piano. "You haven't been paying attention," Marc said, annoyed. "All through the movie, our character, Diane, has been trying to get the performers to make the notes come out of the piano, and now they're finally supposed to do it perfectly, except that you haven't taught them how to do it. I'm very disappointed in you, Diane."

He was right. My mind had been on the Diane Dupuy character — what she was saying, what she was wearing, her motivation — and nothing else that was happening in the movie. "I'm very sorry, Marc," I said, and immediately called the performers together to show them how to do the sequence the way Marc wanted.

When the filming was over, I told the performers we would stay in Las Vegas for the weekend, as a treat. "You've worked hard, so let's celebrate."

Back in Toronto, there was more partying — with the production crew. After the gift-giving — Marc got a bronzed hankie because he had become very emotional while shooting certain scenes, and the performers each got a monogrammed quilted vest from Brooke Adams — I sat down to chat with Joe Cates, Bernard, and our lawyer, Joseph Fodor. "Well, there doesn't seem to be much left for you to do with Famous People Players," Joe said. "You've been to Vegas, Radio City Music Hall, China. You've done a movie. So why don't you do other things? Direct films. Write. Produce." And Joseph enthusiastically agreed.

What is this? I asked myself. Is there something wrong with what I'm doing? Do you people really think there's nothing left for Famous People Players to achieve? And I decided, right then and there, what we were going to do. We would tour the United States and then we would perform on Broadway. But I didn't say anything to anyone — yet. There were some ideas germinating in my mind — ideas for numbers, for places to perform them — and I wanted these thoughts to grow quietly for a while, until they were fully formed.

Meanwhile, all of us waited eagerly for the premiere of our movie, *Special People*, which came while we were on tour. We arrived in Sault Ste. Marie well before the air time of 8 P.M. and everyone gathered around the TV in our hotel — but there was a baseball game on. "We've got to find a place that has a satellite dish and pick it up on an American channel," I said. "We're not going to miss this movie."

The only place we could find was a private Italian club — but my greeting to the owner in Italian didn't do the trick: A wedding reception was under way. Extreme measures were called for: I phoned back holding a cloth over the receiver. "Hello, this is Mrs. Richards calling for Knowlton Nash of 'The National,' " I said. "Could I speak to the owner, please?"

"Yes, may I help you?" the owner said, coming on the line promptly.

"This is Mrs. Richards of 'The National' calling. There's a theatre company called Famous People Players in Sault Ste. Marie tonight, and a movie about them is being shown on CBS right now, but they need to see it in a place with a satellite dish. And we'd like to do an interview with them afterward, to get their reactions, so naturally the name of your establishment would be mentioned on the air . . . ."

"That sounds very good," he said. "No problem." So we watched the show, laughing and pointing as Renato, Sandra, and the others appeared, and crying at the disappointments. Eventually, the guests at the reception wandered over, started to recognize us and began buying us drinks. By the end of the evening, everyone seemed to have forgotten about the interview on "The National," and before we left, the owner even gave us a videocassette he had made of the movie.

As we traveled west, the reviews for *Special People* began to reach us, and people began to recognize us wherever we went. This was a wonderful feeling, but what made us even happier was what one of the reviews said. *People* magazine felt that the performers who played themselves were "often more appealing than the professional actors hired to play the other mentally handicapped people." It's not that I wanted to take anything away from the other actors, but it meant a lot to the performers to hear praise for their acting.

In July we were invited to perform for the Special Olympics in Baton Rouge, Louisiana. I had some misgivings about accepting the engagement. It would be getting close to our next gala, and the performers had qualms about segregating disabled athletes from the community. But the organizers were very persuasive; they even offered to pay for the shipment of the props as well as airfare, accommodation, and meals. So we decided to go.

I wasn't able to go to Baton Rouge ahead of time, so I sent Ida and Renato as an advance team to make sure we had everything we needed. The evening they arrived, I got a phone call from Ida. "You'd better get down here in a hurry," she said, "because I don't think this is what you had in mind."

"What happened?"

"Well, to begin with, the accommodations. We'll forget about the cockroaches, okay? And we'll forget that there's no bedding; I'm sure we can get sheets somewhere. But when I have to share a bathroom with forty other people, that's where I draw the line."

"Look, Ida, just book a hotel and send the bill to the Special Olympics committee," I said. "We'll be there as soon as we can." We took off the next day, and when we landed we found Eddie Drake, the Special Olympics representative, waiting for us. The first thing he said to me was that the accommodations, at a university, were just fine.

"Eddie, let me explain something to you," I said. "We're a professional theatre company, and these performers are very vocal. If they walk into a place where they have to share a bathroom with dozens of other people, they're very unhappy. And if they're unhappy, they don't do a good show. And you want a good show, don't you?"

"Well, all I can say is that if you move them into a hotel, that's your responsibility," he retorted. "We're not paying for it."

"I have news for you, Eddie," I said. "They are going into a hotel and you are paying for it." We did check into a hotel — tripling up to reduce costs.

Needless to say, I had trouble getting to sleep and had bad dreams all night. Early in the morning, I awoke to see Ida tiptoeing into my room. "What's the matter?" I asked.

"Just stay calm," she replied. I was scared out of my mind; I thought my mother had died. After an agonizing pause, Ida told me the puppet heads had been stolen: Liberace, Barbra Streisand, Liza Minnelli, Anne Murray, Kenny Rogers, Frank Sinatra, and the newest additions, Rod Stewart and Dolly Parton. "I went back to the theatre last night because I was worried about the props," she said. "I thought I'd bring the heads back to the room, along with some other props and suitcases, so I drove back to the hotel and left the heads in the trunk while I moved the other stuff into the lobby, and when I got back, the heads were gone." She burst into tears. "I couldn't have been more than ten minutes!"

She was almost hysterical with worry and exhausted after talking to the police for the rest of the night. But did I comfort her? No. I just sat there, feeling as if we'd lost eight members of the family. "Don't just stare like that, Diane!" she said. "Hug me or something!" I finally did hug her, and then I started yelling, and then I cried while she yelled. When we finally calmed down, we went and told the others.

There was nothing more to do but go to rehearsals, where we found Eddie still talking about not paying for our accommodations. "This theft would never have happened if we had had proper accommodations from the start," I said. "We would have kept our puppets in my hotel room."

"I don't see why you're so upset," he said. "They're just puppets." I looked at him in disgust and didn't even bother responding.

Ida was beside herself with guilt over the puppets; the performers were miserable — and angry with Ida because they thought it was her fault — and I was upset because everyone was at odds with each other. It seemed unlikely that we would ever see those puppets again.

I left Benny and Renato in charge of setting up the stage and went back to the hotel to wait for the police, who wanted to talk to us again. The theft was mentioned on television, and I posted a reward notice in the hotel lobby — neither of which did any good, as it turned out. While I was talking to them, Benny called to say the company had set up the stage but were told they had to move to another theatre. Then he called back and told me none of the performers had eaten. I raced over to the second theatre, and Eddie calmly informed me that when we left the university residence, we lost the meals that went with the accommodations. I was furious, but Eddie held his ground. So I ended the conversation, got the rental cars organized, and took everyone back to the hotel for supper.

I was angry now, and fired up. "I know we haven't got half our numbers, but we're professionals, so let's do a professional show!" I told the performers as we got up to leave for the theatre.

Since the loss of our Famous People puppets not only shortened the show but altered the transitions between numbers, I decided to give the performers more time by telling little anecdotes about the company after each number. At the end of "Goldfinger," I looked out in the audience to see Jean Kennedy Smith, who was the Kennedy family member on the Special Olympics committee. I aimed my remarks directly at her, hoping for a response that might generate some action.

"When Liberace first saw this company, he didn't know who we were, and he treated us as professional performers," I said. "At Radio City Music Hall, we were treated as professionals. Now we're here, doing this benefit for you: We've lost eight of our puppets — the heart of our family — but as professionals, we believe the show must go on. And we thank you for bearing with us through this tragedy."

After the show, Mrs. Smith made no move toward us, and she was near the exit when I tapped her on the shoulder and suggested she come backstage to meet the cast. "Oh yes," she said. "I suppose that would be a good idea." Backstage, we all told her about the theft of the puppet heads. "Are you looking into this situation?" she asked Eddie. He replied that the police were working on it. And that was it. No one offered any further help — or even a word of sympathy — except for some audience members who expressed their concern for our predicament. We deeply appreciated their kindness.

The next day, we had to accept that the puppet heads were gone forever, so I got on the phone to Bob Baker in Hollywood and asked him to start making replacements. It would be an expensive and difficult process, because each head was unique. When I got off the phone, I was crying again, and it didn't take long for everyone else to chime in. "That's it!" I finally said, wiping my eyes. "We're all going to New Orleans for a wake."

"What's a wake?" asked Sandra.

"You'll see," I replied.

In New Orleans, we spent most of the day reinventing the wake, courtesy of the birdbath-size margaritas served at Pat O'Brien's bar. New Orleans in July was noisy, dirty, and sweltering, but it somehow suited our mood, and we had a properly maudlin day weeping into our drinks and wandering through the narrow streets of the French Quarter. We all felt much better as we headed to the airport.

The puppet heads were eventually found — abandoned in a swamp just outside Baton Rouge. But they were damaged beyond repair. Luckily, we did get the new heads in time for our next show, but what we never did receive was a check for our hotel and meals.

Replacing the puppet heads had decimated our shaky budget, but fortunately the gala at the Royal Alex was sold out, and the audience response to "That's Entertainment" (a new number we'd been creating over the summer) gave a much needed boost to our morale.

The theme song, which composer Victor Davies had arranged for the show, gave the perfect upbeat rhythm to a dazzling sequence of rapid-fire images: garbage cans dancing; a flasher flashing; a mugger fleeing a burly Manhattan cop; Ginger Rogers in the arms of Fred Astaire; Peter Pan on the run from Captain Hook on the run from a crocodile; Little Orphan Annie with her dog Sandy; and Sweeney Todd, the demon barber of Fleet Street. Performers and audience alike responded to the electricity. Seeing we'd struck a spark, I decided immediately to extend the Broadway concept to other numbers as soon as we got back from a forthcoming tour of Western Canada. The seed had flowered!

Reviewers were equally responsive to the liveliness of our newer creations. "The Superman Theme," said *The Toronto Star*, "brought colliding space ships, asteroids, planets, satellites and space monsters in and out of view with excellent precision. The audience applauded through this scene that looked like it came straight out of George Lucas' Star Wars factory."

The day after the show, I sat in my office and leafed through the program, which I hadn't yet had a chance to read. I came across something I had nearly forgotten: a poem Cathy Camp wrote about life on the road. Here's the last verse:

> The night is cold and airless
> as the troupe rolls down the road.
> The players share a laugh or two
> to ease some of the load.
> And down below and silent
> 'neath the chatter, warmth and glow,
> The magic waits for morning
> and another town and show.

Just before we headed out West, we lost one staff member and gained another. Ida was bound for Africa to work on a mission, a challenge she had been seeking for some time. And the new kid on the block was Neil Thompson. Despite his youth, Neil had the maturity to work effectively with the performers and a quiet charm that quickly endeared him to all of us. He sang and played the guitar very well, entertaining us all, particularly Benny and Renato, with whom he roomed on the road. Neil started out as a roadie, traveling in the truck and keeping track of 3,001 props, 22 sets, more than 75 boxes, 42 black-light tubes and hundreds of costumes. A lot of responsibility — and Neil rose to it.

Before our show in Winnipeg, I got a call backstage from a doctor at an institution for the handicapped in Portage la Prairie, Manitoba. "There's a young man here I'd really like you to see," he said. "Could you come up and visit him?" I explained that we were on tour and couldn't take any side trips, but he wouldn't take no for an answer. "Please come, if only for a short time," he pleaded. "It would mean so much to him." We decided to leave early the next morning to gain some time, and when we arrived, the doctor was waiting out front for us, waving.

After a long walk down the gleaming, silent corridor of the institution, we met the man, Clarence Asham. In his late twenties, retarded and blind, he had been in the institution since he was a toddler. Incapable of learning Braille, and unable (or unwilling) to speak for the past few years, he lived in a world of his own — except for one remarkable lifeline: Music. The doctor led him to the upright piano near the window of the cozy lounge, and we listened in awe as he played classics, pop tunes, and ballads, all perfectly, and all by ear. "He can play anything the first time he hears it," the doctor said, "and he's done the same thing on the accordion, the guitar, and the xylophone."

I handed Clarence my cassette player, which contained a tape of Broadway songs; he listened to the entire tape, then took off the headset and played every tune, note for note. "I really want to do something for Clarence," I told the doctor. "Somehow, we're going to get him to Toronto as our guest."

In the spring of 1984, I invited Clarence to Toronto. Courtesy of Tommy Ambrose and Doug Riley — who has done many of our musical arrangements — he played at their restaurant, Jingles. After this very successful professional debut, he also performed at a show we were doing for Imperial Oil at the Sheraton Centre. The Sheraton gave free accommodation to Clarence and his companion from the institution during their week-long stay; the businessmen attending our performance put up $2,500 for him to study at the Winnipeg School of Music; and he was interviewed on several television programs.

But what meant even more to me was that, by the end of the week, Clarence was not only talking but eating with a knife and fork. I just kept asking him questions, and didn't let him eat with his hands. I knew that cutlery wasn't allowed at the institution — as a protection for the residents — and that the staff couldn't put in the kind of consistent time needed to compel Clarence to speak, but I wanted him to prove to himself that he could do these things. Today, Clarence is still in the institution, but I'm convinced that he could live in the community and make great progress — even have a musical career — if a loving and dedicated family made a commitment to him.

That western tour, unfortunately, also had its down side. In Victoria, a vicious hate letter was delivered to me at the theatre. It said that because the company photograph in the lobby showed us on the Great Wall of China, we weren't Christians. The inclusion of *Sorcerer's Apprentice* in our program proved that I was a witch and the puppets were demons. The letter writer went on to say that, as a Christian, he was obliged to destroy witches. The police were sympathetic and agreed that we were dealing with a real sicko, but they said there was nothing they could do unless he took more direct action.

We were so frightened that we didn't wear our company uniforms or sign autographs that night. After the show, I was still so upset that I couldn't sleep. I felt like going somewhere, so I woke up Dave Balinsky and asked him to come and eat sushi with me. "Are you out of your mind, lady?" he demanded. "Where are we going to get sushi at this time of night?" We drove around in the bus for quite a while, but we finally found a Japanese restaurant. The sushi was great, and Dave's irascible good humor was even better. By the time we got back to the hotel, I was laughing about the letter. (I've had a number of those letters since then, and there are even people who come up to me at receptions and lecture me about my heathen ways. When I tell them I'm a Catholic and go to Mass every day, it really throws them for a loop!)

The worst calamity of the tour — although we all laugh about it today — was the trip home. I conned Dave into driving straight through from Calgary to Toronto so we could get home in good time for Christmas. But somewhere between Calgary and Brandon, the heating system on the bus broke down. December in Manitoba is no joke, and in no time we were all shivering. It *was* an old bus with cracks at the bases of most of the windows, but it had always done us proud — until then.

As we continued our chilly journey, I think Benny and I came close to driving Dave over the brink. I was the worst culprit. Every five minutes, I'd ask how much farther we had to go and complain about the cold. "I am aware that the heat isn't working," he'd say, "and we're five minutes closer than we were the last time you asked me. Now would you kindly shut up and let me drive?"

By the time we got to Winnipeg, the heat was completely gone. As we all numbly got off the bus, I scolded: "Dave, don't you dare come back until you get this bus fixed!" He looked at me as if to say it wouldn't take much for him to stay away permanently, and drove off.

While he was trying to get the heating system fixed (or so we hoped!) the rest of us went looking for some extra layers of clothing and sleeping bags — just in case — and then walked downtown. As we passed a beauty parlor, I suddenly became conscious that I hadn't had a shower in 48 hours. We had been so eager to start for home that we hadn't even washed our faces after the show in Calgary. Darlene, Sandra, and I had our hair done, then went across the street to a hotel to see about a shower. The desk clerk said we'd have to rent a room, but I put up such a vocal protest that he let us take showers just to shut me up!

Just as we were leaving the hotel, Dave pulled up. "Is the heat fixed?" I asked.

"Just get on the bus," he said as the performers filed past me.

"But is the heat fixed?" I asked.

"*Just get on the bus!*"

A few miles down the road, I ventured a comment that the heating system didn't appear to be functioning. Dave favored me with an "*oy veh*!" and a long-suffering glance.

But we did get home in plenty of time for Christmas!

In early 1984 I started adding to our repertoire of Broadway-style pieces. I was more certain than ever that the Famous People Players would get to Broadway, but I rarely expressed this belief to anyone. I just gradually started to build a Broadway medley. Including "That's Entertainment," there were about twenty numbers in the medley, some of which only saw one or two performances because they didn't pass the ultimate test — turning on an audience.

Among the most popular were "Oklahoma," with a big horse leaning on a rail and singing; "The Night They Invented Champagne," with two enormous champagne bottles and two oversized glasses in an inebriated quartet; "Get Me to the Church On Time," featuring a cavorting, strutting Alfred Dolittle; "Can-Can," with a chorus of five plump cancan dancers; and "The Wiz," with Dorothy, Toto, the Scarecrow, and the Tin Man. What distinguished these and our other Broadway numbers from our former productions was the extensive use of costumes as well as puppets. The performers were expected not only to manipulate puppets but also to dance and use theatrical gestures, which meant a lot of extra work.

We also added two new Famous People: Cyndi Lauper, singing "Girls Just Want to Have Fun," and Michael Jackson doing "Billie Jean." Kids in our audiences really loved these two puppets. They stomped their feet and cheered loudly to accompany Cyndi's wild movements and Michael Jackson's loose-limbed moonwalk. But I think the greatest hit of all was Stevie Wonder's "Part-Time Lover," as wildly spinning, glowing orange records appeared carrying a reclining Stevie illuminated by a twirling sun.

I also felt it was time we had our own theme song. Since we had been saying on our posters that Famous People Players was "a little like magic," I asked Victor Davies if he could compose a song for us that used that phrase. "A Little Like Magic" was such a terrific song that it has become our opening, an accompaniment to the top hat-cane-and-gloves character that introduces the show. Many people say they find themselves humming the catchy tune weeks after seeing our show.

So much of our repertoire was inspired by American culture that it seemed natural to organize our first tour of the United States, which might also be a perfect stepping-stone to Broadway. But this proved difficult: despite our appearances in Las Vegas, we weren't very well known in the States. We finally found a promoter, Arthur Katz, whose company, Katamount Productions, was the major investor in the Broadway show *Big River*. Our tour would start late in 1984 and take us to the Beacon theatre in New York, the Shubert theatre in New Haven, Connecticut, and cities in North Carolina, Florida, and Ohio.

As soon as plans for the tour were complete, we decided to form an American board of directors, which included Joseph Cates, the producer and Mark Daniels, director, of *Special People*; Seymour Heller (whom we had nicknamed "Our father who art in Las Vegas"); Robert Jani of Radio City Music Hall; Jimmy Macdonald (the voice of Mickey Mouse) and Tom Sullivan, who had hosted our special for the TV newsmagazine "Good Morning America." These were show-business people who knew the company and would be there to help us if anything went wrong on our tours.

As excited as the company was about touring the United States, we had something more immediate to celebrate: the tenth anniversary of Famous People Players, to be marked by a benefit at the Royal York Hotel. Nancy Lawrence (yes, the same Nancy with whom I had so many arguments when she was a performer in the company) helped organize the event and she did herself and all of us proud. Nancy wrote letters to hundreds of corporations and individuals, talking about how much the company had helped her, and asking them to buy a table for the $100-a-plate dinner — which sold out a month in advance.

All our friends were there to help us celebrate, but it was the pride and self-sufficiency of Nancy Lawrence — who left the company for a job as a clerk in an office — and the other performers, past and present, that made it a memorable occasion. We all basked in the praise of goodwill messages from all the heads of municipal, provincial, and federal governments. The message we received from Prime Minister Trudeau was particularly special to us:

"In a decade of portraying famous people through the magic of black light theatre and puppetry you have added a new star to our entertainment galaxy. Your achievement is a beacon of hope and inspiration to all.

"Long may your light shine!"

We had to sustain this initiative, because we were still well short of our fund-raising goal, so we had a company meeting to toss around ideas. Renato suggested a major drive to sell Famous People Players T-shirts, and Greg thought we might be able to sell them at Swiss Chalet restaurants, for which his dad was an executive. We set up booths at every Swiss Chalet in Toronto and made an astounding $25,000.

Everyone — all the performers, their parents, and the board of directors — got into the act, and for a few weeks there was no one but me to run the office. One morning I came in to work and found several hundred dollars missing from the filing cabinet we used as a safe. The police came and made out a report, but they said it would be almost impossible to find the culprit because there had been no sign of a break-in. Whoever had stolen the money had used a key to get into the building. When the performers came in after the day's fund-raising, I lined them all up and asked them about the missing money.

From the expression on his face, I guessed it was Andy, and he finally broke down and confessed. We were all heartbroken. Just when everyone was pulling together and proving to themselves what they were capable of, one of our veterans betrayed himself and all of us. It seemed so stupid!

I called Mrs. Thomas and told her we would have to let Andy go.

Through Reg Bovaird, one of our board members, Andy was able to get a job at the Elephant and Castle Restaurant in the Eaton Centre. I remember standing out in front of the restaurant with him on his first day, talking to him. "There's not going to be any more Diane Dupuy to bail you out, Andy," I said, and he listened intently. "You have to make it on your own." Today, I'm proud to say that Andy is an assistant chef at the restaurant.

For me, a highlight of our western tour came in Calgary, where I was honored to attend a dinner for recipients of the Ernest C. Manning Award, instituted by the former Alberta premier in 1980 to recognize Canadian inventors. In 1984 a second category of awards was added for Canadians who have developed a unique idea without a laboratory or research facility. I was one of the first winners of a $25,000 Award of Merit. The award money enabled me to select three people who I knew wouldn't make it into the company, invite them to live with me, and teach them everything from balancing a budget to doing the laundry. Even if they weren't going to be in Famous People Players, they could still develop self-sufficiency in their lives.

Just before Thanksgiving, we bumped and shook over gravel roads en route to Yellowknife in the Northwest Territories. On Thanksgiving Day, we went to a huge dinner at the Royal Canadian Legion Hall. There were 400 guests, and the array of turkey and fixings was a formidable (and delicious) sight. Everyone treated us as if we'd lived in Yellowknife all our lives, and we felt at home, too.

Just before we left on our fall tour of Western Canada, I got a phone call from a woman who said she wanted to talk to me about a "possible" donation; I suggested she come to our office. When she arrived, she heard a few of my choice remarks at rehearsal — the performers were having some trouble with "Oklahoma" — and picked up a copy of our financial statement. Then she left, and it wasn't until months later that I found out whom she represented.

Back in Toronto for a few weeks before heading out on our U.S. tour, I decided to try to get a copy of *Special People* to Paul Newman. I was determined that we would somehow connect. I phoned his agency and spoke to his assistant. "He wouldn't be interested," she said and hung up on me.

But shortly afterward, we got a check from Newman's Own company — for $10,000 in American funds. It was only then that I made the connection with the mysterious visitor who had come to see us about a "possible" donation!

A few days before we headed south, I got a call from A.E. Hotchner, Newman's business partner and the author of Ernest Hemingway's biography, *Papa Hemingway.* I told him how much we appreciated the donation, "But what's even more important is that you and Mr. Newman see what you've funded — at the Beacon Theatre in New York City on December 17th."

"Well, Paul is very supportive of what you do, but I'm not certain he can come," Hotchner said. I left it at that for the moment, but I asked everyone I knew to put on the pressure, then added my own phone calls. Finally, we were out of time. We had to head out on the road.

The American audiences were great; I only wish there had been more of them. When we were in Florida, literally hundreds of people approached Greg, Sandra, and Renato to ask for autographs and talk about *Special People.* But they weren't lining up in the same kind of numbers for the shows. On the other hand, the reviews were great. There were ten reviews during the week we were in New Haven — all of them glowing. One writer, in the *Trumbull Times*, said: "The dazzling puppetry that has the sorcerer's apprentice clashing swords on horseback with an army of magical brooms, is worth a few thousand oohs-and-aahs."

The Beacon was a wonderful old theatre. I felt as though we

were on Broadway — if only for a night. "We'll be back," I vowed to Greg. "I promise."

"I know," he said, smiling calmly.

A few minutes before curtain, I peeked out front for the hundredth time to see if Paul Newman had arrived. No. He wasn't coming. My heart sank as I scanned the crowd . . . . And there he was at the bar, holding a Budweiser! I dashed backstage, shrieking out the good news, and suddenly he appeared, walking across the stage, his teeth and hair glowing in the fluorescent light. "I can't stay for the show," he said apologetically, "but I was driving by and I wanted to congratulate all of you on your tremendous success. I'm very proud of all of you."

He shook hands with all the performers, and I escorted him back out front. As I pushed open the door, I hissed at the stage manager: "Hit the tape!" The music started, the curtain went up, and, as he neared the exit, I said: "Paul, just turn around and look for a second."

The music of "A Little Like Magic" played; the huge top hat, cane, and gloves, glowing in the velvety blackness, came dancing across the stage; Paul Newman stared, transfixed. Then, very slowly, he took a seat at the back of the theatre as the strains of "Aruba Liberace" wafted compellingly into the audience, and the Liberace puppet, in sequined finery, floated down to the keyboard of his magnificent glittering piano. Paul stayed for the whole show, and afterward he came backstage again, this time with Mr. Hotchner ("Hotch," he insisted) and his wife, Ursula. They were all tripping over the props in the dark, but when they got to us, they were all smiles.

"We've got to thank you," Paul said. "I've got the easy job: I just sign checks. You've got to do all the work. And it is wonderful."

Magic on Broadway

JANUARY 1985 - DECEMBER 1986

When we came home from our U.S. tour in the winter of 1985, it was clear that our next goal was a Broadway show. We all got together in the warehouse kitchen one afternoon and talked about what this challenge would mean.

"We'll be so good that I'll never have to work in a sheltered workshop or live in a group home," Debbie Lim said. "Broadway isn't like all our other shows, because you can't get any higher than Broadway. It means you're really a success, and nobody can say you're not."

"I think we'll be *great*," said Debbie Rossen. "We can show so many people what we can do."

"It's like being a star," said Greg. "We can be stars."

"And nobody could put us down anymore," added Renato.

For each person, Broadway represented something different, but, in a way, they were all saying the same thing: if we make it on Broadway, we'll be free forever from the label "*retarded* performers." Las Vegas, Radio City Music Hall, China, a feature film: these were all steps on our journey toward acceptance as top-level entertainers. But Broadway symbolized a degree of accomplishment we had yet to attain. And we wanted it.

The agents who hired us for the first U.S. tour loved the show we took across the States, but when I mentioned Broadway they were highly skeptical. Black light isn't for Broadway, they said; you need more variety, like film clips, white light, silhouettes. Other theatrical people agreed, and, closer to home, even Mom thought at first that it was too ambitious a dream. But the more skeptics emerged, the more determined we became. I sometimes thought we thrived on opposition. After all, we had been fighting for acceptance and respect for a long time.

We threw ourselves into preparing our Broadway program. We had a lot of numbers from which to choose and all kinds of ideas about how to do the show. As we tried them out in performance, we began to see which ones worked and which didn't. For example, we developed a routine called "Pops Goes to the Movies" which used the themes from movies such as *Gone with the Wind*, *The Magnificent Seven*, and others. The twenty-minute medley, which was intended for the second half of our Broadway production, was played out in front of a huge screen lit with colored gels (films of plastic that fit over a spotlight). Set against the screen, the performers, clad in black, looked like living silhouettes as they acted out the stories. We worked hard on the medley. Mom and her talented staff even rebuilt a Mennonite carriage for the escape from Atlanta in a scene from *Gone with the Wind.* But there were problems. The screens cracked easily and were very expensive and the choreography was too complex. Most significantly, the medley was inconsistent with the rest of the show: What we were trying to bring to Broadway was our essence: black-light theatre. As spectacular as it was, "Pops Goes to the Movies" had to be dropped in favor of the magic — and audience appeal — of black light.

Audience appeal was also the criterion when we decided which of our many numbers to include in our tribute to Broadway, but at one point I almost went against this popularity principle. Several people suggested we omit "Send In the Clowns," and I agreed — after all, we *had* done the number hundreds of times. But when I asked our arranger, Doug Riley, to cut the Sondheim music from the tape, he protested. "You're the one who's always talking about audience reaction," he said. "That's what you should go by — that and your own instincts." So the number stayed.

When we finished the painful selection process — there was always at least one champion for each number on the cutting block, and almost half of them had to be left out — there still remained an impressive array of Broadway melodies, and black-light magic to go with them. There was everything from "New York, New York" to "Give My Regards to Broadway," from "The Wiz" to our newest piece, "Don't Rain On My Parade," with a Barbra Streisand puppet sailing toward a sixteen-foot mobile mock-up of the Statue of Liberty. And to let audiences in on the secret of black light, we would go to white light for just a moment during "Give My Regards to Broadway," revealing the black-swathed performers racing across the stage, hoisting huge champagne glasses and oversized Dom Perignon bottles before the spell was restored and the bottles and glasses commanded the stage again.

We would also include our most popular Famous People: Liberace, Kenny Rogers, Michael Jackson, Elvis, and Stevie Wonder, as well as the Superman and James Bond sequences, *Sorcerer's Apprentice* and two numbers from *Carnival of the Animals.* Since we weren't doing "Pops Goes to the Movies," we needed a full-length number in the second half to provide a balance for *Sorcerer's Apprentice* in the first half of the show.

I had long considered staging Mussorgsky's *Night On Bald Mountain,* and this was an ideal opportunity. I listened to the music at home, on the way to work, and in the empty rehearsal hall, playing it again and again until the ideas started to come. I imagined myself as a huge Satan, a pair of ferocious black panthers, a tiny, terrified bird. I could see flames surrounding me, giant, hulking trees glowing in the firelight, Satan's impish demons scampering through the forest. Even the ending came to me quickly: An Indian, symbolizing spirituality, defeats Satan and throws down his spear in triumph; the bird flies to freedom; and the white, winged horse — Pegasus — soars into a sunlit sky. We got to work rehearsing the piece immediately, and, to give Mom an idea of the kind of creatures I had envisaged, I combed through some dusty volumes in an occult store until I found appropriately gruesome illustrations. Mom and the prop department went all out designing the Satan puppet: sixteen feet tall, bright red, and utterly terrifying.

Our Broadway project was in good shape artistically, but the business end took a huge amount of effort and planning by Judi Schwartz and the Board of Directors to get off the ground. More than a year before our targeted opening date, I went to New York to talk to Frank Verlizzo, a commercial artist with a major advertising agency. We were supposed to discuss a new logo and poster which Frank was designing for us, but I was more interested in his opinion of our playing Broadway.

"I think it's a great idea," Frank said. "Famous People Players will be like nothing else that's ever appeared on Broadway. And don't pay attention to anyone who says it's not right for Broadway. We do 90 percent of the Broadway shows, and if anyone knows what'll work, we do."

Frank told me what we could expect to pay for advertising and promotion — I tried not to blanch at the figure of more than $400,000 — and introduced me to Barbara Darwall, one of Broadway's most influential general managers. With Barbara, I went to see three of the theatres owned by the Shubert organization. All of them looked fine, but the one that captured my imagination was the Lyceum, a 900-seat theatre and Broadway's oldest.

The moment we walked in, I knew this was the theatre for us. In the lobby were portraits of some of the legendary performers who had graced this stage: Judy Holliday, Charles Laughton, Leslie Howard, Maurice Chevalier. And in the auditorium, with its rich woods, crystal chandeliers, deep purple seats, and generous stage, there was a remarkable feeling of theatrical presence — as if the very walls held the magic that had been this theatre's legacy for eighty years.

"This is the theatre I want," I told Barbara.

"Well, that's not exactly how it works," she said, smiling at my eagerness. "First, we put a proposal together, and then the

Shuberts decide which theatre would be best. Now, have you decided yet when you're going to come?"

"In October of 1986," I answered.

"Okay, and do you know how you're going to raise the funds? Will there be an investment package of some sort?"

"No. I'm just going to raise the money up front and then come and do the show."

Little did I know just how much money we would have to generate. Barbara and I spent several hours figuring out the bill: theatre rental; salaries for stagehands, carpenters, electricians; production costs; accommodation for the company for two months. Added to the advertising and promotion costs, the total was about a million dollars.

"With that kind of cost, it might be better if you went with one of the larger theatres we saw," Barbara suggested.

"No, I want the Lyceum," I insisted. "I know it's the theatre for us."

Soon afterward, the Famous People Players were invited to appear on the Phil Donahue show. The invitation came after Donahue's producer, Gail Steinberg, saw a half-hour documentary on our company. The documentary, *A Little Like Magic*, was made by Peter Rosen, one of our board members and was hosted by Ann-Margret and broadcast on CBS in the summer of 1985, coming to Gail's attention after it was nominated for an Emmy Award. At first, we were asked to be part of a segment on mental retardation, but after Gail and I discussed what the company was trying to accomplish — our integration into society — she decided we merited a one-hour special and offered us free transportation and accommodations.

We flew into New York late at night, and first thing in the morning, we gathered in the living room of our suite to talk about the show. "Do we make the announcement about Broadway to Phil Donahue?" I asked.

"*Yes!*"

We put our heads together like football players, joined hands, and made an oath: We were bound for Broadway, and we would give 200 percent to get there. The TV was on, and someone on "The Today Show" was talking about the great Canadian success story of the year: the Toronto Blue Jays. "This year the Blue Jays," I said. "Next year the Famous People Players!"

Right at the beginning of the Phil Donahue show, I announced that the Famous People Players would hit Broadway in 1986. I can't even remember what else we talked about — the interview seemed to roll by like a wave — but Phil was very pleased and very impressed with the clips that were shown from our movie and shows. Afterward, we all floated home, knowing we were committed to what would be the biggest challenge of our lives.

Back in Toronto, we got to work right away to plan a series of TV commercials to draw attention to our Broadway project. A group of young film makers, who had produced a terrific half-hour documentary on the company for CBC Television, came up with an engaging concept for a commercial done in black light: The sorcerer's book from *Sorcerer's Apprentice* opens to reveal the apprentice, who soars from the pages as a narrator talks about the show. Don Francks did the narration, and the commercial did well in Canada, but it didn't get much notice in the States. Part of the problem was that black light loses much of its impact when televised, especially since TV is capable of such dazzling special effects.

Sid Kessler, the owner of Sounds Interchange, suggested that instead of trying to replicate the effect of black light, we could create an illusion that would convey the same feeling. A spokesman for the show would dress entirely in black; only his head would be visible. "Do you want to see something wonderful?" he would ask. "Something so wonderful that you have to see it to understand it?" And then a two-second flash of black light would be shown.

I loved the idea, and I was ecstatic when Liberace, Paul Newman, and Jack Lemmon (on the recommendation of Seymour Heller and Joe Cates, the producer of *Special People*) agreed to appear in the commercials, which were shown across Canada and the United States.

Jack Lemmon, like Liberace and Paul Newman, extended his involvement with the company beyond doing the commercials. He sent a letter and a videocassette of excerpts from our shows to a number of prominent show-business people, many of whom wrote to tell us their reactions. We treasure the letters — like this one: "Viewing the tape was one of the most emotionally satisfying experiences I've had in a long, long time," wrote composer David Foster.

Or this one: "Your work is the highest order and is deserving of everyone's support and recognition," said Sean Connery.

And director Steven Spielberg's letter left us speechless with delight. "Bravo to you all!" he wrote. "Your talents are resplendent and your show is uniquely original."

Shortly after the commercials went on the air, I headed to New York to make final arrangements for the theatre rental — it *was* the Lyceum! — and meet with Maria DiDia, who was to become our company manager on Broadway. I also dropped in on Frank Verlizzo to discuss newspaper, radio, and television ads, and as I was leaving his office the enormity of our fund-raising challenge hit me. We had to start raising money — *fast.*

The entire history of Famous People Players had been a search for money. We had done fund-raising in a pinch before, but this wasn't a question of a few hundred dollars, or even a few thousand. We would have a budget of about one million, and Judi was determined to raise most of it before we got to Broadway so that ticket sales would be a bonus for us.

But we had only eight months to raise the money: How would we accomplish this objective? We couldn't just hold a fund-raising dinner or start a telephone campaign or do a mailing or sell a few T-shirts. We had to use all these techniques — and more — if we were ever going to make it.

The involvement of Patrick Keenan, a member of the board of Brascan Ltd., who chaired our gala in September 1985, enabled us to attract leading members of Canada's corporate community, in an event that included a performance as well as a dinner. The host for the evening was film director Norman Jewison, and I'll never forget the thrill of hearing him describe us as "Canada's ambassadors of goodwill to the world."

With that kind of impetus, emotional as well as financial, our fund-raising had a good head start. But we had a long way to go.

One of the most obvious ideas to raise money was to do another tour or two. Even though we had just returned from a tour of Western Canada, we arranged another one, as well as a tour of the Maritimes and Newfoundland, for the winter of 1985-86. The tour promoter was a tough negotiator, but Judi was tougher — our Broadway show was on the line! — and he agreed to a $150,000 contract. At work, we had set up a giant paper thermometer with a big sign — $1 MILLION — at the top so that we could record our drive toward the goal. As I entered the rehearsal room after Judi clinched the deal, Renato took one look at my face, pointed at the thermometer, and yelled: "She shoots!"

"She scores!" everyone else chorused as I marked in the amount. Only $850,000 to go!

Then we sat down and talked about other ways to raise money: I mentioned Newman's Own popcorn; Benny suggested T-shirts; and Sandra's idea was buttons. We ended up selling all of them. And we sold them everywhere we went, from Stephenville, Newfoundland, to Vancouver, British Columbia; from Charlottetown, Prince Edward Island, to Winnipeg, Manitoba. We even sold them on our U.S. tour the following spring.

All the buttons bearing the top hat-cane-and-shoes logo, arrived just before we left on the eastern tour. We also had thousands of T-shirts and jars of popcorn. And we lost no time in selling all the loot: we opened for business at the airport. As Kim Hansen, our newest performer (usually a member of the props department) reached onto the luggage conveyor to open a box of buttons, the woman behind him in line moved closer. "What's in there?" she asked.

"They're buttons," he said. "Do you want to buy one? They're only a dollar."

She eagerly reached into her purse, and the other passengers crowded in closer, opening their wallets. "Way to go, Kim!" Greg exulted as we made our way toward the gate, leaving behind a bemused ticket agent.

At the gate, we carried on the button sale — with some unexpected assistance. I happened to tell a fellow passenger about our Broadway plans, and the man promptly stood up on a chair and shouted: "Hey, everybody! Do you know who these people are? They're the Famous People Players, and they're one helluva good group of performers who deserve our support!" I stared at him in disbelief as people started circling us. "Don't be shy, Diane!" he urged. "Go on and get those buttons moving." Anyone who didn't buy one in the departure lounge had a second chance on the plane: One of the stewardesses sold sixty — ten of which she bought for herself. Then, during our layover in Halifax, we sold hundreds of them.

Newfoundland was even better. Somewhere between Stephenville and Cornerbrook, we met a truck driver who took a bag of 100 buttons and later drove all the way to St. John's just to give us the $100.00. In St. John's, a twelve-year-old boy took a bag of buttons and returned only a day later with the money. And one afternoon, I came back to our hotel in St. John's to find a note and a cheque for $100.00 from a lady who had accepted a bag of buttons from one of the performers and sold them out on the street in the bitter January wind. "I didn't mind the cold," she wrote, "because it made me feel warm just to think of how wonderful your company is. I wish you the best of luck on Broadway."

And it was the same thing everywhere we went. People opened their hearts — and their pocketbooks. In Winnipeg we made almost $2,000 in one night from T-shirt, popcorn, and button sales, and by the end of the tour we had taken in more than $15,000.

Back home, Don Harron drafted a letter to about 2,500 people, asking them to help sell buttons and attend an open house at the rehearsal hall during the spring. We also offered a free trip to New York for anyone selling a whole box of buttons (1,500). The reaction was wonderful: thousands of buttons were sold. Some people sold a whole box and didn't even take the free trip. Others donated the $1,500 and let us sell the bag again. Several schools held their own button campaigns. We sold a multitude of buttons. But today there are still bags and bags of buttons at the bottom of the packing crate we use to transport T-shirts and other novelties we sell on tour between shows. Every time I see one of those bags, I'm reminded of the generosity of the people who participated in Buttons for Broadway.

Each of us in the company also contributed whatever we could, and no one had to be urged to give a few cents here, a few dollars there. One day, during lunch break, Greg came in with a burger, and before sitting down to eat he asked me for a big glass jar. There just happened to be an empty peanut butter container in the kitchen, and, at Greg's request, I labeled it BROADWAY MONEY. Greg started things off by dropping in the change from his purchase, and we all followed his example, filling that jar a dozen times as the weeks went on. It doesn't sound like much when your goal is a million dollars, but every little bit counts. It especially counts when it comes to self-confidence.

In May, Maureen McTeer organized a fund-raising gala for us, choosing her committee from the ranks of all three political parties, as she had for our earlier Ottawa gala. The committee raised more than $50,000, but even more important was the wonderful way we were treated by Maureen and her husband, Joe Clark.

As always, they were delightfully unpretentious. My daughters were with me, and we shared Joe and Maureen's limo to the National Arts Centre for the performance. During the ride, Joanne suddenly stuck her foot into the front seat. "How do you like my new shoes, Mr. Clark?" she asked. I just about died of embarrassment, but Joe simply smiled and said the shoes were lovely.

At the gala, they avoided the spotlight, saying that the event should focus on the company, not the dignitaries. Not only did they choose to sit in the second balcony, but Maureen insisted that I forget about calling her on stage for any kind of thanks.

Finally, just a few months before we were to go to New York, our Board of Directors, headed by Dorothy Spencer, organized one last fund-raising event: an off-Broadway show for people who weren't going to have the opportunity to see us on the Great White Way. In the audience were many of the people who had shared our triumphs and failures over the years, from our disastrous five-minute debut at the St. Lawrence Centre to the $150-a-plate benefit hosted by Norman Jewison. A standing ovation from *this* crowd was a real honor, and we were delighted with the financial contribution the event raised.

By the end of the summer, we had raised most of our backing. Clearly, our Broadway ticket sales would have to cover part of our expenses, but we figured we would still break even. Besides, making money wasn't what our Broadway venture was all about. It was about acceptance and the kind of generosity that prompted the woman in St. John's to stand out in the cold, selling our Broadway buttons.

But there were other problems to solve — problems that, at one stage, threatened the entire project. The difficulties, as in the past, began with a group of relatively inexperienced staff members who couldn't handle the challenge of performing, traveling, and developing close relationships with performers who were retarded. During our April tour of the United States, these internal problems escalated into utter chaos, as they had during our first trip to Las Vegas.

You would think that after a decade of hiring — and firing — staff members, I would have developed a sure-fire method of weeding out those who just weren't willing or able to invest the time and effort necessary to communicate with the performers effectively. But potential staff members usually show great aptitude and enthusiasm at the outset, only to become disappointments later. Over the years, there have only been a few people, such as Warren Quinn and Ida Colallilo who have demonstrated the qualities needed to work with our performers.

One performer forgot all the tapes for the show in Kingston, New York, as he recalled only an hour before curtain. Three of the so-called normal performers were spending most of their time bad-mouthing and harassing the retarded performers. One of them actually called Renato "ugly" to his face. A fourth "norm," whom we had hired to spend time with the female performers, was ignoring them. One night Debbie Rossen, Darlene, and Sandra came to my room weeping that she had told them outright to keep away from her. Nasty scenes were even developing in the wings during shows. One night, after one of the performers left a prop on the floor, a kicking and shoving match ensued, and someone used a word I hadn't heard in Famous People Players in years: "retard!"

The April tour dragged on and on, going from bad to worse as we left New York State and traveled through Colorado and Florida. By the time we got back to Ohio, everything was falling apart. Our acting stage manager went home to Toronto for a funeral, but he couldn't get back into the States because he didn't have his work permit. I was in Los Angeles for a speaking engagement and couldn't get back in time to step in, but luckily we were able to bring in Kim Hansen in his stead, just in time to supervise the staging of the show in Akron, Ohio.

It was time to take some action. Judi Schwartz, the Board of Directors, and I decided to turn the bus around and bring everyone home. There was still a week until our May show in Brooklyn — we called it our Broadway dress rehearsal, because the Shubert representatives and our Broadway manager were going to attend — and the mess had to be straightened out before we jeopardized everything we had worked so hard to attain.

The next morning, our board of directors met to discuss the

situation, and when the meeting was over, the five people who had caused all the trouble were no longer part of Famous People Players. (Four of them were fired, and the acting stage manager quit when he was told he would have to go back to the prop department.)

There was a chasm to fill, and we were very fortunate to have people in our lives who were willing to come to the rescue. All of them were former Famous People Players: Neil Thompson, his sister Mary, Cathy Camp, Leslie Danyliw and Ida, who had just returned from working in a mission in Africa. If they hadn't bailed us out, we never would have made it to Brooklyn, let alone Broadway. Not only did they perfect their new parts in time for the show, but, more important, the effect of their presence was so strong that the company was reunited as a family from the moment they walked in the door.

The Brooklyn show was as smooth as silk: *Sorcerer's Apprentice*, the James Bond medley, the Broadway musical sequence — everything went without a hitch. After it was over, Philip Smith of the Shubert organization came backstage with Maria DiDia, our Broadway manager, and Donald Pippin, the composer who had arranged the music for *A Chorus Line*. Donald made some suggestions about musical transitions, but he, Philip, and Maria were thrilled with the show. "That's the best Broadway preview I've ever seen," Donald said. "But I do have one more bit of advice."

"What's that?" I asked.

"I think you should get someone else to do 'The Stripper.' Those bumps and grinds are more like twitches!" The stripper had been yours truly; I had lost a lot of weight worrying about the past months' problems. I laughed in agreement and passed the number over to Cathy Camp, who was much more curvaceous!

As the weeks and months flew by, I frequently felt the urge to reach up and hold back the hands of the clock. Everything was happening so fast, and before we knew it, we were on the bus and pulling up to the 46th Street entrance to the Lyceum. It was raining hard, and as I said hello to Sam Ellis, our production coordinator, who was standing at the entrance, I shook a fist at the downpour. "This is a disaster!" I complained.

"Oh, don't worry about the rain," Sam said. "Rain means you're gonna have a big hit."

But the first indications weren't promising. As we unloaded the props — they looked so funny, all sprawled out in the elegant velvet seats of the theatre — the stagehands summoned me. It seemed we couldn't use the trap door to bring out the huge Satan puppet in "Night On Bald Mountain"; the puppet would have to enter from the wings like all the others. And there were a few other problems in the number. There was no way to create the illusion of fire erupting from the floor or, at the end, the impression of a sky opening to allow the good guys, Pegasus and the Indian, to soar heavenward. Instead, they too departed via the wings.

As well, Ken Billington — the award-winning lighting director we had met at Radio City Music Hall — had to revise some of his lighting. There were flies to hang, technical rehearsals to conduct, and run-throughs to supervise. And the previews were to begin in only two days.

I was worried that we would get off to a bad start; so worried that I started to wonder whether it had been such a good idea to come to Broadway in the first place. Was it fair to subject the performers to this level of pressure? My friends kept reminding me that I had to believe in my company — and myself. Seymour Heller, who was in New York for Liberace's performances at Radio City Music Hall, Peter Rosen, the producer of our CBS documentary, and singer Catherine McKinnon — they were always there for us. And even after the dour box-office manager, whom we nicknamed "Dick Depressed," told me that the tickets weren't moving very quickly ("This certainly isn't another *Cats*," he moaned), Catherine kept coaxing me back on the bright side. "It doesn't matter about the tickets," she said. "The important thing is that you brought the company to Broadway. You *know* that, Diane. You just have to *believe* it."

But the rain kept falling and falling, and I couldn't hold on to that optimism for long — or the belief that the showers spelled success. I could only think about the internal divisions the company had endured. The increasing effort of getting ready for the show would come to nothing if we bombed. Without my friends' reassurance, which at least showed me that there *was* another side, I might have opened in Bellevue instead of Broadway.

It was also fortunate for my sanity that there were some pleasant diversions in that period before the previews began. Our Broadway press agent, Mark Goldstaub (who had also represented Shirley MacLaine) had arranged for a number of interviews and photo sessions, and many of the photographers wanted to shoot us outside with the puppets. For one photographer, I took the whole company out on Times Square, and there, right under the Coca-Cola sign, with a huge crowd watching, we jumped rope — double-dutch, yet! — with the Stevie Wonder puppet. Then, *The New York Times* wanted a shot of the Famous People walking across Broadway. Kim Hansen escorted Liberace, Mary Thompson promenaded arm in arm with Kenny Rogers, and Stevie Wonder had two companions, Renato and Debbie Lim.

We even did a little Famous People Players-style renovation to the front of the theatre, which was under repair when we arrived and looked terrible because of a scaffolding that had been erected. We asked Maria DiDia to phone the Shubert organization about getting us some paint, which was donated to us: green, pink, and yellow fluorescent colors that glowed in the dark under the lights of Broadway, just as I prayed *we* would dazzle audiences inside.

Finally, the previews began, and I remember that we all walked, in the ever-present rain, from our hotel to the theatre. The house was only about 75 percent full, and I had a seat in the fourth row (much too close; the outlines of the puppeteers are often visible from the front rows). But there I was anyway with my palms sweating and stomach churning, prepared for the worst. Well, it was rough — especially the transitions — but I could also see the magic: the glowing, vibrant colors; the vanishing and reappearing animals, pianos, monsters, spaceships, stars; the roller coaster pacing. And despite the fact that I sweated through every little mistake, I couldn't help noticing that everyone around me was gasping and giggling with delight.

"It's marvelous, isn't it?" one woman asked me at the end as she pulled on her coat to leave. "Those tap shoes dancing in midair were a scream! And that little clown on the tightrope — so sad . . . . And those black panthers! They looked like they could jump off the stage and go on a rampage!"

Smiling at her thankfully, I rushed backstage, where we all collapsed in each other's arms, weak with relief that the first show was finally over. But there was still a week of previews — and the gala — before we reached our ultimate test: opening night.

The Broadway gala had been organized to raise funds toward the purchase of a building for Famous People Players. It was wonderful even to contemplate having our own home after fourteen years of scraping together the rent for dank church basements and drafty warehouses.

The proceeds would also go toward our building fund and sharing our philosophy with others, and the event, which was to include a short version of our Broadway show and a dinner at New York's Lincoln Center, had attracted a very impressive guest list, including Prime Minister Brian Mulroney and his wife, Mila.

There were more than sixty people involved in the organization of the gala, headed by Ken Taylor, the former Canadian ambassador who helped six American hostages escape from Iran in 1979, and Joan Sutton Straus, former *Toronto Sun* columnist. The committee list read like a Who's Who of the arts, big business and politics: Honorary patrons included Joe Clark and Maureen McTeer, Opposition Leader John Turner, Ontario Premier David Peterson, and Robert Johnston, Consul-General of Canada; well-wishers for the Broadway run included entertainers Jack Lemmon, Ann-Margret, Stevie Wonder, Alan Alda, Anne Murray, Paul Newman and George Burns.

It was quite a task to get ready for our gala performance. Everyone had got used to the full production after all the previews, and it wasn't easy to cut the show down to 45 minutes from two hours and still maintain the timing and flow between numbers. But we managed, and the final rehearsal was great.

The day of the gala, I went to the Lyceum to discuss the details of the evening with the stage manager. After our talk, I wandered down the aisle, brooding. Suddenly, there was a tap on my shoulder, and there stood Maureen McTeer. I was delighted.

"Well, what do you want me to do?" Maureen asked crisply after we had hugged. "Flags. Where are the flags? You've got to have flags outside the theatre: The prime minister's coming." And she told a theatre employee to phone the consul-general's office and arrange for the flags. And finally, she took Ida and me to her hotel for a drink.

"You know, Maureen," I told her, "it's people like you who make us want to do a great show. I promise you that we'll do it for you."

"Great!" said Maureen, and then looked anxiously at my face. "What's wrong, Diane?" But I couldn't tell her what had been bothering me for days, and what the stage manager had just reminded me. I had to let the performers know that, at the end of the show, they would be sharing the stage with a whole crowd of gala organizers and VIPs. There would also be speeches and congratulatory telegrams delivered — on stage. When I got back to the Lyceum, I took aside Benny, Renato, and Debbie Lim and broke the news.

"Why can't they do that stuff later?" demanded Renato.

"At the dinner," added Debbie.

"I know," I said. "That's the way it should be."

"This was supposed to be our night," Benny said.

For one horrible moment, I thought they were going to refuse to perform. You see, all the performers feel very strongly about their bows, their one moment to shine after working entirely in the dark to make magic for others. And this moment was being taken away from them. "I know this isn't right," I finally said, "but let's just do it. Let's do it and get it over with. And let's remember that a lot of people are coming from Canada who care about us — like Maureen. Let's do it for them."

We talked to the others, and once again we huddled together like a football team: "*Let's go!*" Everyone's adrenalin was coursing like crazy as we waited for the call to start the show. But it didn't come: ten minutes passed, then twenty. It was fifty minutes before the curtain went up. In the entertainment business, you hurry up and wait! I casually strolled out into the lobby to find that a receiving line had been set up for the audience to meet Prime Minister and Mrs. Mulroney. There's nothing wrong with a receiving line, but we were almost an hour late going on. As any performer will tell you, the nervous energy that powers a great performance can vanish as quickly as it comes.

Because of the performers' professionalism, there were no major problems in the show — except a technical one in the second half. The stage fog that is supposed to billow on stage during "Night On Bald Mountain" instead poured out into the audience in a thick cloud. In a way, it foreshadowed the events to come.

When the show was over, I stood in the wings, surrounded by the stage crew and Catherine McKinnon, and went over the speech the organizers had asked me to deliver before presenting a sculpture to Prime Minister Mulroney. Meanwhile, Ken Taylor read some of the telegrams — they were wonderful — and Joan Straus, at the end of a long speech, announced that the gala had raised sufficient funds, a major portion of which went to the building fund.

But the good news got lost in the events that followed. I never did deliver the speech. One of the ladies from the committee, which assembled on stage with the Mulroneys, presented the sculpture to the Prime Minister. And after the presentation, everyone left the stage.

"What's going on here?" hissed Sam Ellis, our production supervisor. "Aren't you supposed to be introduced?" I shrugged my shoulders and gulped hard.

Suddenly, Ken Taylor ran back on stage and blurted: "Oh, we forgot the next best thing to the Mets score — Diane Dupuy!"

Catherine grabbed my hand and whispered, "Okay, so they did it wrong. Now you get out there and do it right!"

I walked out to center stage, lifted my head high, and began, "I want to thank you all for being here tonight, and now, I'd like to ask you to look beyond what you've seen on this stage. I'd like to ask you to look beyond black light and see that we've accomplished something more, that we have made a lasting contribution. And now you, the audience — the corporate leaders of this country and the world — are in a position to do something even greater, to open up your companies and employ handicapped people."

When I was finished, there was dead silence. No one knew how to handle what I'd said — no one outside the company, that is — except for the reporters sitting with Mark Goldstaub. They stood up and cheered. And Bill Davis came over and congratulated me on my speech. Everyone else left so fast that you might have thought the theatre was on fire.

Back in the dressing room, Maureen was waiting for me; it was the first time I had ever seen tears in her eyes. We didn't speak, but we looked at each other with the same question in mind: How did this happen?

It wasn't over, either. There was still the dinner. A few of the performers and Famous People Players staff ducked out of the theatre and went out on the town on their own. But the rest of us pulled ourselves together and got ready to go to the Lincoln Center, where the dinner was being held.

Only one problem: the bus was nowhere in sight. Maureen, nothing daunted, dashed out on the street in her high heels and evening dress and hailed one of the buses returning after delivering audience members to Lincoln Center. Murphy's Law then went into overdrive. First, the bus let us off at the wrong entrance and we wandered around Lincoln Center for half an hour trying to figure out how to get inside. Then the security guard at the door wouldn't let us in. Our names, he said, were not on the guest list. "Would you please go upstairs," Catherine said, "and tell them that the guests of honor have arrived?"

At last we were inside. The television cameras gathered around us as we raised our champagne glasses. "I'd like to propose a toast," I said, "to the best chairperson of the best gala that's ever been held for Famous People Players. Here's to Maureen McTeer!" It might have been blunt to praise Maureen's gala in the middle of another function, but what I said was the truth.

Although a number of people attending the dinner came over and sympathized with us about the delay in starting the show and the confusion on stage afterward, we were all still too upset to enjoy the event. After less than an hour, we left and met the other performers at a disco, where we danced and laughed hard enough to at least take the edge off our feelings of frustration and hurt.

I have to say that we were all extremely grateful for the contributions made by so many individuals and corporations on our behalf. We were honored to perform for them and delighted to see them after the show. But none of us could pretend that most of the events of the evening had been anything other than an excruciating experience.

"You know the best part about the gala, Mrs. Dupuy?" Renato asked as we made our way home in the wee hours.

"No, what?"

"It's over," he said. "And we have our own gala. It's called *opening night*!" Everyone cheered wildly.

When October 26 arrived, I spent it alone. I didn't want the performers to see my nervousness. An important last-minute task kept me occupied: a trip to Tiffany's to pick up gifts for the performers — sterling silver bookmarks, each engraved with the title of a song that had become our motto, "Fighting the

Odds to the End." I had also intended to walk to the theatre alone, but Benny and Debbie Lim were waiting for me, so we went together.

It was still raining.

As we approached Shubert Alley, I noticed, as if for the first time, our billboard, sandwiched between *42nd Street* and *La Cage Aux Folles*, and for the first time my heart told me that everything we had been through was worth it, just for this moment.

"You know something, Diane?" said Benny. "If we bomb, it doesn't matter. Because look at us, next to those big shows. That's *us*, Diane!" I hugged him hard, the tears flowing again — I swear I've never cried as much in my life as on Broadway — and we continued toward the theatre.

"Don't cry, Diane," Debbie coaxed. "We're going to do a really great show for you tonight."

"For *you*, Debbie," I said. "Do it for you, too."

How can I even begin to describe the show? Never, in the fourteen years of the Famous People Players, had I ever seen such a magnificent performance. Every transition was perfect; every prop and puppet seemed more glowing, bright, colorful, magical than ever before. The standing ovation, led by Liberace, lasted ten minutes.

I came racing backstage, and all of us hugged and laughed, cried and screamed, danced and cavorted like crazy people. "You did it! You really did it!" I said again and again.

The first person to arrive backstage was Liberace. There were tears in his eyes as he hugged and congratulated us, and he didn't speak for a moment.

"I'm so proud of you," he finally said. "Of all the people I've introduced over the years, you are the first who have really made a big name for yourselves on you own. Other than Barbra Streisand, of course!" Then he looked more serious. "Now, there's just one thing I want to tell you, Dora. And this is: Don't tamper with success. Don't let people convince you to jazz up the show or change it in a way you don't want. Because people will try to convince you to do just that, and you've all got to fight that. You've got to stick together."

Just then, I felt a hand pluck at my sleeve. It was Sandra, and right behind her, Darlene. "Can we talk to you for a second, Diane?"

"Sure, but . . ." They were pulling me back on stage. With an apologetic smile for Lee — who beamed back at me understandingly — I let myself be hauled to center stage.

"We have something for you, Diane," Darlene said.

"Yeah," Sandra confirmed. "It's a review."

"It's a review of you, Diane," continued Darlene, pulling a crumpled piece of paper out of her purse. "We just finished it." She handed it to me, but for some reason, I couldn't look.

"Read it to me, okay?" I looked out at row upon row of empty seats and back at the bare stage, where two solemn-looking young women were about to tell me about myself. "Go ahead; read it."

"Dear Diane," Darlene began:

> "Things are great here on Broadway. I really are having a wonderful time. So much things to do and see. Thank you for bringing me here. You are a good director. You make us learn wonderful parts and you put a great show together for Broadway. It's not black light or puppets that's important, it's everything you taught us that's important. You are a good friend. If I have a problem, you would be there when I need you. And Diane you are the nicest sweetest friend that I could ever ask for . . . ."

"My turn," said Sandra, taking the paper:

> "But as the old saying goes if you can't stand the heat get out of the kitchen. Because you have given me a new life and I am not lazy any more and I don't watch soaps anymore and that's what I think of you and Diane thanks for all the consideration but when the going gets tough the tough get going."

"So what do you think of our review?" Sandra demanded.

"Sandy, if the critics hate us — every single one of them — we'll still be a smash," I said, moved beyond tears. "*That's* what I think of your review. Now let's go party!"

We were all on cloud nine at our opening night party. The champagne flowed and the food was out of this world: patés, chicken cooked in wine, fiddleheads flown in from New Brunswick . . . . What a feast!

As midnight approached, the oldest of Broadway traditions came to a climax: the wait for the media reviews. Finally, with Maria DiDia and Mark Goldstaub in tow, I headed for the ad agency where the reviews were being assembled in a locked room that wouldn't be opened until every article had arrived. I was ready to explode by the time I was allowed into the office. The first person who saw me started waving *The New York Times* in my face: "You're a hit!"

I leaped onto the conference table and started jumping up and down as I was handed review after review, rave after rave. Finally, I just couldn't stand it anymore, and, grabbing as many reviews as I could, I headed back to the party.

The music stopped as I walked into the room, and everybody looked up at me expectantly. The tension was so thick you could almost see it. I forced my expression into a frown and held the pose for what seemed like eternity. Then I exploded: "*We're a hit!!!*"

I swear I don't know how the walls stayed intact after the cheer that erupted in that room. Renato was dancing Sandra around the table; Debbie Rossen and Greg were in each other's arms; Mom, Debbie Lim, and Kim were jumping up and down. I climbed onto yet another table, this time sending champagne glasses flying in all directions. "*Listen!*"

And I started to read. First, *The New York Times*:

> Here are a pair of dancing feet, a hat and hands — identifiably human but disembodied. Now the insistently pervasive music shifts to Liberace, and a very large Liberace

— a caricature — pounds a piano that is also a caricature. It all emerges from the dark. There are mammoth chickens sawing fiddles to a Celtic tune, and scenery of a desolate sort floats in as the backdrop for the enactment of "The Sorcerer's Apprentice." Now our attention is riveted by country singers and rock stars as well as animals struggling to the death to the strains of Mussorgsky.

"*Go on! Go on!*" everyone shrieked as I paused for breath.

Black light is the secret of this viewer-friendly, iridescent spectacle that drenches the senses in sight and sound for almost two hours . . .

"Magic" is clever, colorful and cute. The colors are loud and so is the music. Sometimes it feels as though you are sitting through some gigantic rock video, with the selections ranging from Saint-Saëns to Kenny Rogers by way of Cole Porter, Rodgers and Hammerstein, George M. Cohan and Stevie Wonder . . . .Everything had a kind of Technicolor brightness . . . .

There are times that "A Little Like Magic" does seem like magic: the magic of theater, the magic of diversion, the magic that impels one to say, "That's entertainment."

Renato noticed me starting to choke up on the last line, and before I could break into tears, he commanded loudly: "Read another one, Mrs. Dupuy!"

"Oh, okay. . . . Hey, listen to this one from the *New York Daily News*!"

Watching the Famous People Players in "A Little Like Magic" at the Lyceum Theater is rather like being Alice in her first few minutes in Wonderland, when everything before her eyes seemed a hallucination.

. . . the best moments are those when the black stage is filled with floating apparitions — mammoth goldfish, an ungainly, spindly-legged ballerina, a clown who ends his tightrope act wafted into space by a balloon, a stripper

> whose body literally disappears with every article of clothing she removes from it.
>
> . . . the stage is like an artist's canvas, every corner of which tingles with delight.

"What about James Bond and Superman?" demanded Renato.

"Well, the *Newsday* guy talked about them, and about the way Liberace soars into the air and floats offstage at the end. And here's what else he said:"

> The arts of stagecraft and puppetry merge to create a delightfully innovative and cheerful theater experience . . . a precisely co-ordinated ballet of intricate movements.

"Read some more, Diane!" insisted Debbie Rossen.

"Okay, what did Clive Barnes say? Here we go. *New York Post.*"

> Life-size celebrity puppets are worked with uncanny skill. No praise is too high for the visual art effects of Mary C. Thornton, the lighting by Ken Billington and the dazzling expertise of the unseen performers.

"Yea, Mary!" And we were off on what had to be the 29th toast of the evening. I read reviews until my voice gave out; then Mark read them, and Maria read them. For days, the media tributes kept streaming in, from the radio and television networks and the out-of-town press. *USA Today* put it succinctly: "Broadway has a little winner here."

With rave reviews, the box office really started to pick up, and we finally began to get sellout houses. As the weeks continued, we were also delighted to welcome some pretty distinguished visitors. One night I was standing out in the lobby when an enormous stretch limo pulled up to the curb, and out stepped the brothers Gibb — better known as the Bee Gees — with all their children! I sneaked up to the first balcony, where they had seats in the front row, and sat behind them. They laughed and cheered all the way through the show, and afterward they came backstage to meet the performers. Everybody flocked around them to talk — except Renato, who introduced himself, asked if they had enjoyed the show, then calmly went back to picking up his props!

Sandy Duncan came to the show, and so did Paul Newman and his wife, Joanne Woodward. One of our Famous People — the real Kenny Rogers — tried to get tickets the day he was in New York, only to find out we were dark that day. It was so disappointing!

As the run came to an end, we realized that our Broadway experience hadn't been everything we imagined: Instead of making money or breaking even, we came out with a deficit. But all the media attention rekindled interest in our touring, which was to expand to such an extent in 1987 and 1988 that today, two years after Broadway, we're in the black again. Most of all, being on Broadway had fulfilled the performers' dream of making it to the top — on talent alone.

In December 1986 we said farewell to the Great White Way. The goodbyes at the Lyceum were difficult, and as the bus pulled away from the theatre, that persistent rain was still falling.

This is where we came in, I thought.

We were all silent for a while. Finally, Benny broke the silence. "It's sad to leave. Did you see all the stagehands crying?"

"Yeah, I was crying too," said Darlene.

"Me too," said Debbie Lim. "But we have to leave. Because we have to start all over again tomorrow."

Epilogue

Our 1987 tour of Western Canada and the United States had really just started when we reached Calgary, Alberta, and the Jubilee Auditorium. One week down, four months to go!

We were in familiar territory. The Famous People Players have performed in the Jubilee for almost ten years, ever since we first started touring. It was reassuring to hear stagehands and house managers call us by name and remind us of funny incidents from times past.

As the truck backed down the loading dock, all the performers gathered at the door to haul in the bags of props, the boxes of black-light tubes and puppet heads. In just a few hours this endless array of crates and cloth-covered foam rubber would be assembled in the wings on prop tables, ready to be transformed into magic by the performers' deft hands and agile bodies and the sorcery of ultraviolet light.

I wandered into a dressing room to throw down my traveling bag, and as I headed on stage to see how everyone was coming on the setup, there was a phone call for me. It was a *Toronto Star* reporter, who told me that Liberace was seriously ill with anemia, emphysema, and heart disease.

I was speechless. We all knew that Liberace had been ill, but we thought he was getting better. Or maybe it was that we *hoped* he was getting better.

"Hello?" It was the reporter's voice.

"Oh, I'm sorry. What were you saying?"

"I was wondering if you might be able to talk a little about Liberace. I understand he's been very close to your company."

Close to our company! There was the understatement of the year. But what could I say about the man who made it possible for us to be in this theatre, who made it possible for all of us to have a career in which our imagination was the only limit of the heights we could reach?

Just talk, Dupuy, I advised myself. "Well, Liberace has been very good to the Famous People Players," I began. "He took us from a church basement in Toronto all the way to Broadway. If he hadn't expressed confidence in our professionalism by inviting us to Las Vegas twelve years ago, we might never have accomplished what we've been able to do in this company. Liberace is a very generous man who always gave more than he could give."

I began to feel strange. It was as if we were talking about someone who had died. I knew he was very sick, but he couldn't die. Could he?

The reporter cut in on my thoughts again. "Liberace came to your performance on Broadway, didn't he?"

"Oh yes; he was tremendous," I said. "He spent a lot of time with us, even though he had his own show at Radio City Music Hall. He's always had time for us, time to give us advice and encouragement. He really taught us the meaning of the word professionalism, and the word humanity too."

By the time the interview was over, my teeth were firmly sunk into my lower lip so I wouldn't cry. I called Seymour Heller in Palm Springs, California — Liberace's home — and asked him to send our love to Lee. Neither of us speculated about the future. We just chatted about this and that as if we could make things all right just by pretending they were.

Out on stage, the performers were arranging their props on the tables and rolling out the gigantic black velvet carpet that would turn the stage into a huge ebony jeweler's box for the gemlike colors of fluorescent paint caught by ultraviolet light. I couldn't interrupt the flow of activity. We had three shows to do this afternoon and evening, and we had to be on the bus by midnight to get to Hope, B.C. on schedule.

That night, as we traveled, the news came out. There were a few questions; then everyone was silent. I turned around to see some of the performers crying quietly to themselves. As I glanced toward Renato, I could see his mouth silently forming words. He was praying.

We were all praying.

On February 4, we reached the Queen Elizabeth Theatre in Vancouver. I was exhausted after being unable to sleep the night before, so I sneaked a catnap in an armchair in the dressing room. In my dream, someone was saying goodbye to me, but I couldn't see who it was. Suddenly, a woman's voice was calling my name on the public-address system.

I knew what was coming before I heard Seymour's soft voice on the line. Lee was dead.

Wladziu Valentino Liberace, 67 years young.

I must have been in shock, because — almost to my surprise — I wasn't crying. I just felt numb as I walked into the wings on stage left, where Renato was grumbling over his Superman props.

"Renato." He looked up from his work. "Liberace just died."

Renato put down the prop he was holding and got to his feet. Huge tears, magnified by the heavy, thick lenses of his glasses, gathered in his eyes and coursed down his cheeks. He made no effort to wipe them away.

We both just stared at each other for a long moment. At last Renato broke the silence. "He was such a good man; he was such a good man," he kept saying. "A *good* man."

Just before curtain, all the Famous People Players gathered in one of the big dressing rooms and talked about what we could do to honor our great mentor — our great friend — during the show.

After the introduction, we brought the white lights up and I came to the microphone. "Ladies and gentlemen, we have all lost a very special person," I said. "Today, Liberace passed away, and with him went our hearts. But, you know, Liberace was always the most dedicated of professionals, and he exemplified that old show-business expression 'The show must go on.' So we will go on, and tonight we offer this tribute to one of the greatest entertainers and finest human beings it has ever been our honor to know — Liberace."

The music started for "Aruba Liberace." There was a total blackout. Then the ultraviolet lights came on to reveal the Liberace puppet sitting motionless at the keyboard; the candelabrum completely still on either side of the piano. The joyous music played on, and the only movement on stage was the flickering of light as it played off the glittering sequins of his costume and the brilliant flash of his smile.

When the music stopped, there was another blackout. And then we went on with the show.

We think of Lee very often now, as our touring schedules get longer and longer, as new dreams beckon in the distance. Being on the road is hard work, but, as Renato says: "We do the shows because it makes people happy, and that makes us happy. That's what Liberace used to say, and he's right."

We also do the shows because touring means earning the income that brings us closer to our greatest goal: a home of our own. We want a building where we can rehearse, build props, conduct the understudy program, and develop ideas to bring more self-sufficiency and meaningful employment to the lives of the developmentally handicapped. We'd like to start a doll and toy hospital where battered (but irreplaceable) old playthings can be restored to their former glory. We want to open a restaurant, and an art gallery displaying the work of handicapped artists from all over the world. And all these facilities would be staffed by people who are handicapped.

Fund-raising, notably from the Broadway gala, has given us a good start. But in a way, what we're able to do ourselves to make this dream come true is even more rewarding. These days we're on tour in Canada and the United States at least five months a year, and in 1988 we were delighted to be invited to perform at the Sea World aquatic centre in Orlando, Florida, where we performed several new numbers, including Famous People puppets Lionel Richie and Willie Nelson.

There are other artistic plans on the horizon, but it's building our new home that consumes most of our attention. Someday, we *will* build it. Soon. So don't be surprised if you're in downtown Toronto some evening in the not-too-distant future and you notice something different about one of the buildings. A huge sign, glowing in the dark: THE HOME OF FAMOUS PEOPLE PLAYERS.